G000139149

INSTANT REFERENCE HISTORY OF THE USA

ty TEACH YOURSELF®

For UK orders: please contact Bookpoint Ltd, 78 Milton Park, Abingdon, Oxon OX14 4TD. Telephone: (44) 01235 400414, Fax: (44) 01235 400454. Lines are open 9.00-6.00, Monday to Saturday, with a 24-hour message answering service. E-mail address: orders@bookpoint.co.uk

For USA and Canada orders: please contact NTC/Contemporary Publishing, 4255 West Touhy Avenue, Lincolnwood, Illinois 60646-1975, USA. Telephone: (847) 679 5500, Fax: (847) 679 2494.

Long renowned as the authoritative source for self-guided learning – with more than 40 million copies sold worldwide – the *Teach Yourself* series includes over 200 titles in the fields of languages, crafts, hobbies, business, computing and education.

British Library Cataloguing in Publication Data
A catalogue record for this title is available from the British Library.

Library of Congress Catalog Card Number: On file

First published in UK 2000 by Hodder Headline Plc, 338 Euston Road, London NW1 3BH.

First published in US by NTC/Contemporary Publishing, 4255 West Touhy Avenue, Lincolnwood (Chicago), Illinois 60646-1975, USA.

The 'Teach Yourself' name and logo are registered trademarks of Hodder & Stoughton.

Copyright © 2000 Helicon Publishing Ltd

In UK: All rights reserved. No part of this publication may be reproduced or transmitted in any form or by any means, electronic or mechanical, including photocopying, recording, or any information storage or retrieval system, without permission in writing from the publisher or under licence from the Copyright Licensing Agency Limited. Further details of such licences (for reprographic reproduction) may be obtained from the Copyright Licensing Agency Ltd, 90 Tottenham Court Road, London W1P 9HE.

In US: all rights reserved. No part of this publication may be reproduced, stored in a retrieval system, or transmitted in any form or by any means, electronic, mechanical, photocopying, or otherwise, without prior permission of NTC/Contemporary publishing.

Picture credits: Ann Ronan Picture Library 47, 111, 195; Sachem 68, 85, 172; Image Select 10, 101, 110, 115, 118, 161, 162, 178, 189, 209; Corbis 105; Library of Congress 105, 113; Ann Ronan at Image Select 151; Excem Publications/Image Select 198.

Text editor: John Wright
Typeset by TechType, Abingdon, Oxon
Printed in Great Britain for Hodder & Stoughton Educational, a division of Hodder Headline Plc, 338 Euston Road, London NW1 3BH, by Cox & Wyman Ltd, Reading, Berkshire

Impression number   10 9 8 7 6 5 4 3 2 1
Year   2006 2005 2004 2003 2002 2001 2000

Contents

Bold type in the text indicates a cross reference. A plural, or possessive, is given as the cross reference, i.e. is in bold type, even if the entry to which it refers is singular.

abolitionism

A movement especially strong in the 19th century to abolish **slavery** in the southern states and to free the 4 million slaves who mostly worked on cotton plantations. Their cause was greatly helped in 1852 when Harriet Beecher **Stowe** published *Uncle Tom's Cabin*, a novel describing how badly some slaves were treated. Other famous abolitionists included Susan B **Anthony** and John **Brown**, who was hanged in 1859 for trying to lead a violent slave uprising. The question of whether new states could allow slavery was a major issue in the break-up of the Union and the formation of the **Confederate States of America**. Slavery was officially abolished in the Confederacy by the **Emancipation Proclamation** announced in 1863 by President Abraham **Lincoln**, but it could not be enforced until 1865 after the Union victory in the **Civil War** and so some Union states allowed slavery until then.

abortion

Abortion in the USA was illegal and often dangerous until 1973 when the Supreme Court ruled in the case of *Roe v Wade* that states could not ban abortions during the first three months of a pregnancy. The ruling said the fetus was not a person, and the decision should be made by a woman and her doctor. Some religious 'right to life' groups strongly oppose abortion, and a few violent acts occurred in the 1990s against people working in abortion clinics, including a sniper who killed a doctor in his home in Amherst, New York, in 1998.

ACLU See *American Civil Liberties Union.*

Adams, John (1735–1826)

The second president of the USA from 1797 to 1801. A member of the **Federalist Party**, he had also been the country's first vice-president from 1789 to 1797, elected twice. He was born in Braintree (now Quincy), Massachusetts, studied at **Harvard**, and became a lawyer in 1758. He successfully defended the British soldiers who fired on civilians during the

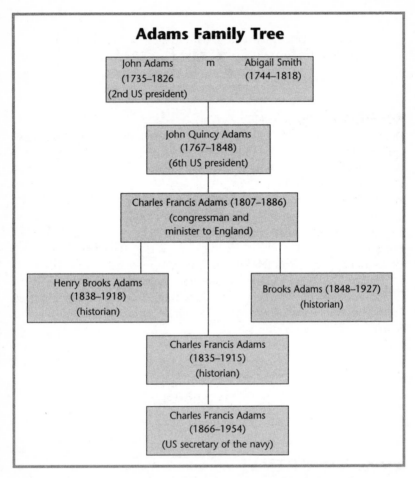

Adams Family Tree

John Adams
(1735–1826
(2nd US president)

m

Abigail Smith
(1744–1818)

John Quincy Adams
(1767–1848)
(6th US president)

Charles Francis Adams (1807–1886)
(congressman and
minister to England)

Henry Brooks Adams
(1838–1918)
(historian)

Brooks Adams (1848–1927)
(historian)

Charles Francis Adams
(1835–1915)
(historian)

Charles Francis Adams
(1866–1954)
(US secretary of the navy)

Boston Massacre. Adams was a member of the **Continental Congress** from 1774 to 1778 and signed the **Declaration of Independence**. In 1779 he went to France and helped negotiate the treaty of 1783 that ended the **American Revolution**. In 1785 he became the first US ambassador to Britain. As president, he became unpopular because he supported the **Alien and Sedition Acts** that made citizenship more difficult and restricted freedom of speech. Adams represented the aristocratic point of view, in contrast to Thomas Jefferson, the champion of democracy, who was his vice-president and the next president. Adam's son, John Quincey **Adams**, was the sixth US president.

> ❝ What a poor, ignorant, malicious, short-sighted, crapulous mass is Tom Paine's *Common Sense*. ❞
>
> **John Adams**, writing to Thomas Jefferson in 1819

Adams, John Quincy (1767–1848)

The sixth president of the USA from 1825 to 1829. Born in Braintree (now Quincy), Massachusetts, he was the eldest son of President John **Adams**. He studied at **Harvard**, becoming US minister to the Netherlands from 1794 to 1796 and to Germany from 1796 to 1801. He was elected to the US Senate in 1803. He negotiated the Treaty of Ghent to end the **War of 1812** against Britain and in 1817 became President James **Monroe's** secretary of state, formulating the **Monroe Doctrine** in 1823. In 1824 Adams, an independent Federalist and later Democratic Republican, was elected president by the House of Representatives despite receiving fewer votes than his main rival, the Democrat Andrew **Jackson**. As president, he was an advocate of strong federal government, but many politicians were opposed to this. The **Erie Canal** was completed while he was in office. In 1831 Adams returned to Congress, where he served until his death.

> ❝ Think of your forefathers!
> Think of your posterity! ❞
>
> **John Quincy Adams**, speech 22 December 1802

Adams, Samuel (1722–1803)

A leader of the **American Revolution** who helped organize the **Boston Tea Party**. He was one of the signers of the **Declaration of Independence**, began the **Committees of Correspondence**, and served in the **Continental Congress**, where he urged independence. Adams took the colonists' side in the disturbances caused by the **Stamp Act** of 1765, and from 1765 to 1774 was a member of the legislature of Massachusetts. He was lieutenant-governor of Massachusetts from 1789 to 1793 and governor until 1797. He was a second cousin of President John **Adams**.

Before Napoleon used the same phrase, Samuel Adams called the British a 'nation of shopkeepers'.

AEF See *American Expeditionary Force.*

affirmative action

A US government policy of positive discrimination that favours women and members of minority ethnic groups in such areas as employment and education. The Equal Opportunities Act of 1972 set up a commission to enforce the policy in organizations receiving public funds, such as universities. Many private institutions and employers adopted voluntary affirmative action programmes at that time. In the 1980s there were allegations of 'reverse discrimination' (individuals receiving preferential treatment solely because they belonged to a particular group). In November 1998 voters in Washington state followed the lead of Californians two years earlier by approving a proposition prohibiting racial and gender-based affirmative action in areas such as employment, education, and public procurement.

AFL–CIO

The abbreviation and popular name for the American Federation of Labour and Congress of Industrial Organizations, which is the largest workers' organization in the USA. The AFL was established in 1886 for craft unions, and some of its members broke away in 1935 to form the CIO for industrial workers. They merged in 1955, and today's AFL–CIO has about 80 trade unions with almost 14 million members. The organization usually supports the **Democratic Party.**

Agent Orange

A selective weedkiller that became infamous in the 1960s when US forces used it in the Vietnam War to eliminate ground cover that could protect enemy forces. It was later discovered to contain highly poisonous dioxin now banned in the USA. About 60,000 US troops who had handled it, along with many Vietnamese people who came into contact with it, later developed cancer, other illnesses, or produced deformed babies. Agent Orange was named after the distinctive orange stripe on its packaging. Seven companies that had manufactured the chemicals faced an increasing number of lawsuits in the 1970s. All were settled in 1984 out of court in a single class action, resulting in the largest ever payment of its kind ($180 million) to claimants.

Alabama

A cruiser of the **Confederate States of America** that captured 65 US merchant ships during the **Civil War** and burned 52 of them. The ship was built in Liverpool, England, and, under Captain Raphael Semmes, began raiding the seas in 1862. It was sunk on 19 June 1864, off Cherbourg, France, by the USS *Kearsarge*, a warship protected by chain armour hidden with wood. Only 9 of the 149 *Alabama* crew members died. After the war, in 1871, the US government sought compensation from Britain through the Treaty of **Washington** for the damage caused by the *Alabama*.

When the *Alabama* sank in the English Channel, Captain Semmes and his officers were rescued by an English yacht, the *Deerhound*, and entertained by London society.

Alamo, the

The mission fortress in San Antonio, Texas. It was besieged from 23 February to 6 March 1836 by Santa Anna and 4,000 Mexicans; they killed the garrison of about 180, including Davy **Crockett** and Jim **Bowie**. After their heroic 12-day stand, Texans who wanted independence from Mexico used the cry 'Remember the Alamo!' The fortress, now surrounded by large city buildings, is preserved as a national monument.

Alger, Horatio (1832–1899)

A US writer of children's books. He was born in Revere, Massachusetts, and known as 'Holy Horatio' as a boy, because his father was a Unitarian minister. He attended **Harvard** and also became a Unitarian minister, but quickly resigned to begin his literary career. Alger wrote over 100 instructive moral tales in which the heroes rise from poverty to riches through hard work, good deeds, and luck, including the series *Ragged Dick* from 1867 and *Tattered Tom* from 1871. It is estimated that his books sold more than 20 million copies. To Americans, a 'Horatio Alger tale' still means any rags-to-riches story, often an implausible one.

> ⁶ Horatio Alger wrote the same novel 135 times and never lost his audience.' ⁹
> **G Juergens**, in his book *Joseph Pulitzer and His New York World*

Alien and Sedition Acts

Four laws passed by the US Congress in 1798, when war with France seemed likely. The acts lengthened the period of residency required for US citizenship, gave the president the power to expel 'dangerous' aliens, and severely restricted criticism of the government. The laws were controversial because of the new degree of power exercised by the central government, and they harmed the popularity of President John **Adams**, who supported them. The Alien Acts were never used, but several newspaper editors were convicted under the Sedition Acts.

Allen, Ethan (1738–1789)
A colonial military leader in the **American Revolution** who founded the **Green Mountain Boys** in 1770. Born in Litchfield, Connecticut, Allen served in the **French and Indian War** (1755–60) before taking up a campaign to protect Vermont from territorial claims by New Hampshire and New York. At the outbreak of the Revolution in 1775, Allen and his Green Mountain Boys joined with Benedict **Arnold** and captured Fort Ticonderoga on 10 May 1775. Captured by the British in the subsequent invasion of Canada, Allen continued his campaign for Vermont's independence after his release in 1778.

❝ Come out of there, you damned old rat. ❞

Ethan Allen, demanding that Lt Jocelyn Feltham surrender Fort Ticonderoga, 10 May 1775

Alliance for Progress
The US programme of assistance to Latin American countries, initiated by President John F **Kennedy** in 1961 under the auspices of the **Organization of American States**. It called for expenditure of $20 billion over ten years and had a charter that set goals for more democracy, land reform, fairer distribution of income, and improved health services. However, economic and political conditions continued to worsen in Latin America, and President Richard M **Nixon** effectively dismantled the programme.

American architecture
The dominant American colonial architecture came from 17th-century English immigrants. Most houses were small with massive chimney stacks, and were timber-framed with brick, clapboard, or wattle-and-daub walls. By the end of the century, more elegant and elaborate examples of Jacobean and Queen Anne styles were built. In the 18th century, the neoclassical

style dominated and was referred to as Georgian architecture. The rough-hewn log cabin also became an American architectural mainstay. Other, finer, buildings included plantation houses and grand public buildings, such as **Independence Hall** in Philadelphia. In the 19th century, Neo-Classicism was introduced by Thomas **Jefferson** at his house at

Notable 20th-century architects working in the USA included Frank Lloyd Wright, Louis Henry Sullivan, Walter Gropius, Ludwig Mies van der Rohe, Eliel and Eero Saarinen, I M Pei, Philip Johnson, Robert Venturi, and Michael Graves.

Monticello, the Federal Capitol at Washington by William Thornton, and the White House by James Hoban. After the **Civil War**, architects turned to Romanesque forms, French Renaissance design, and a Romantic revival of Gothic architecture. The 20th century saw the rise of modern architecture, with the skyscraper as the fundamental US contribution to world architecture. By the 1980s a reinterpretation of earlier styles was promoted by Post-Modernists.

American art

Painting in colonial America began with the work of artist-explorers and naturalists, such as the 16th-century watercolourist, John White. The early 18th century saw a reflection of European portraiture in John Smibert, Robert Feke, and others. In the later 18th century, London called to American-born painters like Benjamin West and J S Copley. A native development in the 18th and 19th centuries was a 'primitive' or folk art by Edward Hicks and others. In the 19th century, Romanticism in landscape developed in the imaginative paintings of Washington Allston, then by those exploring the vast continent artistically, for example Thomas Cole of the 'Hudson River School'. The later 19th century saw artists again turning to London, such as James McNeill Whistler and John Singer Sargent, while a host of others studied in Paris and Munich. The early 20th century saw determined efforts to look at the USA in an American way. The 'Ashcan School' took its name from its depiction of city squalor, and this realism expanded into the 'regionalism' of the 1930s, as in the work of Grant Wood. Enthusiasm for modern art was quickened by the celebrated Armory Show of 1913. In the mid-20th century, abstract expressionism was exemplified by the 'action painting' of Jackson Pollock. The pop art movement, led by artists such as Andy Warhol and Roy Lichtenstein, dominated the 1960s and fostered multimedia works and performance art in the following decades.

American Civil Liberties Union (ACLU)

An organization established in 1920 to defend US constitutional freedoms. In 1998, it had about 250,000 members. It has been involved in famous and controversial cases, including the 1925 '**Monkey Trial**' to overturn a ban on teaching the theory of evolution in Tennessee schools and the 1954 *Brown v. Board of Education* case in which the **Supreme Court** ruled segregated schools to be illegal. The ACLU has been criticized for supporting freedoms for anyone, including hate groups. In 1978 it defended the American Nazi Party's right to march in Skokie, Illinois.

American Expeditionary Force (AEF)

The US force sent to fight in Europe under Gen John **Pershing** after the USA entered World War I on 6 April 1917. Although initially only one division went to France, by November 1918 the AEF comprised three armies each of three corps, a total of 1,338,000 combat troops. The greater part of this force was infantry, with only small detachments of cavalry. A considerable force of artillery was also deployed but was armed entirely with British or French guns since US production had not geared up. A strong tank force was planned but only three battalions, using British and French tanks, saw action. In all, some 2 million US troops eventually served in France.

❝ Lafayette, we are here ❞

US colonel Charles E Stanton, standing before Lafayette's tomb after the first American units landed in France

---

American Federation of Labor and Congress of Industrial Organizations See *AFL–CIO*.

American Indian

The first colonists in America found a land already occupied by hundreds of different native groups that they called Indians from Columbus's mistaken belief that he had reached the Indian subcontinent. Some of the main groups were:

- Eastern: **Cherokee, Creek,** and **Seminole**
- Plains: **Sioux**, **Cheyenne**, **Comanche**, and **Blackfoot**
- Southwest: **Apache**, **Navaho**, and **Pueblo**.

Contact with the European settlers proved to be disastrous to all the native peoples, who were exposed to new diseases and superior weapons. Their uncoordinated resistance in the **Indian Wars** led only to the humiliation of being forced west to **Indian Territory** and restrictive reservations. Most of today's American Indians, now often termed Native Americans, continue to live in virtual poverty on the same reservations, although many individuals have left their traditional culture to seek a better living in large US cities.

American literature

Early US literature began with the colonial writing that was mainly theological. The post-Revolutionary period produced political writing by Thomas **Paine**, Thomas **Jefferson**, and Alexander **Hamilton**. In the early 19th century, the influence of English Romantics was seen in the poems of William Cullen Bryant, Washington Irving's tales, and James Fenimore Cooper's novels. From 1830 to 1860 intellectual life in New England produced the essayists Ralph Waldo Emerson and Henry Thoreau, the poet Henry Wadsworth Longfellow, and the novelist Nathaniel Hawthorne. Outside the New England circle were the novelists Edgar Allan Poe and Herman Melville. After the **Civil War**, Stephen Crane wrote realistic war stories, Mark Twain dealt with Western life, and Henry James developed the psychological novel. The dominant poets were Walt Whitman and Emily Dickinson. The short story flourished with Hawthorne, Poe, James, Harte, and O Henry. In the 20th century, the powerful group of dramatists included Eugene O'Neill, Arthur Miller, Tennessee Williams, Edward Albee, and Sam Shepard. Traditional poets like Carl Sandburg and Robert Frost were joined by the modernists Ezra Pound and T S Eliot. Post-**World War II** poets included Robert Lowell and Sylvia Plath. The novel became realistic in the hands of Upton Sinclair, Ernest Hemingway, William Faulkner, F Scott Fitzgerald, Henry Miller and, since World War II, John O'Hara, Truman Capote, John Updike, Norman Mailer, Philip Roth, and Thomas Pynchon.

American Revolution

The revolutionary war from 1775 to 1783 between Britain and its North American colonies, resulting in the establishment of the United States of America. Colonial resentment was caused by high-handed British legislation, like the **Stamp Act** of 1765, and the **Townsend Acts** of 1767. At the **Boston Tea Party** of 1773, protesters emptied 342 chests of imported tea into the harbour. Fighting broke out on 19 April 1775 at **Lexington** and **Concord**, Massachusetts, and that year saw George **Washington** appointed commander in chief of the American forces. Two days later, the British won the Battle of **Bunker Hill**. The **Declaration of Independence** was approved by the **Continental Congress** on 4 July 1776. A decisive American victory at the battles of **Saratoga Springs** on 7 October 1777, prompted the French to enter the war on the American side. Britain's **Yorktown** surrender on 19 October 1781 signalled the war's end, with American independence recognized at the Peace of Versailles on 3 September 1783.

American Revolution *American Revolution Uniforms: American Rifleman (left) and American General (right)*

MAJOR BATTLES OF THE AMERICAN REVOLUTION

- 19 April 1775: American victories at Lexington and Concord
- 17 June 1775: British victory at Bunker Hill
- 30 August 1776: British victory at Long Island
- 26 December 1776: American victory at Trenton
- 3 January 1777: American victory at Princeton
- 11 September 1777: British victory at Brandywine
- 17 October 1777: American victory at Saratoga
- 12 May 1780: British victory at Charleston
- 16 August 1780: British victory at Camden
- 17 January 1781: American victory at Cowpens
- 19 October 1781: British surrender at Yorktown

Amish

A strict Christian group based on the Mennonite Church, found today in the states of Pennsylvania, Ohio, and Indiana, as well as in Canada. They were named after their leader, Swiss bishop Jakob Amman (*c.* 1644–*c.* 1730), who rejected the Mennonite Church as too secular. The Amish Church was formed between 1693 and 1697, and when its members were persecuted many migrated in the 18th century to North America. The Amish live in

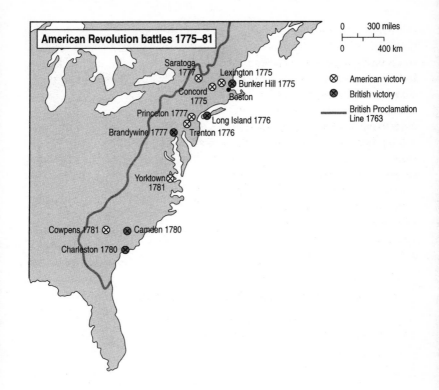

German-speaking farm communities and are distinctive for their pre-20th-century dress and a simple lifestyle, making no use of modern inventions such as cars and electricity. They are pacifists whose main concern is the freedom to worship God, known to them through piety and personal religious experience. Anyone marrying out of the community is cast out for ever. **See also:** *Pennsylvania Dutch.*

Andersonville Prison

An infamous military prison for US soldiers captured by Confederate troops in the **Civil War**. Located near Andersonville, Georgia, it was 26 acres in the open surrounded by a 20-foot fence of tree trunks. More than 33,000 prisoners were packed into the area,

Andersonville had a 'dead line', a railing that ran parallel to the prison fence and 20 feet away from it. Any prisoner going beyond the railing, or even reaching past it, was shot dead.

and they received little food, water or medical care because the **Confederate States of America** could hardly provide for its own soldiers. There were more than 12,000 prisoners in Andersonville during the war, and the prison's commander, Swiss-born Maj Henry Wirz, was the only 'war criminal' executed after the war.

Anthony, Susan B(rownell) (1820–1906)

A US pioneering campaigner for women's rights who also worked for the antislavery and temperance movements. She supported the **Underground Railroad** that helped slaves escape. Born in Adams, Massachusetts, she was first a school teacher. In 1869, with Elizabeth Cady Stanton, she founded the National Woman Suffrage Association and was its president from 1892 to 1900. Anthony edited and published a radical women's newspaper, *The Revolution* from 1868 to 1670,

Susan B Anthony was the first American woman to have her image on a coin, the Anthony dollar that was minted between 1979 and 1981.

and co-edited with Elizabeth Cady Stanton the four-volume *History of Woman Suffrage* from 1881 to 1886. She organized the International Council of Women in 1888 and founded the International Woman Suffrage Alliance in Berlin 1904.

Antietam, Battle of

The bloodiest battle of the **Civil War**, on 17 September 1862 at Antietam Creek, off the Potomac River in Maryland. The Confederates called it the Battle of Sharpsburg, after the village there. The battle was indecisive, but Maj-Gen George McClellan of the Union blocked the advance on Maryland and **Washington** of the Confederate forces under Gen Robert E **Lee**. This paved the way for Abraham **Lincoln** to issue his **Emancipation Proclamation** freeing the slaves, and also persuaded the British not to recognize the **Confederate States of America**. The Confederates lost 2,700 dead, 9,024 wounded, and about 2,000 missing out of 51,844 troops; the Union forces lost 2,108 dead, 9,549 wounded, and 753 missing out of 87,000 troops.

Anti-Masonic Party

The first 'third party' in US political history, existing from 1827 to 1836. It wanted to force Freemasons out of public offices. The party was established as a reaction to the disappearance in 1826 of William Morgan who had written a book revealing Masonic secrets. Rumour said he had been murdered by Masons. The party's first national convention in 1832 nominated William Wirt as its candidate for president in a futile effort to defeat President Andrew **Jackson**, who was a Mason.

antitrust laws
US laws that prevent or restrain trusts, monopolies, or any other business practices considered unfair or uncompetitive. The first important law was the Sherman Antitrust Act of 1890, which banned mergers and acquisitions that restrained trade. The Clayton Antitrust Act of 1914 prohibited unfair price cutting, exclusive contracts, and other schemes to isolate competitors; it was strengthened in 1936 by the Robinson-Patman Act. Today's US antitrust laws have sometimes been de-emphasized, because they might restrict American companies from competing internationally, but 1999 saw a federal suit charging the computer giant Microsoft with creating a monopoly and another against vitamin makers for fixing prices.

Anzio landings
Landings made at the small port of Anzio, Italy, during World War II. About 50,000 US and British troops were landed on 22 and 23 January 1944, capturing it from the Germans and making it a beachhead. German troops were initially taken by surprise but soon moved their full forces to contain the Allies at Anzio. It was not until 23 May that the US-British force was able to begin a slow offensive that, by 1 June, approached Rome.

ANZUS
An acronym for 'Australia, New Zealand, and the United States', a military alliance established in 1951 and put into effect the following year. It was a mutual defence pact in the Pacific, protecting the three countries and the islands under their jurisdictions. No integrated ANZUS military force has been established. In 1985, New Zealand refused to allow American warships into its waters if they were nuclear powered or carried nuclear weapons. In retaliation, the USA suspended its defence obligations to New Zealand in 1986. Since then, the USA and Australia have continued the ANZUS alliance.

Apache
A member of an **American Indian** people who now live mostly on reservations in Arizona, southwest Oklahoma, and New Mexico. There were about

50,330 Apaches in 1990. They are descendants of Athabaskan-speaking Indians who migrated to the southwest from Canada about AD 1000. They lived by hunting bison, gathering wild plant foods, and farming maize, but were known as fierce raiders and horse warriors in the 18th and 19th centuries, raiding other Indian groups in what is now Arizona, and parts of Colorado, New Mexico, Texas, and north Mexico.

- Apache leaders such as **Cochise** and **Geronimo** led their warriors against US cavalry troops during the second half of the 19th century.

- Many Apaches surrendered between 1871 and 1873 and moved to reservations in Arizona. A large number refused to settle, however, and intermittent raids continued until 1886 when the last great Apache chief, Geronimo, surrendered.

- Today, their enterprises on the reservations include casinos, tourism, ski resorts, and cattle ranches.

Apollo moon landing

The greatest space venture of the 20th century, when two US astronauts landed on the moon on 20 July 1969. Neil Armstrong landed the lunar module (named *Eagle*) manually because the automatic navigation system was heading for a field of boulders. On landing in an area called the Sea of Tranquillity, Armstrong announced 'Tranquillity base here. The *Eagle* has landed.' Armstrong was the first to set foot there. He was accompanied on the moon's surface by 'Buzz' Aldrin, and they collected rocks, set up experiments, and mounted a US flag. The module remained on the moon for 22 hours, while the third astronaut, Michael Collins, stayed in the orbiting command module. The return flight went without a hitch, but after splashdown the astronauts were quarantined as a precaution against any diseases which may have been contracted from the lunar surface.

- The Apollo programme was announced in 1961 by President Kennedy.

- The world's most powerful rocket, *Saturn V*, was built to launch the Apollo spacecraft.

- The first mission, *Apollo 1*, ended in disaster on 27 January 1967 when the three crew members were killed by a fire during a preliminary check on the ground.

- After the first landing on the moon, five more followed.

- The total cost of the programme was over $24 billion.

> ❝ That's one small step for man,
> one giant leap for mankind. ❞
>
> **Neil Armstrong**, on first stepping on the moon

Appomattox Court House

The former village in Virginia where Confederate general Robert E **Lee** surrendered to Union general Ulysses S **Grant** on 9 April 1865, effectively ending the **Civil War**.

Grant allowed the Confederates to keep their horses, gave them food, and permitted them to return safely to their homes. The surrender was signed in Wilmer McLean's house, and soldiers then bought or stole most of the furniture. A reconstruction of the two-storey brick house is now a museum in the 972-acre Appomattox Court House National Historical Park, 5 km/3 mi from today's town of Appomattox.

Strangely, Wilmer McLean's houses featured at both the beginning and the end of the war. His first house was shelled during the war's first battle at Bull Run. To move his family away from the conflict, he bought the house in Appomattox Court House where the surrender eventually took place.

Arnhem, Battle of

A major battle of **World War II** from 17 to 26 September 1944 in the Netherlands city of Arnhem. An Allied airborne operation tried to secure a bridgehead over the Rhine, thereby opening the way for a thrust towards the Ruhr and a possible early end to the war. It was only partially successful, with 7,600 casualties. US troops were assigned bridges to the south of the city, while Arnhem itself was to be taken by the British. Unfortunately, two divisions of the SS Panzer Corps were refitting in Arnhem when the British landed and penned the British troops in, while the US force captured the bridge at Nijmegen but were unable to secure the bridge at Elst. Despite the arrival of Polish reinforcements on 21 September, Britain's Gen Montgomery ordered a withdrawal four days later.

Arnold, Benedict (1741–1801)

An American soldier in the **American Revolution** who won the turning-point battle at **Saratoga** in 1777. He is chiefly remembered, however, as a traitor to the American side. Arnold was a merchant in New Haven, Connecticut, who joined the colonial forces and fought well in the Battles of Ticonderoga and Quebec. He was a major general and one of the most trusted officers of Gen George **Washington**, but he felt bitter at having been passed over for promotion. Arnold was put in charge of West Point on the Hudson River in 1780 and later began to send military information to the British, ultimately offering to surrender his garrison to them. Maj John André was sent by the British to discuss terms with him, but was caught and hanged as a spy. Arnold escaped to the British lines, where he was given an army command. He went to England in 1782 and stayed there until his death.

Articles of Confederation

The first written plan of government for the USA. The full name was the Articles of Confederation and Perpetual Union. They were drafted by the **Continental Congress** in 1776 and 1777 but not approved by all 13 states until 27 February 1781. The Articles limited the powers of a central government, giving 'sovereignty, freedom, and independence' to the states. It allowed Congress to control foreign affairs and do such jobs as coin money and run a post office, but many weaknesses became evident: Congress could not enforce its laws, no federal court was provided for, and no revenue was set aside for government. The Articles were therefore replaced in 1788 by the **Constitution of the United States.**

> ❝ The stile of this confederacy shall be the United States of America. ❞
>
> **Articles of Confederation**, first article

Atlanta, Battle of

An important battle in the **Civil War,** because Atlanta, Georgia, was the major railway centre for the **Confederate States of America**. It occurred outside the city on 22 July 1864, between about 100,000 Union troops of Maj-Gen W T Sherman and about 60,000 Confederate troops of Gen John Hood. Neither side won but both suffered some

Union soldiers manning the cannons that bombarded Atlanta would often yell 'There goes the Atlanta Express' as a large shell was fired.

30,000 casualties, heavy losses that the Confederates could not afford. Sherman began to siege and bombard the city on 28 July, and it did not surrender until 2 September. He had it burned before he began his destructive march through Georgia on 16 November.

Atlantic Charter

A declaration issued during **World War II** by the US president Franklin D **Roosevelt** and British prime minister Winston Churchill after meetings in August 1941. It stressed their countries' broad strategy and war aims and was largely a propaganda exercise to demonstrate public solidarity among the Allies. Among the Atlantic Charter's stated goals were that the USA and UK:

- Sought no territorial gains
- Desired no territorial changes not acceptable to the peoples concerned
- Respected the rights of all peoples to choose their own form of government
- Wanted self-government restored to the occupied countries
- Desired international cooperation to raise economic standards
- Hoped to see a peace affording security to all nations.

This charter was incorporated into the Declaration of the United Nations in 1941.

atomic bomb

The powerful nuclear-fission bomb developed in the 1940s in the USA into a usable weapon. Research began in the UK in 1940 and was transferred to the USA after its entry into World War II the following year. Known as the **Manhattan Project**, the work was carried out under the direction of the US physicist Robert Oppenheimer at Los Alamos, New Mexico. After one test explosion, two atomic bombs were dropped on the Japanese cities of Hiroshima (6 August 1945) and Nagasaki (9 August 1945); the Hiroshima bomb was as powerful as 12,700 tonnes of TNT, and the Nagaskai one was equivalent to 22,000 tonnes of TNT. The USSR first detonated an atomic bomb 1949 and the UK in 1952. **See also:** *Rosenberg, Julius and Ethel Greenglass.*

Australia, New Zealand, and the United States See *ANZUS.*

Bacon's Rebellion

A rebellion in 1676 in colonial America led by a newly arrived planter, Nathaniel Bacon, against the Virginia governor, Sir William Berkeley. Because the governor failed to defend the frontier from Susquehannock Indians, Bacon organized and led an unauthorized militia that defeated the Indians on 10 May. After Berkeley proclaimed Bacon a traitor and briefly arrested him, Bacon marched on 23 June with 500 men on Jamestown and inspired the Virginia House of Burgesse to pass democratic reforms. He returned with a force on 13 September, driving the governor out, and six days later burned the town. When he died suddenly of malaria on 18 October, the rebellion collapsed.

Barton, Clara (1821–1912)

A US health worker who founded the American Red Cross in 1881 and became its first president from 1882 until 1904. Born in Oxford, Massachusetts, Barton was trained as a teacher before becoming involved in projects for the welfare of American soldiers. A volunteer nurse, she tended the casualties of the **Civil War,** and in 1864 Gen Benjamin Butler named her superintendent of nurses for his forces. Nicknamed 'The Angel of the Battlefield', she served at many battles, including **Antietam** and **Fredericksburg**. Once as she was tending a wounded man, a Confederate bullet nipped her sleeve and killed him. After the war, Baron nursed in the Franco-Prussian War before returning to create the American Red Cross.

> ❝ While our soldiers stand and fight,
> I can stand and feed and nurse them ❞
>
> **Clara Barton**, 1861

Battle Hymn of the Republic, The

The rousing battle hymn that became the unofficial anthem for the Union during the **Civil War**. After Julia Ward Howe, a well-known author, visited

Washington, DC, she wrote the new lyrics for the tune of a pre-war song, 'John Brown's Body'. It was published in 1862 by the *Atlantic Monthly* magazine, which paid her only $5.

> ❝ Mine eyes have seen the glory of the coming of the Lord;
> He is trampling out the vintage where the grapes of wrath are stored;
> He has loosed the fateful lightning of his terrible swift sword;
> His truth is marching on. ❞
>
> **The Battle Hymn of the Republic**

Bay of Pigs

A bay on the southwest coast of Cuba that was unsuccessfully invaded on 17 April 1961 by about 1,500 Cuban exiles living in the USA. They had received training and support from the **CIA**, and their defeat within 48 hours by Cuban troops was a great embarrassment to the US government and President John F **Kennedy** who had approved the operation and took full public blame for the fiasco. The exiles had wrongly expected the local population to join their invasion. Results of a CIA internal investigation in the 1960s were released in February 1998 and blamed the agency, rather than President Kennedy, for the failure.

> ❝ There's an old saying that victory has a hundred fathers and defeat is an orphan. ❞
>
> **John F Kennedy**, speaking after the Bay of Pigs failure

Beauregard, Pierre Gustave Toutant (1818–1893)

The Confederate general who ordered the attack on **Fort Sumter** on 12 and 13 April 1861 that started the **Civil War**. Beauregard was born in New Orleans, Louisiana, and graduated from the military academy of West Point in 1838. He distinguished himself during the **Mexican War** and in 1861 was appointed superintendent of West Point, but resigned after four days to join the South. After achieving fame as the 'Hero of Sumter', Beauregard played a leading role in the Confederate

Gen Beauregard's nicknames during the war were 'Old Bory', 'The Little Creole', and 'Little Napoleon'.

victory at the 1st Battle of **Bull Run** in 1861 and prevented disaster at the Battle of **Shiloh** in 1862. From September 1862 until May 1864, he defended Charleston, South Carolina. In 1865 he helped delay the Union advance on Petersburg, Virginia. He spent his post-war years in New Orleans, where he was a railway president and prominent in politics. **See also:** *Confederate States of America.*

Bell, Alexander Graham (1847–1922)

A Scottish-born US scientist, and the inventor of the telephone, first transmitting speech by this electrical means in 1876. Later he invented a photophone to send words in a beam of light, the first wireless transmission of speech. Bell was born in Edinburgh and educated at the universities of Edinburgh and London. In 1870 he went to Canada and then to the USA, where he opened a school for teachers of the deaf in Boston. With the money he had made from his telephone system, Bell set up a laboratory in Nova Scotia, Canada, and in 1880 also established the Volta Laboratory in Washington, DC. There, he patented the gramophone, which was a commercially successful improvement on Thomas **Edison's** first phonograph.

- Bell's invention of the telephone stemmed from his interest in hearing defects. His wife was profoundly deaf.

- Bell's laboratory also experimented with flat disc records, electroplated records, and permanent magnetic fields impressed on records, an embryonic tape recorder. Bell also built hydrofoil speedboats and invented an air-cooling system, a method of desalinating sea water, the forerunner of the iron lung, and a sorting machine for punch-coded census cards.

- On the day Bell was buried in 1922, the entire telephone network in the USA was closed down for one minute in tribute.

❝ Mr Watson, come here; I want you. ❞

Alexander Graham Bell, first sentence spoken
over the telephone, March 1876

Berlin Airlift

A humanitarian operation by the US and UK air forces to drop food and other needed supplies to citizens of West Berlin, Germany, when the USSR blockaded the city by land and water from 23 June 1948 to 12 May 1949. The combined airlift, which lasted until 30 September 1949, dropped nearly 2 million tons of supplies in 250,000 flights at a cost of $224 million.

Bill of Rights

The first ten amendments to the **Constitution of the United States**, guaranteeing important basic freedoms to Americans. Twelve were originally proposed by **Congress** in 1789. The amendments, added to avoid any abuse of power by the government, were passed in 1791 to help encourage states to ratify the Constitution. The Bill of Rights went into effect that year on December 15. The guarantees of the amendments are:

1 freedom of worship, of speech, of the press, of assembly, and to petition the government;

2 the right to keep and bear arms;

3 a ban against keeping soldiers in private homes in peacetime without the owner's permission;

4 protection from unreasonable search and seizure;

5 protection from being 'deprived of life, liberty or property without due process of law', tried twice for the same crime, or compelled in a criminal case to be a witness against himself or herself;

6 the right to speedy trial, to call witnesses, and to have a defence counsel;

7 the right to trial by jury of one's peers;

8 protection against excessive bail or fines, or 'cruel and unusual punishment';

9 and **10** a safeguard to the states and people for all rights and powers not specifically given to the central government.

'Billy the Kid' (1859–1881)

The nickname of William H Bonney, a US outlaw in the **Wild West**. He also used the name of William Wright. A leader in the 1878 Lincoln County cattle war in New Mexico, he allegedly killed his first victim at age 12 and was reputed to have killed 21 men by age 18. Born in Brooklyn, New York, Bonney moved west with his family to Kansas and then New Mexico. He was sentenced to death for murdering a sheriff, but escaped (killing two guards) and was finally shot dead on 4 July 1881 by Sheriff Pat Garrett, his former drinking partner, while trying to avoid recapture.

> ❝ He ate and laughed, drank and laughed, rode and laughed, talked and laughed, fought and laughed, and killed and laughed. ❞
>
> **Pat Garrett**, on Billy the Kid, in *The Authentic Life of Billy the Kid*.

'Blackbeard' (d. 1718)

The nickname of Edward Teach, a vicious English pirate who attacked ships along the middle Atlantic coast of the American colonies. His warship, *Queen Anne's Revenge*, had 40 guns. In earlier years, Teach had been a privateer in the War of the Spanish Succession and then a pirate in the West Indies. The governor of North Carolina, Charles Eden, gave him protection in exchange for part of his spoils. Teach was eventually captured by troops from Virginia led by Lt Robert Maynard. On 22 November 1718, they shot him dead and then beheaded him.

Black Codes

Laws that were passed by southern states after the **Civil War** to deny black people equal rights. At best, the codes gave them rights with restrictions during their transition from slavery to freedom. Despite the 14th and 15th Amendments to the **Constitution of the United States** to provide blacks with full civil rights, the Black Codes persisted into the 20th century through **segregation** and by various laws favouring whites, such as the educational qualifications needed to vote.

Blackfoot

A member of an American Indian people who live on reservations in Montana and in Canada. They number about 32,000 (1990) and consist of three subtribes: the Blackfoot proper, the Blood, and the Piegan. Their name came from the black moccasins they wore.

The Blackfoot originally lived in the Great Lakes region, but in the early

1700s they migrated westwards as far as Montana. Initially they hunted buffalo on foot but in about 1750 they acquired both guns and horses. An extremely aggressive tribe, they drove weaker Indian groups from their lands and warred with their neighbours, taking scalps. They prevented the white settlers from establishing a settlement in their territory until well into the 19th century. After the buffalo disappeared in the early 1880s and there were many Blackfoot deaths from starvation, they were forced to take up farming.

Black Hawk War

A bloody war from April to August in 1832 between the US Army aided by the Illinois militia and two **American Indian** peoples, the Sauk and Fox, who were led by Black Hawk (1767–1838), also known as Black Sparrow Hawk. The Indian warriors were defeated and almost all killed at the Battle of Bad Axe River. Opposing the cession of his lands to the US government, Black Hawk had sided with the British during the **War of 1812** and joined his people in their removal to Iowa in 1831. The next spring, he led a large contingent back to Illinois to resettle their lost homeland and plant corn. Defeated and captured in the resulting Black Hawk War, he was permanently exiled to Iowa.

Fighting in the Black Hawk War were Capt Abraham Lincoln in the Illinois militia and Lt Jefferson Davis in the US Army. They would become the opposing presidents in the **Civil War**.

Black Muslims

A religious group founded 1930 for black Americans, formally known as The Lost-Found Nation of Islam. Members adhere to Muslim values and believe in economic independence for black Americans. 'Prophet Fard' (Wallace D Fard) founded the organization. It was led from 1934 by Elijah Muhammad (then Elijah Poole), who renounced whites and preached separatism. Its growth from 1946 as a black separatist organization was due to **Malcolm X** who, in 1964, broke away to found his own Organization for Afro-American Unity. Under the leadership of Louis Farrakhan from 1977, the movement underwent a resurgence of popularity. In October 1995, it organized the largest civil-rights demonstration in US history when more than 400,000 black males joined a 'Million Man March' to Washington, DC.

Black Panthers

A political movement for black Americans that was founded in 1966 by Huey Newton and Bobby Seale. Formally named the Black Panther Party, its declared aim was the creation of a separate black state in the USA. Stokely Carmichael, a US civil-rights activist and leader of the Black Panthers (1967–69), advocated the exploitation of political and economic power and the abandonment of nonviolence, moving towards the separatism developed by the **Black Muslims.** Such leaders as Martin Luther **King** rejected this approach.

- The Black Panther name was chosen because the panther is not usually aggressive but will fight to the death under attack.
- One of the party's leaders was the writer Eldridge Cleaver, who wrote *Soul on Ice* (1968).
- The Black Panthers tried to involve and care for the black community with health clinics, free breakfasts for poor children, and classes in political education.
- The movement disintegrated when it was targeted by **FBI** undercover operations.

Black Power

The rallying call of many black Americans in the 1960s and 1970s. The idea was begun by Stokely Carmichael who later joined the **Black Panthers.** The Black Power activists sought more political and economic power, and some of this was realized. Supporters of the movement held up one fist as a Black Power salute, and this was given at the 1968 Olympic Games in Mexico City by two black winners when they received their medals.

blockade runners

Confederate ships during the **Civil War** that transported goods past the US Navy's blockade of southern ports. There were at least 250 such steamers, most of them travelling to Bermuda, Nassau, or Havana for desperately needed food, clothes, and war materials. Among the major ports for blockade runners were Wilmington, North Carolina; Charleston, South Carolina; Savannah, Georgia; Mobile, Alabama; and Galveston, Texas. When these were captured by the Union forces, the romantic era of blockade running ended, and this contributed to the defeat of the Confederacy.

Bonnie and Clyde

The infamous duo of Bonnie Parker (1911–1934) and Clyde Barrow (1909–1934) who killed 12 people and carried out a series of small-scale robberies in Texas, Oklahoma, New Mexico, and Missouri between August 1932 and May 1934. They were eventually betrayed and then killed in a police ambush in Louisiana. Much of their fame came from their elusive encounters with the police and their coverage by the press. Their story was filmed as *Bonnie and Clyde* (1967) by the US director Arthur Penn.

> ❝ They're punks. They're giving bank-robbing a bad name. ❞
>
> **John Dillinger**, US bank robber, discussing Bonnie and Clyde

'Bonus Army'

A march on **Washington, DC**, by some 15,000 unemployed ex-serviceman in the spring of 1932 during the **Great Depresssion**. Officially called the Bonus Expeditionary Force, the group went to the nation's capital to lobby **Congress** for immediate cash payment of a promised war veterans' bonus. The 'Army' camped by the River Potomac or squatted in disused government buildings. They were eventually dispersed by troops authorized by President Herbert **Hoover**. Congress approved the payments in 1936, overturning a veto by President Franklin **Roosevelt.**

Boone, Daniel (1734–1820)

A US frontiersman who became an American legend. In 1775, he cleared a forest path called the Wilderness Road from Virginia to Kentucky through the **Cumberland Gap** for the first westward migration of settlers across the Appalachian Mountains. In 1775 he led a party of settlers who founded the town of Boonesborough, Kentucky. During the **American Revolution**, he led militias against Indians allied with the British. He was captured by a Shawnee war party in 1778 and so impressed the chief that he adopted Boone. He later escaped to warn the Boonesborough settlers of a planned British–Indian attack that they successfully repulsed. Boone later sat in the Virginia legislature as the representative of Kentucky, which was then only a county.

> ❝ I had not been two years at the licks before the damned Yankee came, and settled down within a hundred miles of me! ❞
>
> **Daniel Boone**, quoted in Henry Nash Smith's *Virgin Land*

Boston Massacre

The killing of five American colonists in Boston by British soldiers on 5 March 1770. Six more Americans were wounded. These were the first deaths in confrontations that happened before the **American Revolution**. The incident began as an unruly crowd of 60 people, upset at seeing British soldiers in their town, harassed the sentry. The overstated 'massacre' helped fuel colonial emotions, and the event was recorded in an engraving by Paul **Revere**. Nine British soldiers were tried, being defended by John **Adams**. Seven were acquitted, including Capt Thomas Preston, and two were found guilty of manslaughter and branded as punishment.

Boston Tea Party

An action by colonists who dumped British-owned tea into Boston Harbour on 16 December 1773 to protest against the tea tax imposed by the British government. It was a significant event leading to the **American Revolution**. When a valuable consignment of tea (belonging to the British East India Company and intended for sale in the American colonies) arrived from England in the harbour, Bostonians disguised as Mohawk Indians boarded the three ships at night and threw all 342 chests of tea overboard. The British government, angered by this and other colonial protests against its policy, took retaliatory measures in 1774, including the closing of the port of Boston.

- The destroyed tea was valued at £15,000.
- The participants used a secret password: an Indian grunt followed by 'me know you'.
- Samual **Adams**, John **Hancock**, and Paul **Revere** were supposedly among the 'Indians'.

Bowie, Jim (James) (1796–1836)

A US frontiersman and folk hero. A colonel in the Texan forces during the **Mexican War**, he is said to have invented the single-edge, curved hunting and throwing knife that became known as the Bowie knife. On 19 September 1827, people in Natchez, Mississippi, watched him use the knife to kill a man armed with a sword as they duelled on a sandbar in the Mississippi River. Bowie had become rich by buying and selling land and slaves. He was killed in the Battle of the **Alamo**.

Bradley, Omar Nelson (1893–1981)

A US general in World War II. In 1943 he commanded the 2nd US Corps in their victories in Tunisia and Sicily, leading to the surrender of 250,000 Axis troops. In 1944 he led the US troops in the invasion of France. His command, the 12th Army Group, grew to 1.3 million troops, the largest US force ever assembled. Born in Clark, Missouri, Bradley graduated from West Point in 1915 and served in World War I. After World War II, he was Chief of Staff of the US Army in 1948 and 1949 and was the first chairman of the joint Chiefs of Staff from 1949 to 1953. He was appointed general of the army in 1950 and retired from the army in 1953.

> ❧ In war there is no second
> prize for the runner up. ❧
>
> **Omar Bradley**, in *Military Review*, September 1951

brainwashing

A technique of mind control first used on American servicemen captured by communist forces during the **Korean War**. Expecting torture, the GIs were surprised to have their North Korean captors resort instead to psychological means to convince them of the American government's 'wrongful action' and of the virtues of communism. While this occurred, they were kept in isolation and subjected to personal humiliations and various punishments and rewards. Some prisoners issued statements agreeing with these ideas, and a few remained in North Korea and China after the war ended. To Americans in the 1950s, brainwashing was a new and feared form of communist indoctrination.

Brandywine, Battle of

A British victory during the **American Revolution** on 11 September 1777 on Brandywine Creek in southeastern Pennsylvania. Some 11,000 soldiers of Gen George **Washington** were protecting Philadelphia by using the steep banks of the Brandywine as a secure defensive position. Gen William Howe, with about 15,000 British troops, surprised the colonials by crossing the creek to the north. The Americans lost about 1,000 men during the battle, and the British only 576. This forced Washington to retreat to Germantown, but his army still blocked the way to Philadelphia.

brinkmanship

A high-risk foreign policy followed by the USA during the **Cold War**. It was first advocated in 1956 by US secretary of state John Foster **Dulles**. Brinkmanship allowed a crisis with the USSR to escalate to the risk of nuclear war. The theory said this pressure would cause the Russians to back down or reach an agreement. President John K **Kennedy** provided the most successful example of brinkmanship in 1962 during the **Cuban missile crisis.**

> ❝ If you are scared to go to the brink, you are lost. ❞
>
> **John Foster Dulles**, quoted in *Life magazine*, 1956

Broadway

A famous avenue in New York whose name is synonymous with American theatre. It runs the length of Manhattan, crossing Times Square at 42nd Street, the heart of the theatre district where Broadway is known as 'the Great White Way'. The first theatres were constructed in the area in 1894 and by the 1920s Broadway plays were making a major impact on international drama. The district began to look sleazy in the 1960s, but a restoration project successfully revitalized it.

Brown, John (1800–1859)

A fanatic American abolitionist, Brown was born in Connecticut and studied briefly for the Congregationalist ministry. In 1856 he was responsible for the 'Pottawatomie massacre' when five proslavery farmers were killed. Then, on the night of 16 October 1859, he led 18 men to seize the government arsenal at Harper's Ferry in Virginia (now West Virginia), apparently intending to distribute weapons to runaway slaves. On 18 October the arsenal was stormed by US Marines under Col Robert E **Lee**. Brown was tried and

> John Brown was married twice and had 20 children. Two of his sons were killed when the US troops stormed Harpers Ferry.

hanged at Charlestown on 2 December, becoming a martyr and immortalized in the popular song 'John Brown's Body'. **See also:** *abolitionism*.

'Buffalo Bill' See *Cody, William.*

Bulge, Battle of the

An important battle during **World War II** that involved US and British troops. On 16 December 1944, the German army launched a surprise counteroffensive against the Allied forces in the Ardennes Forest in Belgium. The purpose was to divide the US and British forces. The centre of the Allied line fell back to create a bulge, leading to the name of the battle, but Americans held Bastogne and the British swung south to confront the Germans. The Allied counterattack, launched on 30 December, did not achieve total success until the end of January 1945. This crucial battle made the German troops realize how helpless they were to stem the Allied advance.

'Bull Moose' Party

The nickname for the Progressive Party founded in 1912 by supporters of the former president Theodore Roosevelt. In 1908, when his presidential term was expiring, **Roosevelt**, a Republican, supported W H Taft as his party's next presidential candidate. After Taft's presidency, however, Roosevelt turned against him. Asked how he felt about the split, Roosevelt replied, 'Like a bull moose'. The name was promptly adopted by his new party. Roosevelt's election platform included legislation for workers' protection and strict regulation of corporations. The Bull Moose ticket split the Republican Party, allowing the Democratic candidate, Woodrow **Wilson**, to win the 1912 election. Roosevelt destroyed the chances of his new party becoming permanent when he declined to stand again.

Bull Run, Battles of

Two battles of the **Civil War**, both won by the Confederate army under Gen Robert E **Lee** at Manassas Junction, northeastern Virginia. The Confederates called them the Battles of Manassas. The first battle on 21 July 1861 was the first real one of the war. Union troops under Gen Irvin McDowell opened it with a determined attack that was firmly resisted by the Virginia brigade of Brig-Gen Thomas **Jackson**, earning him the title of 'Stonewall' Jackson. Confederate reinforcements under Gen Joseph E Johnston arrived to turn the balance, and the Union troops fled the field in disorder.

In the first Battle of Bull Run, some of the society and politicians of Washington, DC, rode in their carriages to overlook the battlefield, taking along picnics to enjoy a Union victory. They ended the day retreating in panic with their defeated troops.

In the second battle on 29 and 30 August 1862, Jackson's troops met those of Union general John Pope's head on at Bull Run. Jackson again held firm and, again in the nick of time, Gen Lee and Maj-Gen James Longstreet appeared with reinforcements. As with the first battle, this second engagement ended with the defeated Union forces running pell-mell for the safety of Washington, leaving more than 10,000 dead and wounded behind them.

Bunker Hill, Battle of

An early engagement of the **American Revolution**, on 17 June 1775 near a small hill in Charlestown (now part of Boston), Massachusetts. The battle actually took place on Breed's Hill, but is named after Bunker Hill, the more significant of the two. The hills had a commanding position over Boston, and so British general Thomas Gage decided to occupy them. Arriving there first, however, was a 1,200-strong American militia who seized Breed's Hill on the night of 16 June. The following morning Gage ordered a 2,000-strong force of infantry to clear the hill. The British made two advances, which suffered heavy losses, but their third attack succeeded in driving off the Americans. The British suffered 1,150 casualties to the Americans' 441. Gage's failure to defeat them soundly resulted in his replacement as British commander.

> ❝ Men, you are all marksmen — don't one of you fire until you see the whites of their eyes. ❞
>
> **Israel Putnam,** colonial soldier, his order at the battle of Bunker Hill

Burgoyne, John (1722–1792)

A British general in the **American Revolution**. His surrender on 17 September 1777 to Gen Horatio Gates at Saratoga, New York, was a major blow to the British cause. He was criticized for this failure, but reenforcements had not arrived as planned. Burgoyne had previously fought at the battle of **Bunker Hill** and in 1777 captured Fort Ticonderoga in New York State. He was also a dramatist whose comedies were great successes in London.

Burnside, Ambrose Everett (1824–1881)

A Union general during the **Civil War** and later a politician. He was born in Liberty, Indiana, and attended West Point military academy, but resigned his commission in 1853 and began manufacturing firearms. Three years later he invented a breech-loading rifle, the 'Burnside carbine'. In the war, he served briefly in 1862 as commander of the Army of the Potomac. Blamed for the Union defeat at Fredericksburg, Virginia, in 1862 and for losing 3,798 men during the siege of Petersburg, Virginia, in 1864, Burnside retired from active service. After the war, he was governor of Rhode Island from 1866 to 1869 and a US senator from 1874 to 1881.

Ambrose Burnside's distinctive side whiskers became popularly known as 'burnsides', and this was later changed to 'sideburns'.

Burr, Aaron (1756–1836)

A Republican vice-president from 1801 to 1805 who is most remembered for killing Alexander **Hamilton** in a duel. He was on the staff of George

Washington during the **American Revolution** and served as a US senator from 1791 to 1797. He and Thomas Jefferson received equal **Electoral College** votes in the presidential election of 1800, but Hamilton influenced the House of Representatives to vote **Jefferson** in, Burr becoming vice-president. In 1804 Burr's ambition to become governor of New York was thwarted, he believed, by Hamilton's opposition, and the fatal duel followed that year. In 1807 Burr was tried and acquitted of treason charges involving a scheme to establish an empire in the southwest. He died in poverty at the age of 80.

Bush, George Herbert Walker (1924–)

The 41st president of the USA from 1989 to 1993, a Republican. The son of a Connecticut senator, Bush moved to Texas in 1948 to build up an oil-drilling company. A congressman from 1967 to 1970, he then served as US ambassador to the United Nations from 1971 to 1973. He was director of the **CIA** from 1976 to 1981 and the US vice-president from 1981 to 1989. As president, his sending of US troops to depose Gen Manuel Noriega of Panama, proved a popular move at home. Success in the 1991 **Gulf War**

In 1994, one of Bush's sons, George W Bush Jr, was elected as governor of Texas, and another, Jeb Bush, won the Florida governorship.

against Iraq further raised his standing, but domestic economic problems helped bring about his defeat in the 1992 presidential elections by Democrat Bill **Clinton**. Prior to handing over to his successor, Bush signed the **START** II treaty with Russia to cut long-range nuclear weapons.

❝ Read my lips: no new taxes. ❞

George Bush, promise made during 1988 presidential campaign
(and not kept)

busing

The controversial US government policy of transporting students by buses from their neighbourhoods to more distant schools in order to help integrate the races. More than 500 of the 16,000 US schools systems are under court orders to bus students. This usually means black students are bused to white schools. The policy began in 1954 and became common after it was upheld in 1971 by the US **Supreme Court.** Forced city busing has resulted in many white families moving into suburbs. In 1999, a federal judge ordered Charlotte, North Carolina, to end busing, and other cities were expecting court challenges.

Cabot, John (Giovanni Caboto) (*c*. 1450–*c*. 1499)

An Italian explorer and navigator who sailed twice from England to mainland North America, in 1497 and 1498, to become probably the first European to land there. England's king Henry VII authorized both voyages. The first, in the ship *Matthew* with 18 men, reached America, probably Newfoundland, on 24 June 1497 and then went south to Maine. The second, with four ships and nearly 200 men (a fifth ship was disabled and left in Ireland), reached Labrador, where he traded with **American Indians**, and then sailed south to Cape Cod, Massachusetts, before returning.

- Cabot thought he could sail west from Canada to Japan where he would find gems.

- After his first voyage, Cabot gave himself the title of 'admiral'. He received a £5 gift from King Henry VII for his discoveries.

- After his second voyage, Cabot received an English annuity of £10 and disappeared from the pages of history.

Cajun

A member of a French-speaking community of Louisiana. They are descended from French-Canadians who, in the 18th century, were driven there from Nova Scotia (then known as Acadia, from which the name Cajun comes). They speak a dialect of French mingled with English, Spanish, German, African American, and American Indian words. Hot, spicy Cajun food has become world famous. Cajun music has a lively rhythm and features the steel guitar, fiddle, and accordion.

- Cajun terms include 'lagniappe' ('a little something extra'), 'Laissez les bons temps rouler' ('Let the good times roll'), 'Ca C'est Bon!' ('It's good!'), and 'coonass' (a slang name for a Cajun).

- Cajun dishes include fried alligator, smothered rabbit, blackened redfish, crawfish etouffee, seafood gumbo, and red beans and rice.

- Some Cajun songs are 'Ma Belle Evangeline', 'Jambalaya', 'Jolie Blonde', 'Mamou Two-Step', and 'La Danse de San Antonio'.

Calamity Jane (*c.* 1852–1903)

The nickname of Martha Jane Burke, a heroine of Deadwood, South Dakota. She transported supplies to the mining camps during the **gold rush** days, adopted male dress and, as an excellent shot, promised 'calamity' to anyone who angered her or wanted to court her. In 1878 she nursed victims of a smallpox epidemic in Deadwood. Many fictional accounts of the **Wild West** featured her exploits. She was a close friend, and possible lover, of 'Wild Bill' **Hickok**. She also claimed to have been a **Pony Express** rider and an aide to George **Custer**.

Calhoun, John C(aldwell) (1782–1850)

The US vice-president from 1825 to 1829 under John Quincy **Adams** and from 1829 to 1832 under Andrew **Jackson**. A great orator, he was a defender of strong **states' rights** and the institution of slavery. Calhoun was born near Abbeville, South Carolina, and was educated at Yale University. He served in the US House of Representatives from 1811 to 1817 and was secretary of war from 1817 to 1825 in President Monroe's cabinet. Calhoun later served in the US Senate from 1833 to 1844 and from 1845 to 1850. In between his times in the Senate, he became President John Tyler's secretary of state in 1844 and 1845 and was responsible for effecting the annexation of Texas.

> ❢ The states themselves ... have the right to enlarge or diminish, at pleasure, the powers of the government, and to amend, alter, or even abolish the Constitution, and, with it, the government itself. ❢
>
> **John C Calhoun**, *Reports and Public Letters of John C. Calhoun*, 1856

Camden, Battle of

The greatest British victory in the **American Revolution**, on 16 August 1780 near Camden, South Carolina. The Americans had sent an army to South Carolina to attack the British headquarters at Camden. Lord **Cornwallis** collected his troops and attacked. Though much inferior in strength, his force was of disciplined regulars, while the American force was largely composed of untrained militia, and the Americans were comprehensively defeated.

They lost over 1,000 killed and wounded and about the same number of prisoners were taken, as well as a large quantity of stores. At the time it seemed that the American cause was doomed.

Camp David Accords

Two framework accords agreed in 1978 and officially signed in March 1979 by Israeli prime minister Menachem Begin and Egyptian president Anwar Sadat at Camp David, Maryland, under the guidance of US president Jimmy **Carter**. They covered an Egypt–Israel peace treaty and phased withdrawal of Israel from Sinai, which was completed in 1982, and an overall Middle East settlement including the election by the West Bank and Gaza Strip Palestinians of a 'self-governing authority'. The latter issue has stalled repeatedly over questions of who should represent the Palestinians and what form the self-governing body should take.

Cape Canaveral

The promontory on the Atlantic coast of Florida used as the rocket launch site by **NASA**. It is 367 km/228 mi north of Miami and was established as a National Seashore in 1975. Cape Canaveral has been a rocket launching facility since 1947. Famous launches include the first American satellite, *Explorer I*, in 1958 and *Apollo 11,* which put the first men on the moon, in 1969. The Kennedy Space Center is nearby, and Cape Canaveral was known as Cape Kennedy from 1963 to 1973.

capital punishment

Capital punishment is retained in 38 US states, but it is a hotly contested issue. Most of those executed are black and poor. A 1995 Gallup poll indicated that 74% of US citizens support capital punishment. The **Supreme Court** declared it unconstitutional in 1972 (as a cruel and unusual punishment) but decided in 1976 that this was not so in all circumstances. The death penalty was therefore reintroduced in some states. In 1989 the

> The method of execution varies by states, and includes lethal injection, the gas chamber, the electric chair, hanging, and the firing squad.

Supreme Court decided that capital punishment could be imposed from the age of 16 for murder and that the mentally retarded could also face the death penalty. In the late 1990s there were over 3,000 prisoners on death row (awaiting execution).

Capone, Al(phonse) (1899–1947)

The best-known US gangster during the era of **Prohibition**. Nicknamed 'Scarface', Capone built a formidable criminal organization in Chicago. In 1927, his profits from bootlegging, gambling, vice, and the protection business were estimated at $165 million. He was brutal in his pursuit of dominance, killing seven members of a rival gang in the **St Valentine's Day Massacre** in 1929. Capone was imprisoned from 1931 to 1939 for income-tax evasion, the only charge that could be proved against him. He died relaxing in the sunshine of Palm Island, Florida.

> 6 Some call it bootlegging. Some call it racketeering. I call it business. 9
>
> **Al Capone** US gangster, newspaper interview, 1927

carpetbagger

An insulting name for any of the entrepreneurs and politicians from the North who moved to the Southern states during **Reconstruction** (1867–77) after the **Civil War**. They were called carpetbaggers because they were supposed to carry their ill-gotten gains in small satchels made of carpeting. They moved South to exploit the chaotic conditions for their own benefit. With the votes of newly enfranchised blacks and some local white people (called **scalawags**), they won posts in newly created Republican State governments and also elected newly freed slaves to high political positions.

Carson, Kit (Christopher) (1809–1868)

A US frontier settler, guide, and Indian agent, who fought in the **Mexican War** and later for the Union side in the **Civil War**, becoming a brigadier general. Carson City, Nevada, was named after him. Carson emigrated from Kentucky to Missouri as a hunter and trapper. His knowledge of Indian languages and habits made him a useful guide (at $100 a month) for John Fremont on his Rocky Mountains explorations from 1842 to 1845. Carson served under **Fremont** during the conquest of California in 1846 in 1847, and settled in New Mexico in 1853, becoming a US Indian agent.

- When Carson helped the Cheyenne Indians fight the **Crow**, they gratefully named him 'Little Chief'.

- His second wife, a Cheyenne, divorced him by placing his possessions outside their teepee, the traditional way of her people.

- Carson's fame came from dime novels, whose writers made up stories about his exploits.
- In 1849 Carson tried to rescue a pioneer woman, Mrs White, from Apaches. He found that they had just killed her with an arrow through the heart. In their camp was a dime novel about Carson killing hundreds of Indians.

Carter, Jimmy (James Earl) (1924–)

The 39th president of the USA from 1977 to 1981, a Democrat. Features of his presidency were the return of the Panama Canal Zone to Panama, the introduction of an amnesty programme for deserters and draft dodgers of the **Vietnam War**, and the **Camp David Accords** for peace in the Middle East. Carter was born in Plains, Georgia, and served in the navy as a physicist until 1953, when he took over the family peanut business. He entered politics in 1962 as a Georgia state senator, and in 1970 was elected governor. In 1976 he won a narrow victory over Gerald **Ford**. When the USSR invaded Afghanistan in 1979, Carter imposed a grain embargo on the Russians and boycotted the 1980 Olympic Games in Moscow. He was defeated by Ronald **Reagan** in 1980 after an economic downturn and his failure to halt the **Iran hostage crisis**. During the 1990s he emerged as a mediator and peace negotiator, being awarded the Presidential Medal of Freedom in 1999.

> ❻ We should live our lives as though Christ were coming this afternoon. ❾
>
> **Jimmy Carter**, speech to Bible class in Plains, Georgia, March 1976

Carver, George Washington (1860–1943)

A US agricultural chemist who devoted his life to improving the economy of the US South and the condition of black Americans. He taught people how to diversify crops, promoted peanut production, and was a pioneer in the field of plastics. At the Tuskegee Institute in Alabama, Carver demonstrated the need for crop rotation and how to use leguminous plants, especially the peanut. Born a slave in Missouri, he was kidnapped and raised by his former owner, Moses Carver. He graduated from Iowa Agricultural College, where he began teaching agriculture and bacterial botany. In 1897 he transferred to Tuskegee, becoming director of agriculture and of a research station.

- Carver developed 325 by-products from the peanut, including milk, cheese, face powder, printer's ink, shampoo, and dyes.
- He discovered 118 products which could be made from the sweet potato and 75 products from the pecan nut.
- He developing a plastic material from soybeans which Henry **Ford** later used in part of his automobile.
- Carver was well known for extracting dyes and paints from the clays of Alabama.

Casablanca Conference

A World War II meeting from 14 to 24 January 1943 of the US and British leaders Franklin D **Roosevelt** and Winston Churchill, at which the Allied demand for the unconditional surrender of Germany, Italy, and Japan was issued.

This demand only served to harden the resolve of the Axis powers and may have lengthened the war. Matters of general strategy were also covered, including agreements to:

- give priority to the Battle of the Atlantic
- continue the supply of aid to the USSR
- make joint preparations for an invasion of France from Britain (which led to the **D-Day** invasion)
- begin planning for an invasion of Sicily.

censorship

Censorship has been difficult to enforce in the USA because the **First Amendment** guarantees freedom of speech and of the press to everyone. Despite this, attempts at censorship are made by government agencies or groups. During the Gulf War in 1991, access to the theatre of war was controlled by the US military: only certain reporters were allowed in and their movements were restricted. Censorship is often tested in the US courts, especially with respect to sexually explicit material. **Supreme Court** rulings in 1973 and 1987 gave states the power to decide what is obscene. Recently, efforts have been made to suppress certain pieces of music and works of art, on such grounds as racial harassment and social depravity. Concerns over the ready availability of material such as bomb recipes and pornography led to the US Communications Decency Act of 1996, but it was overturned in 1997 by the Supreme Court.

> ❦ You can cage the singer but not the song. ❧
>
> **Harry Belafonte**, US singer and civil-rights activist, quoted in the *International Herald Tribune*, 3 October 1988

Central Intelligence Agency See *CIA*.

Chancellorsville, Battle of
A major Confederate victory during the **Civil War** on 4 May 1863 at Chancellorsville, Virginia. The forces of Gen Robert E **Lee** intercepted an intended attack by Brig-Gen Joseph **Hooker** on Richmond on 1 May and in three days had shattered the Union forces. Lee secured a remarkable victory, defeating a force three times the size of his own, but 'Stonewall' **Jackson**, perhaps his best general, was accidentally shot dead by one of his own men during the battle. The next day, Confederate major general Jeb Stuart's troops split Hooker's army in two. Hooker yielded and on 5 May withdrew across the Rapahannock River to safety.

> ❦ My God, my God, what will the country say? ❧
>
> **President Abraham Lincoln**, after hearing the news of his army's defeat at Chancellorsville, 4 May 1863

Charleston, Battle of
The name of a victorious British attack and siege of Charleston, South Carolina, during the **American Revolution** from 1 February to 12 May 1780. It was the largest American surrender of the war. The 8,000 troops of Gen Sir Henry Clinton lost only 255 men as they captured Fort Moultrie and its 5,400 American

Americans called the Charleston defeat **'Saratoga** in reverse', because it hurt their cause as much as their victory at Saratoga had devastated the British.

defenders under Maj-Gen Benjamin Lincoln. Other prizes included four ships and a fully stocked arsenal. The Charleston attack heralded the new British strategy of turning the war to the South, hoping to receive support from loyalists there.

Charleston, Siege of

The long Siege of Charleston, South Carolina, beginning in 7 April 1863 during the **Civil War**. This was two years after Charleston had fired the first shots of the war at **Fort Sumter,** and Union forces were determined to punish the city. The Northern forces besieged and bombarded the city for nearly two years. A Union land attack from 5 to 7 July 1864 was successfully repulsed. The city was not taken until 19 February 1865 (seven weeks before the war's end), and the American flag was again raised over Sumter on 14 April, four years to the day it had been taken down.

Chautauqua Movement

A US adult education movement of the late 19th and early 20th centuries. John H Vincent, a Methodist minister, and Lewis Miller began it in the summer of 1874 at Fair Point, New York, on the shores of Lake Chautauqua. The participants lived in cabins and tents, often fishing in the daytime and in the evenings attending opera or concerts under a wooden amphitheatre or gathering around campfires to discuss culture. Chautauquas based on this original idea soon appeared throughout the USA until there were about 60,000 people attending their centres. The movement declined by the 1930s, overtaken by the popularity of radio and the cinema.

> ❝ We may divide the whole struggle of the human race into two chapters. First the fight to get leisure, and then the second fight of civilization: what shall we do with our leisure when we get it. ❞
>
> **US president James A Garfield**, speaking at Lake Chautauqua, summer, 1880

Chavez, Cesar Estrada (1927–1993)

A US labour organizer who almost single-handedly founded the National Farm Workers Association in 1962. With the support of the **AFL-CIO** and other major unions, Chavez embarked on a successful campaign to unionize California grape workers. This later became the AFL-CIO's United Farm Workers of America under Chavez's leadership. He led strikes and boycotts of citrus fruits, lettuce, and grapes in the early 1970s, and these efforts led to better pay and conditions for the migrant farm labourers, although their exploitation later continued.

- Cesar Chavez was especially influenced by the autobiography of Mahatma Ghandi.

- Chavez's influence led to California enacting an Agricultural Labor Relations Act in 1975 that permitted farm workers to organize collectively.

- The main opposition to Chavez's union came not from growers but from the Teamsters Union, which competed with it.

Cherokee
A member of the largest group of **American Indian** people, numbering 308,000 (1990) and now living on a reservation in North Carolina and in Oklahoma. They originally lived around the Great Lakes, but were driven by the Delaware and Iroquois into the southern Appalachian Mountains. The Cherokee were one of the **Five Civilized Tribes** and had adopted the white man's methods of farming. They had a written constitution modelled on that of the USA and a written language invented in 1821 by their scholarly leader **Sequoyah**. The Cherokee sided with Britain in the **American Revolution**, but after 1800 relations with the US government were peaceful. However, when gold was discovered on Cherokee land in Georgia in the early 1830s, settlers called for their removal. In the winter of 1838–39 over 15,000 Cherokee were forced to march more than 1,000 miles to Indian Territory (Oklahoma) in what became known as the 'Trail of Tears'.

Cheyenne
A member of an **American Indian** people who number about 11,500 (1990). One of the most warlike of the Plains Indians, the Cheyenne joined with the **Sioux** in the Battle of **Little Bighorn** in 1876. The Cheyenne were originally farmers and hunter-gatherers living in Minnesota, but after about 1700 they moved westward into North Dakota where they acquired horses and guns and became increasingly dependent on buffalo. Towards the end of the 18th century, smallpox and wars with the Chippewa and Sioux decimated the tribe. They now live on reservations, established in 1878, in

Montana, Oklahoma, and South Dakota. Their language belongs to the Algonquian linguistic family. Like other Plains Indians, they believed in the vision quest to acquire a guardian spirit, and their main ceremony was the snake dance.

Chicago Great Fire
A devastating fire that burned down most of Chicago on 8 and 9 October 1871. It killed 250 people and left 98,500 homeless as it destroyed 17,450 buildings and 2,124 acres of the city. The fire followed a year-long drought, and people said it began when Mrs O'Leary was milking a cow in her barn on De Koven Street, and it kicked over a kerosene (paraffin) lamp. (Mrs O'Leary later testified she was in bed at the time.) The wind in the 'Windy City' immediately expanded the destructive flames. The estimated damage was nearly $200 million, but Chicago soon rose again, inventing the skyscraper for a more impressive skyline.

Chickamauga, Battle of
A Confederate victory in the **Civil War** on 20 September 1863 at Chickamauga Creek in northern Georgia. Union major general William Rosecrans had driven the Confederates under Gen Braxton Bragg out of middle Tennessee, forcing them to abandon Chattanooga and withdraw into Georgia, where Bragg regrouped his army. Rosecrans mistakenly thought the Confederates were in a disorganized retreat and advanced. He soon discovered his error and hurriedly prepared a defensive position behind Chickamauga Creek. The Confederates attacked the Union flanks on 19 September, and on the following day part of the Union army was routed, but Maj-Gen George Thomas's troops put up a firm defence for six hours before retiring in good order to Chattanooga. Thomas was thereafter known as the 'Rock of Chickamauga'.

* President Lincoln said his defeated Maj-Gen Rosencrans was 'confused and stunned, like a duck hit on the head'.

* Johnny Clem, a 12-year-old Union drummer, survived the battle and was thereafter called 'the drummer boy of Chickamauga'.

* The Union hero of Chickamauga, Maj-Gen Thomas, had virtually panicked earlier in the battle, causing a gap to open in the Union lines.

Chisolm Trail
A route used in the late 19th century to drive cattle from south Texas past Dallas to Abilene, Kansas, for the eastern markets. The first 35,000 Texas

longhorns arrived on 5 September 1867. The 1,609-kilometre/1,000-mile trail, called 'the long drive', was suggested by an Abilene businessman, Joseph M McCoy, and named after the scout, Jesse Chisholm. About 2 million cattle made the drive before the trail fell into disuse in 1881. Farmers had begun to fence in their lands, and the new railway offered an easier means of transport.

'THE OLD CHISHOLM TRAIL'
Well, come along, boys, and listen to my tale;
I'll tell you of my troubles on the Old Chisholm Trail.
  Coma ti yi yippy, yippy yay, yippy yay,
  Coma ti yi yippy, yippy yay.
I woke up one morning on the Old Chisholm Trail,
Rope in my hand and a cow by the tail.
  Coma ti yi yippy, yippy yay, yippy yay,
  Coma ti yi yippy, yippy yay.

Christian Science
A sect established in the USA by Mary Baker Eddy in 1879 and formally titled the Church of Christ, Scientist. Christian Scientists believe that since God is good and is a spirit, matter and evil are not ultimately real. Consequently they refuse all medical treatment. There is no ordained priesthood, but a body of public practitioners of Christian Science healing who are officially authorized. Their headquarters is in Boston, Massachusetts, with branches in most parts of the world. The textbook of Christian Science is Eddy's *Science and Health with Key to the Scriptures* (1875). The church publishes a respected daily newspaper, the *Christian Science Monitor*, which is known for its outstanding coverage of international news.

church and state
The **First Amendment** of the **Constitution** assures that church and state are officially separated in the USA, but religion often seems closer to the US government than in European countries having state religions. Congress traditionally opens its sessions with prayers and the US National Motto is 'In God We Trust', appearing on all coins and paper money. Yet, there is a continuous controversy about the importance of religion in public life. Many Americans were shocked when the **Supreme Court** ruled in 1962 that

schools could not force students to say prayers. Recent individual cases include an Alabama judge who refused an order to remove the Ten Commandments from his courtroom and Texas high schools that refused in 1999 to drop the traditional prayer before football games.

CIA
The abbreviation and common name of the Central Intelligence Agency, the US spy organization established in 1947. It has actively intervened overseas, generally to undermine left-wing regimes or to protect US financial interests, for example, in the Democratic Republic of Congo (formerly Zaire) and Nicaragua. From 1980 all covert activity by the CIA had by law to be reported to **Congress**, preferably beforehand, and to be authorized by the president. George Tenate became director in 1997 and that year released the government's budget for spying for the first time in its history, announcing that the US government spends $26.6 billion annually on national intelligence.

- The CIA was set up by Congress as part of the National Security Act, on the lines of the British Secret Service.
- The CIA was involved in the restoration of the Shah of Iran in 1953, the coup against Chile's president Salvador Allende, and the Bay of Pigs.
- CIA headquarters is in Langley, Virginia.
- Past directors include William Casey, Richard Helms, and George Bush.

civil rights movement
The general term for efforts by black Americans to affirm their constitutional rights and improve their status in society after **World War II**. The sustained campaign especially challenged racial discrimination and segregation in the 1950s and 1960s. Tactics included boycotts, 'sit-ins' at shops refusing to serve blacks, and **freedom rides** into the South. One of its highlights was the 1963 civil rights march to **Washington, DC**, led by Martin Luther King. The movement led to favourable legislation, such as the Civil Rights Act of 1957 that created the Civil Rights Commission, the Civil Rights Act of 1964 and the Voting Rights Act of 1965. Other results were **busing** and **affirmative action.**

Civil War
The war from 1861 to 1865 between the **Confederate States of America** in the South and Union states in the North. The Confederacy, led by President

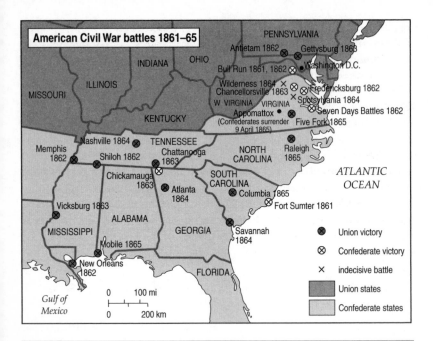

American Civil War battles 1861–65

⊗ (filled)	Union victory
⊗ (outline)	Confederate victory
×	indecisive battle
■ (dark)	Union states
■ (light)	Confederate states

MAJOR BATTLES OF THE CIVIL WAR

- 21 July 1861: Confederate victory at Bull Run
- 6 and 7 April 1862: Union victory at Shiloh
- 29 and 30 August 1862: Confederate victory at Bull Run
- 17 September 1862: Union victory at Antietam
- 13 December 1862: Confederate victory at Fredericksburg
- 1 to 4 May 1863: Confederate victory at Chancellorsville
- 1 to 3 July 1863: Union victory at Gettysburg
- 19 and 20 September 1863: Confederate victory at Chickamauga
- 23 to 25 November 1863: Union victory at Chattanooga
- 15 and 16 December 1864: Union victory at Nashville
- 1 April 1865: Union victory at Five Forks

Jefferson **Davis,** wished to maintain states' rights and slavery, while the North, under President Abraham **Lincoln,** fought mainly to preserve the Union. The industrial North had great advantages, with a population four times larger then the South. The war began on 12 April 1861 when Southern forces bombarded **Fort Sumter** off Charleston, South Carolina. The first battle came on 21 July 1861 at **Bull Run**, with the Union forces routed. Other Rebel victories followed, but the Confederate army of Gen Robert E **Lee** was defeated on 3 July 1863 in the vital battle at **Gettyburg.** Lee eventually surrendered to Gen Ulysses S **Grant** at **Appomattox Court House** on 9 April 1865. The Union was preserved and slavery abolished. The conflict had cost over 620,000 lives, more than any American war ever.

Clay, Henry (1777–1852)

A US politician known as 'the Great Compromiser' because he tried to hold the Union together on the question of slavery. His efforts included the **Missouri Compromise** of 1820 and the **Compromise of 1850.** Born in Virginia, Clay stood unsuccessfully three times for the presidency: as a Democratic Republican 1824, as a National Republican 1832, and as a Whig 1844. He supported the **War of 1812** and in 1814 represented the USA in peace negotiations with Britain to end it. A powerful orator, he was elected to the US Senate in 1806, 1831, and 1849, and to the House of Representatives from 1811–21 and from 1823–25 where he served as its speaker. He was secretary of state from 1825–29 and devised a controversial 'American system' for the national economy.

> ❛I had rather be right than be President. ❜
>
> **Henry Clay**, remark to Senator Preston of South Carolina, 1839

Clinton, Bill (William Jefferson) (1946–)

The 42nd president of the USA from 1993, a Democrat. Born in Hope, Arkansas, he graduated from Georgetown University in 1968, won a Rhodes scholarship to Oxford University from 1968 to 1970, and graduated from Yale University Law School in 1973

He served as governor of Arkansas from 1979–81 and from 1983–93, establishing a liberal and progressive reputation. As president he implemented a 'New Democrat' programme, combining social reform with economic conservatism, to bring the country out of recession. He introduced legislation to reduce the federal deficit and cut crime, and he successfully repositioned himself on the centre-right to become, in November 1996, the first Democrat since Franklin D **Roosevelt** to be elected for a second term. His foreign policy successes have included the **North American Free Trade Agreement** (NAFTA), the Israeli–PLO accord on the West Bank, the **Dayton peace accord** for Bosnia and Herzegovina, and the Northern Ireland cease-fire. Following accusations of perjury and obstruction of justice, concerning mainly his improper relationship with a White House intern, Monica Lewinsky, Clinton underwent an impeachment trial (the second in US history) in early 1999 and was acquitted.

> ❝ There is nothing wrong with America that cannot be cured by what is right with America. ❞
>
> **Bill Clinton**, inaugural speech as US president, 1993

Cochise (*c.* 1815–1874)
An **American Indian** leader who campaigned relentlessly against white settlement of his territory. Cochise, born in Arizona, gained a large number of followers in his long and bitter dispute with the US government and conducted repeated raids on American posts. Unjustly arrested by US authorities in 1850, he escaped from custody and took American hostages, whom he later executed. A Chiricahua **Apache**, Cochise joined forces with the Mimbrëno Apache and successfully fought off a large force of California settlers in 1862. Finally apprehended by Maj-Gen George Crook in 1871, he made peace with the US government the following year and settled on a reservation.

Cody, William Frederick (1846–1917)
A US scout and performer who was popularly known as 'Buffalo Bill'. From 1883 he toured the USA and Europe with a **Wild West** show that featured the re-creation of Indian attacks and, for a time, the cast included Chief **Sitting Bull** as well as Annie **Oakley**. Cody's nickname derives from a time when he had a contract to supply buffalo carcasses to railway labourers (over 4,000 in 18 months). Born in Scott County, Iowa, in the 1860s he was one of the chief riders for the **Pony Express** and during the **Civil War** was

In 1893, William Cody and members of his Wild West show went to Thomas Edison's new motion-picture studio to make Bucking Bronco, a 30-minute film that was shown in US 'Kinetoscope parlors'.

a scout for Union troops operating in the Midwest. He was a heavy drinker and died in poverty after seeing his exploits recounted and exaggerated in novels of the West.

Coercive Acts See *Intolerable Acts*.

Cold War

The tensions lasting from 1945 to 1989 between the USA and Western Europe on the one hand and the USSR and Eastern Europe on the other. The term 'Cold War' was first used by Bernard Baruch, advisor to US president Harry **Truman**, in a speech made in April 1947. The Cold War was fuelled by propaganda, undercover activity by intelligence agencies, and economic sanctions. Arms-reduction

Cody *'Buffalo Bill' (William Frederick) Cody is shown shooting an American Indian with a revolver.*

agreements between the USA and USSR in the late 1980s, and a reduction of Soviet influence in Eastern Europe eased the Cold War. It was formally declared over in December 1989 at a summit meeting in Malta attended by Soviet president Gorbachev and US president George Bush.

Columbus, Christopher (1451–1506)

Italian navigator and explorer who has been credited as the first person to visit America. His Spanish name is Cristóbal Colón. Born in Genoa, Columbus went to sea at an early age, and settled in Portugal in 1478. Believing that Asia could be reached by sailing westwards, he eventually won the support of King Ferdinand and Queen Isabella of Spain and set off on his first voyage from Palos on 3 August 1492 with three small ships, the *Niña*, the *Pinta*, and his flagship, the *Santa Maria*. Land was sighted on 12 October, probably Watling Island (now San Salvador Island), and within a few weeks he reached Cuba and Haiti, returning to Spain in March 1493. His other three voyages to the New World were:

- 1493–96 to Guadaloupe, Montserrat, Antigua, Puerto Rico, and Jamaica
- 1498 to Trinidad and the mainland of South America
- 1502–04 to Honduras and Nicaragua.

Columbus died in poverty and is buried in Seville Cathedral. The US cele-brates Columbus Day as a holiday on the second Monday in October.

Comanche

A member of an **American Indian** people largely responsible for introduc-ing horses to the Plains Indians. They number about 13,300 (1990) and mostly now live in western Oklahoma. Their language belongs to the Uto-Aztecan language family. Originally, the Comanche were hunter-gatherers living in the Rocky Mountains of Wyoming. In the 1700s they were pushed south by the **Cheyenne** and **Sioux** into Kansas, Oklahoma, and Texas. In the early 1800s, hostilities developed with white settlers moving into Comanche territory. In 1864 Kit **Carson** led US forces in an unsuccessful campaign against the Comanche. A year later they signed a treaty with the US government granting them much of western Oklahoma. Further hostili-ties ensued when whites continued to move onto their land, and it was not until the 1880s that the last Commanche bands settled on reservations.

Committees of Correspondence

Local town groups that helped unify the colonial struggle of independence before and during the **American Revolution**. They had been established in 1772 to correspond with British colonial agents but quickly developed, under the direction of Samual **Adams**, into a communication network to support independence. Paul Revere was the official courier for the Boston Committee of Correspondence. Before Benedict **Arnold** and Ethan **Allen** led troops to seize Fort Ticonderoga in 1775, the Committee of Correspondence of Hartford, Connecticut, took £300 from the colony's treasury to fund the attack.

communism

An ideology that seemed to present an idealistic vision to some Americans immediately after the Russian Revolution. The Workers Party of America was established in 1921 and changed its name in 1929 to the Communist Party of the United States. Those who joined or supported it suffered greatly in the **Cold War**, especially during the 'communist witch hunts' of Senator Joseph **McCarthy** and the **House Committee on Un-American Activities**. Restrictions on communists were also added by Congress in 1954, and some party leaders were imprisoned. The party began normal operations again in 1966 but has had little influence to date.

Compromise of 1850

A legislative attempt by **Congress** to resolve the conflict between North and South over the admission of California to the Union in 1850. The compromise was the result of a series of resolutions sponsored by Senator Henry **Clay**. The sticking point was the issue of slavery. In order to admit California without slavery, concessions had to be made to the slavery states. The Compromise of 1850 agreed that:

- California should be admitted as a state under a constitution that prohibited slavery

- New Mexico and Utah should be organized as territories without any regulation about slavery, leaving it to the settlers whether there should be slaves or not

- the slave trade should be excluded from the District of Columbia, but be interfered with nowhere else by federal law

- the whole judicial and administrative machinery of the federal government should be put at the disposal of the Southern slave-owners to help recover fugitive slaves found in the free states.

The Senate debate on the compromise lasted nine months, and its acceptance temporarily revitalized the Union.

Concord, Battle of

The first major engagement of the **American Revolution**, on 19 April 1775 at Concord, Massachusetts. It followed the smaller engagement of **Lexington** earlier in the day to attempt to halt British soldiers from marching on Concord to destroy military stores. With the approach of the 700 British under Lt-Col Francis Smith, the colonial militia retreated, hiding their stores in village homes. When they saw smoke from wooden gun carriages the British had set light, the Americans led by Maj John Buttrick returned to confront the enemy, inflicting 14 casualties and routing them. The British retreated to Boston, enduring sniper fire from farmers along the way. The Concord victory greatly raised American morale. The two battles that day cost the British 73 killed and 174 wounded; the Americans had 49 killed and 41 wounded.

Confederate States of America (CSA)

The union of 11 Southern states, commonly called the Confederacy, that seceded in 1860 and 1861 from the United States, initiating the Civil War.

The states, in their order of secession, were South Carolina, Florida, Alabama, Georgia, Mississippi, Louisiana, Texas, Arkansas, Virginia, Tennessee, and North Carolina. They all allowed slavery, which influenced their decision to leave the Union. The Confederate constitution was based on the US **Constitution**. The only Confederate president was Jefferson **Davis**, and the capital was first established at Montgomery, Alabama, on 4 February 1861 and then moved on 29 May that year to Richmond, Virginia. When the war was lost in 1865, the Confederacy ended.

> ❝ But most impartial people, at least in New York, are of opinion that the South has shaken the dust off her feet, and will never enter the portals of the Union again. She is confident in her own destiny. She feels strong enough to stand alone. ❞
>
> **William Howard Russell**, correspondent, *The Times* of London, 16 April 1881

Congress

The national legislature of the USA, which has two chambers. The upper house, the Senate, has 100 senators, two for each state, elected for six years, with one-third elected every two years. The lower house, the House of Representatives, has 435 members, apportioned to the states of the Union on the basis of population, and elected for two-year terms. Both senators and representatives are elected by direct popular vote. Congress meets in **Washington, DC**, in the Capitol Building. An act of Congress is a bill passed by both houses. Congress convenes each year on 3 January for two sessions, normally ending its year in the autumn. The Congress of the United States met for the first time on 4 March 1789. It was preceded by the Congress of the Confederation representing the several states under the Articles of Confederation from 1781 to 1789.

Congressional Medal of Honour See *Medal of Honour.*

Connecticut Compromise

The compromise reached during the Constitutional Convention of 1787 that ended a deadlock blocking approval of the **Constitution of the United**

States. The Virginia Plan had proposed that the number of a state's representatives to both houses of **Congress** should be based on its population. Smaller states opposed this, arguing that the more populated states could control Congress. The compromise was suggested on 16 July by a Connecticut delegate, Roger Sherman, and is still in effect: each state has an equal number of representatives (two) in the Senate and a number proportional to its population in the House of Representatives. (In 1999, for example, California had 52 representatives and Idaho had 2.)

conservation

The USA was a leader in recognizing the need to conserve nature. The idea of national parks began in the USA with Yellowstone National Park, established in 1878. **Congress** passed the Forest Reserve Act in 1891, and the nation's first conservationist president was Theodore **Roosevelt** whose administration passed the Newlands Reclamation Act of 1902. The world's first private conservation group also began in the USA with the Sierra Club in 1892. Recent successes in the conservation of endangered wildlife include the bison, alligator, and peregrine falcon. The USA now has 54 national parks and has also set aside national preserves, seashores, lakeshores, reserves, and rivers. The National Park Service administers more than 33 million hectares/83 million acres of federal land.

> ❝ The man who would so handle his forest as to cause erosion and to injure stream flow must be not only educated but he must be controlled. ❞
>
> **Theodore Roosevelt**, special message to Congress, 22 January 1909

Constitution of the United States

The document that defines the organization and power of the US government, the powers and rights of the individual states, and the rights of the people. The US **Supreme Court** can invalidate a new law passed by **Congress** by deciding it is 'unconstitutional'. The document, with seven articles, was drafted in 1787 at the Constitutional Convention in Philadelphia, mainly written by James **Madison**, who was called 'the Father of the Constitution'. It was ratified by the states in 1789 and has been amended 27 times.

> ❧ The Constitution of the United States was made
> not merely for the generation that then existed, but
> for posterity - unlimited, undefined, endless,
> perpetual posterity. ❧
>
> **Henry Clay**, US senator, speech to the Senate, 1850

containment

The US policy adopted in 1947 that was designed to prevent the spread of **communism**. It was first stated in July that year by George F. Kennan, then a state department official, and later the US ambassador to Moscow. In an anonymous article in *Foreign Affairs*, he wrote that the US policy towards the USSR should be 'a long-term, patient but firm and vigilant containment of Russian expansive tendencies....' This policy evolved into the Truman Doctrine that included economic and technical aid to countries threatened by communism.

Continental Congress

The federal legislature of the original 13 colonies (states after 1776), acting as a provisional government before and during the **American Revolution**, from 1774 to 1789. It was responsible for drawing up the **Declaration of Independence** in 1776 and the **Articles of Confederation** in 1777. The First Continental Congress was convened in Philadelphia on 5 September 1774 to force 'the British Parliament to come to proper terms'. It ended on 26 October 1774, and the Second Continental Congress was convened on 10 May 1775 after the first battles of the war. It appointed George **Washington** as commander in chief of the army, maintained the military forces throughout the war, and was in charge of foreign policy. The Continental Congress was replaced by the US Congress in 1789.

Copperhead

A term of abuse applied by people of the Northern states during the **Civil War** to Northern Democrats who opposed the Union government's war policy. Copperheads preferred the name of 'Peace Democrats'. Many supported peace through negotiation because they did not believe it possible to conquer the Confederacy or because they were Southern sympathizers. Copperheads managed to have a peace plank inserted in the

Democratic Party platform in the election of 1864, but their candidate, the former US major general George McClellan, refused to support it. The term implies a comparison with the poisonous copperhead snake.

The US congressman Clement Vallandigham was a Copperhead who even encouraged Union soldiers to desert. He was arrested for treason in 1863 and banished to the South. After the war, he practised law in Ohio, but died when he shot himself in court while demonstrating a gun in a murder case.

Coral Sea, Battle of the
A World War II battle in the Pacific Ocean from 4 to 8 May 1942 in which the US Navy checked the Japanese advance towards New Guinea. The entire battle was fought with planes launched from aircraft carriers on both sides. The US sustained the most casualties but achieved its goal of stopping the Japanese.

The Battle of the Coral Sea was the first sea battle ever fought in which each navy never saw the other's ships.

Cornwallis, Charles, 1st Marquis and 2nd Earl (1738–1805)
A British general in the **American Revolution** until 1781, when his **Yorktown surrender** ended the war. He had earlier won victories over Gen Horatio **Gates** at Camden, South Carolina, in 1780, and Gen Nathanael Greene at Guilford near Greensboro, North Carolina, in 1781. After the war, Cornwallis served twice as governor-general of India and once as viceroy of Ireland. He succeeded to the earldom in 1762, and was made a marquis in 1792.

Coronado, Francisco Vásquez de (c. 1510–1554)
The Spanish explorer who sailed to the New World in 1535 in search of gold. In 1540 he set out with several hundred men from the Gulf of California on an exploration of what are today the Southwestern states. Although he failed to discover any gold, his expedition came across the impressive Grand Canyon and introduced the use of the horse to the indigenous Indians.

consumerism
The protection of the consumer began in the USA mainly in the late 20th century. More than 1,000 national, state, and local bodies now exist to

benefit the consumer. The US Food and Drug Administration was established in 1940, the US Office of Consumer Affairs in 1971, and the Consumer Product Safety Commission in 1972. Private organizations also conduct research and campaigns, such as Ralph Nadar's Public Citizen Foundation established in 1980.

counterculture
The US youth movement beginning in the 1960s that questioned and defied the Establishment. Members of the counterculture protested against the **Vietnam War** and challenged the authority of corporations, universities, churches, and the police, among others. The movement created several positive ideas that still exist, such as the concern for the environment, ecology, and organic foods, but the counterculture was hurt by its association with the hippy culture that supported noncommitment, drugs, and free love.

> 6 Turn on, tune in, drop out 9

Dr Timothy Leary, psychologist and advocate of drugs, lecture, 1967

cowboy
One of the men in the Western states who herded and watched over cattle. He is also called a 'cowpuncher'. Cowboys were most numerous after the **Civil War** for about two decades when they drove herds east on long trails. Americans admire their image of independence, honesty, and justice portrayed through books and films. The real cowboy, however, was different from Hollywood's hero version. He normally worked long days for poor pay, wore rugged clothes, slept in a dirty bunkhouse or under the sky, and was seldom involved in romance, saloon gambling, or honourable gun battles. Today's cowboy often rides in a Jeep rather than on a horse. **See also:** *Chisholm Trail*.

> 6 Yet what other job lets a man ride alone under the wide sky or gives a sense of freedom, however illusory, like that which belongs to the cowboy? 9

Louis L'Amour, US author of Westerns, introduction to Martin Schreiber's *Last of a Breed* (1982)

Cowpens, Battle of

An American victory during the **American Revolution** on 17 January 1781 near Cowpens, South Carolina. A colonial army of about 1,000 men led by Gen Daniel Morgan defeated an equal number of British troops under Col Banastre Tarleton. The British forced the battle and when the Americans seemed to withdraw, the Redcoats charged and found themselves surrounded and attacked by bayonets. They surrendered, suffering 100 killed and 700 captured. Total American casualties numbered 72.

Crazy Horse (*c.* 1849–1877)

An **American Indian** leader who led his Ogala **Sioux** warriors to victory at the Battle of **Little Bighorn** on 25 June 1876. Crazy Horse, whose Sioux name was Ta-Sunko-Witko, had begun battling settlers in 1865 when a road was built into the goldfields of Montana. In June 1998, the mountain sculpture of Crazy Horse, by Korczak Zilolkowski, was unveiled – 50 years after it was begun.

Creek

A member of an **American Indian** people numbering about 44,000 (1990). They were Mound Builders and lived in large towns in Georgia and Alabama, but are now found mainly in Oklahoma. In the early 1700s they attacked Spanish settlements in a series of raids and organized a Creek Confederacy. During the **War of 1812** they allied themselves with the British and on 30 August 1813 massacred over 500 settlers at Fort Mims north of Mobile, Alabama, beginning the Creek War. In retaliation, Maj-Gen Andrew **Jackson** and 5,000 militia, including Davy **Crockett**, wiped out several Creek villages and on 27 March 1814 killed over 800 Creek warriors at the Battle of Horseshoe Bend. In the 1830s they were forcibly relocated to a reservation in Indian Territory, where they became one of the **Five Civilized Tribes**.

- The Creek men tattooed their entire bodies, beginning when a boy became a warrior.

- They were agriculturalists growing maize, beans, and squash, supplementing their diet with fish and meat.

- They lived in mud houses around a community square in which a dome-shaped temple set upon a mound was located.

Crockett, Davy (David) (1786–1836)

A Tennessee frontiersman and politician who became a US folk hero. He served under Andrew **Jackson** in the war with the **Creek** Indians in 1813 and 1814, then entered politics, serving on the state legislature from 1821 to 1824. He was a Democratic Congressman from 1827–31 and from 1833–35. A series of books, which he may have co-authored, made him into a mythical hero of the frontier, but their Whig associations cost him his office. He clashed with Jackson, whom he claimed had betrayed his frontier constituency, and left for Texas in bitterness. He died in the Battle of the **Alamo** during the Texas rebellion.

❝ We shot them like dogs. ❞

Davy Crockett, after a massacre of Creeks at Tallushatchee, Alabama, in which all 186 Creek men were killed, November 1813

Crow

A member of an **American Indian** people living in Montana and numbering about 8,600 (1990), one of the Plains Indian groups. Their language belongs to the Siouan family. The Crow originally lived around the Yellowstone River and its tributaries but in the early 18th century moved westward. They lived primarily by hunting buffalo, which provided them with food, clothing, teepee covers, and most material needs. They suffered losses from smallpox and cholera in the first half of the 19th century and also at the hands of the **Blackfoot** and **Sioux**. During the **Indian Wars** of the 1860s and 1870s they allied themselves with the US government. In 1868 they accepted a reservation in southern Montana. Today about half the Crow raise cattle, while a large percentage live largely by leasing their land.

CSA See *Confederate States of America*.

Cuban missile crisis

A dangerous confrontation in 1962 when Soviet rockets were installed in Cuba. US president John F **Kennedy** then compelled Soviet leader Nikita Khrushchev, by military threats and negotiation, to remove them. Following reports that the USSR was constructing launching sites for nuclear missiles in Cuba, the USA imposed a naval 'quarantine' around the island on 22 October 1962, and the two superpowers came closer to possible nuclear war than at any other time. Soviet inferiority in nuclear weapons forced a humiliating Russian capitulation on 2 November, when Kennedy announced that Soviet missile bases in Cuba were being dismantled.

> 6 I have directed the armed forces to prepare for any eventuality. 9
>
> **John F Kennedy**, television address to the nation during the Cuban missile crisis, 22 October 1962

Cumberland Gap

A pass cut by the Cumberland River through the Cumberland Mountains range of the Appalachian Mountains. It is at an altitude of 518 m/1,700 ft between southwest Virginia and southeast Kentucky, including part of northeast Tennessee. This route was followed by the pioneer Daniel **Boone**, who drove his Wilderness Trail through the mountains into Kentucky, paving the way for the early settlers migrating to the west. Its position gave it strategic importance during the time of the **Civil War**, when it was held alternately by the Confederates and the Union forces. The area has been a National Historical Park since 1940.

Custer, George Armstrong (1839–1876)

A US **Civil War** general and Indian fighter who is most famous for his death. Custer became the Union's youngest brigadier general in 1863 as a result of a brilliant war record. He was made a major general in 1865, but following the end of the Civil War, his rank was reduced to captain. He took part in an expedition against the **Cheyenne** in 1867 and 1868, and defeated several other American Indian groups in the West. He campaigned against the **Sioux** from 1874, and was killed with all of his troops on 25 June 1876 in Montana by the forces of Sioux chief **Sitting Bull** in the Battle of **Little Bighorn**, also known as 'Custer's last stand'.

Custer's last stand See *Little Bighorn, Battle of.*

D

Dakota See *Sioux.*

Davis, Jefferson (1808–89)
The only president of the **Confederate States of America**. Born in Kentucky, he was a US senator from Mississippi from 1847 and 1851 and 1857 to 1861, and was known for his defence of **states' rights** and slavery. He fought in the **Mexican War** and in 1853 became the US secretary of war. Davis hoped to lead Mississippi forces during the **Civil War** and was dismayed to be selected as the Confederacy's president. He was a popular leader but lost some support when his government began conscription and taxation. When the Confederate capital of Richmond fell at the end of the war, Davis and his cabinet fled south, but he was captured in Georgia and imprisoned for two years. He then retired to Mississippi.

> ‘The man and the hour have met!’
>
> **William Yancey**, Alabama secessionist, introducing the newly elected Jefferson Davis to the crowd in Montgomery, Alabama, 16 February 1861

Dayton peace accord
The peace agreement initiated on 21 November 1995 outside Dayton, Ohio, by leaders of Bosnia, Croatia, and Serbia. The opposing sides were brought together by President Bill **Clinton**. The agreement was signed on 14 December of that year in Paris, France, and the accord was then policed by about 60,000 NATO troops, including about 20,000 US soldiers.

D-Day
The day of 6 June 1944 during **World War II** when the Allies invaded Normandy, France, under the command of Gen Dwight D Eisenhower. This began Operation Overlord, the liberation of Western Europe from German occupation. The Anglo–US invasion fleet landed on the Normandy beaches

on the stretch of coast between the Orne River and St Marcouf. Five beaches – Utah, Omaha, Gold, Juno, and Sword – were selected. The landings commenced at 0630 hrs, and by midnight 57,000 US and 75,000 British and Canadian troops and their equipment were ashore and the captured beachheads were being linked into a continuous front. Although the operation was a success, casualties were heavy: Allied losses during the day amounted to 2,500 killed and about 8,500 wounded. After overcoming fierce resistance, the Allies broke through the German defences. Paris was liberated on 25 August, and Brussels on 2 September.

- The operation was preceded by a month-long bombing campaign to disrupt communications and prevent reinforcements from arriving. This was accompanied by airborne landings to destroy vital bridges and gun positions.

- The German response was hampered by a rigid command structure that required a personal directive from Hitler before any significant move could be made, and by the belief that the landing was a feint – a mock attack designed to foil the enemy.

- Allied air forces flew 14,000 sorties in support of the operation and lost 127 aircraft.

- D-day has become military jargon for any day on which a crucial operation is planned.

Decatur, Stephen (1779–1820)

A US naval hero who distinguished himself in the war with the Barbary pirates at Tripoli (1801–05) when he boarded and burned the *Philadelphia*, a US frigate captured by the enemy. During the **War of 1812**, he commanded three vessels and captured the British frigate *Macedonian*. In January 1815, unaware that the war was over, he battled with four British ships, taking one but surrendering to the three pursuers. Decatur was killed in a duel with Commodore James Barron, whose return to duty he had opposed.

> 6 Our country! In her intercourse with foreign nations, may she always be in the right; but our country, right or wrong. 9
>
> **Stephen Decatur**, offering a toast, April 1816

Declaration of Independence

The historic US document stating the theory of government on which the USA was founded. The statement was issued by the **Continental Congress** on 4 July 1776, renouncing all allegiance to the British crown and ending the political connection with Britain. Following a resolution moved 7 June, by Richard Henry Lee, 'that these United Colonies are, and of right ought to be, free and independent States', a committee including Thomas **Jefferson** and Benjamin **Franklin** was set up to draft a declaration, Jefferson being the main author. The Declaration was adopted by the representatives of 12 colonies on 4 July; the date that has ever since been celebrated as **Independence Day**.

> ❛ We hold these Truths to be self-evident, that all Men are created equal, that they are endowed by their Creator with certain unalienable Rights, that among these are Life, Liberty, and the Pursuit of Happiness. ❜
>
> **Declaration of Independence**, 4 July 1776

Democratic Party

One of the two main political parties of the USA. It tends to be the party of the working person, as opposed to the Republicans, the party of big business. Briefly called the Republican Party, and then named the **Democratic Republican Party**, it was founded by Thomas **Jefferson** in 1792 to defend the rights of the individual states against the centralizing policy of the **Federalist Party**. In the 20th century, under the presidencies of Grover Cleveland, Woodrow **Wilson**, Franklin D **Roosevelt**, Harry **Truman**, John F **Kennedy**, Lyndon B **Johnson**, Jimmy **Carter**, and Bill **Clinton**, the party adopted more liberal social-reform policies than the Republicans. In 1993 Clinton became the first Democrat president for 13 years and in 1996 was the first Democrat since Roosevelt to be elected for a second term.

Democratic Republican Party

A US political party established in 1792 that became, in about 1830, the **Democratic Party**. It was first briefly called the Republican Party and was set up to oppose the **Federalist Party**. Thomas **Jefferson** founded it after resigning as secretary of state under the Federalist president George

Washington, and Jefferson was the first Democratic Republican president, elected in 1800. The party's other two presidents were James **Madison** and James **Monroe**.

Depression See *Great Depression.*

de Soto, Hernando (*c.* 1496–1542)
A Spanish explorer who was made governor of Cuba and Florida in 1538 and spent the next two years exploring Florida and the Southeast. Moving west, he was the first to visit the Mississippi River in 1541. He went as far as eastern Oklahoma but died while returning the next year, and his body was buried in the Mississippi River. De Sota first sailed with Pedro Arias Avila to Darien, Central America, in 1519, he explored the Yucatán Peninsula in 1528, and travelled with Francisco Pizarro in Peru from 1530 to 1535.

détente
The reduction of political tension and strained relations between the USA and USSR in the late 1960s and 1970s. It first led to trade agreements and cultural exchanges and then to the **SALT** treaties limiting nuclear weapons. Détente weakened in the late 1970s because of American mistrust of Soviet promises and disappeared after the Russian invasion of Afghanistan in 1979. It returned as communism began to collapse and the Cold War ended in 1989. The French word détente means 'relaxation'.

Dewey, George (1837–1917)
A US naval officer in the **Civil War** and **Spanish–American War**. He was born in Montpelier, Vermont, and graduated from the US Naval Academy in 1858. In the **Civil War** he saw action on the Mississippi River and in the blockade of Southern ports. As a commodore after the war, he was dispatched to the Pacific in 1896. Without losing a man, he destroyed the Spanish fleet in Manila harbour at the outbreak of the Spanish–American War in 1898. The following year, Dewey was promoted to admiral of the navy, the highest naval rank ever awarded. In 1910 he became president of the General Board of the Navy Department and held that position until his death.

Dillinger, John Herbert (1903–1934)
A US bank robber and murderer of 16 people. In 1923 he was convicted of armed robbery and spent the next ten years in state prison. Released in

1933, he led a gang on a robbery spree of 20 banks throughout the Midwest, staging daring raids on police stations to obtain guns. Named 'Public Enemy Number One' by the **FBI**, Dillinger led the authorities on a long chase. He was finally betrayed by his mistress, the mysterious 'Lady in Red', and was killed by FBI agents in Chicago as he left a cinema.

> ❦ Age, 32 years; Height, 5 foot 7-1/8 inches; Weight, 153 pounds; Build, medium; Hair, medium chestnut; Eyes, grey; Complexion, medium; Occupation, machinist; Marks and scars, 1/2 inch scar back left hand, scar middle upper lip, brown mole between eyebrows. ❧

Detail from an FBI poster, description of **John Dillinger**, offering $10,000 reward for his capture, 1934

Dixie

A nickname for the Southern states, especially those that formed the **Confederate States of America**. The word may derive from the **Mason-Dixon Line** defining the North-South boundary. Another explanation refers to the paper money printed in Louisiana before the **Civil War**, which had one side inscribed in French: on ten-dollar bills *dix*. The song 'Dixie' (1859) by Daniel Emmett popularized the term. Emmett himself was born in Ohio and worked in a minstrel troupe.

'DIXIE'

I wish I was in de land ob cotton,
Old times dar am not forgotten;
Look away, look away, look away, Dixie land!
In Dixie land whar I was born in,
Early on one frosty mornin',
Look away, look away, look away, Dixie land!

Dixiecrats

Southerners who left the **Democratic Party** to form the States' Rights Party for the 1948 presidential election only. Their third party was commonly called the Dixiecrat Party. They were against the Democratic platform that supported civil rights. The Dixiecrat presidential candidate was Strom Thurmond, governor of South Carolina. The party won the states of Alabama, Louisiana, Mississippi, and South Carolina, receiving 1,169,000 votes and 39 **Electoral College** votes.

Strom Thurman is still a US senator and, at the age of 98 in 2000, the oldest one ever. In 1954, he became the first senator to be elected by a write-in vote. In 1964, he changed from the Democratic to the Republican Party.

domino theory

An idea popularized by US president Dwight **Eisenhower** in 1954 that if one country came under communist rule, adjacent countries were likely to fall to communism as well. The domino theory was later used in the USA and Australia to justify intervention in Southeast Asia and was invoked in reference to US involvement in Central America.

❝ You have a row of dominoes set up, you knock over the first one, and what will happen to the last one is the certainty that it will go over very quickly. ❞

Dwight Eisenhower, news conference, 7 April 1954

Douglas, Stephen Arnold (1813–1861)

A US Democrat from Illinois who engaged in the **Lincoln-Douglas Debates** with Abraham **Lincoln** in the 1858 Senate race. It was won by Douglas who had urged a compromise on slavery. Lincoln later defeated him in the 1860 presidential race. He served in the US House of Representatives from 1843 to 1847 and as a US senator for Illinois from 1847 to 1861. Douglas helped draft the **Compromise of 1850** and the **Kansas-Nebraska Act** of 1854. He acquired the nickname 'Little Giant' for his support of westward expansion.

Douglass, Frederick (1817–1895)

A US slave who became an antislavery campaigner before and during the **Civil War**. Born Frederick Augustus Washington Bailey, he escaped from his Maryland master in 1838 and fled to Britain. He returned to the USA after securing sufficient funds to purchase his freedom. His autobiographical *Narrative of the Life of Frederick Douglass* (1845) aroused support for **abolitionism**. Douglass issued a call to blacks to take up arms against the South and helped organize two black regiments for the Union army. After the war, he held several US government posts, including minister to Haiti from 1889 to 1891.

draft
The US name for military conscription, first introduced by the **Continental Congress** in 1777 for the **American Revolution**. The draft caused controversy during the **Civil War**, leading to refusals to serve on both sides and draft riots in the North, the worst killing at least 105 people in New York City from 11 to 13 July 1863. It proved effective during the two world wars, but draft dodging and the burning of draft cards were problems during the **Vietnam War**. The draft was ended in 1973, and President Jimmy **Carter** pardoned most draft evaders in 1977.

Drake, Francis (c. 1540–1596)
An English buccaneer and explorer who rescued the survivors at the Roanoke colony in Virginia in June 1586. Drake had already enriched himself as a pirate against Spanish interests in the Caribbean from 1567 to 1572 and sailed round the world from 1577 to 1580 in the *Golden Hind* as far north in the Pacific as California. He sailed into San Francisco Bay and claimed the area for Queen Elizabeth. He returned to England and helped to defeat the Spanish Armada in 1588 as a vice admiral on the *Revenge*. Drake sailed on his last expedition to the West Indies in 1595 and died of dysentery off the town of Puerto Bello (now Portobello), Panama.

Dred Scott case
The US **Supreme Court** decision of 1857 dealing with citizenship and legal rights of slaves. Dred Scott (c. 1800–1858), a slave from Missouri, sued for freedom from his owner John Sanford in the Missouri courts, arguing that he had lived with his owner in Illinois, a free state, and the Wisconsin Territory, where slavery had been outlawed by the **Missouri Compromise**. The case reached the Supreme Court, which ruled that:

- black people were not US citizens
- slaves did not become free by entering a free state and
- the Missouri Compromise was illegal as it interfered with the right to own

slaves, guaranteed by the Constitution.

drugs

The first US drug law, the Harrison Drug Act, was passed in 1916 under President Woodrow **Wilson**, requiring pharmacists to register stocks with the Internal Revenue Service (IRS). Since recreational drug use began to become popular in the 1960s, however, the enforcement of drug laws has proven to be expensive and often inadequate. The Drug Enforcement Administration (DEA) was established in 1973, and the **FBI** was given joint jurisdiction with DEA in 1982 as the US government declared a 'War on Drugs' programme. Other agencies now involved include the US Coast Guard and the US Customs Service. The FBI said that in 1997 federal police agencies spend about $16 billion a year on enforcement.

Dulles, John Foster (1888–1959)

The US secretary of state from 1952 to 1959 who initiated **brinkmanship** to force communists into agreement by threatening to go to the brink of a nuclear war. A lawyer and the senior US adviser at the founding of the **United Nations**, Dulles largely drafted the Japanese peace treaty of 1951. As secretary of state, he was an architect of the US **Cold War** foreign policy. Dulles presided over the creation of the CENTO (Central Treaty Organization) alliance in the Middle East and **SEATO** (Southeast Asia Treaty Organization). He also secured US intervention in support of South Vietnam following the expulsion of the French in 1954.

Dust Bowl

An area in the south Great Plains region of the USA (Texas to Kansas) that suffered extensive wind erosion as the result of drought and poor farming practice in once-fertile soil. Much of the topsoil was blown away in the droughts of the 1930s, adding to the misery of the **Great Depression**, and many families moved to other areas. Serious wind damage occurred again in the 1980s.

The Grapes of Wrath, the 1939 novel by John Steinbeck, was about a family that had to escape the Dust Bowl and move to California, the 'promised land'. A film version was made in 1940.

Earp, Wyatt Berry Stapp (1848–1929)

A US frontier law officer. With his brothers Virgil and Morgan, Doc Holliday, and the legendary 'Bat' **Masterson**, he was involved in the famous gunfight at the OK Corral in Tombstone, Arizona, on 26 October 1881, killing the Clanton brothers. Renowned as a scout and buffalo hunter, he also gained a reputation as a gambler and brawler. Born in Monmouth, Illinois, Earp went to Wichita, Kansas, in 1874, where he was employed by the US marshal. He was appointed assistant marshal in Dodge City, Kansas, in 1876. Leaving Tombstone in 1882, a year after the gunfight, he travelled before settling in Los Angeles.

Earhart, Amelia (1898–1937)

A US aviation pioneer who in 1928 became the first woman to fly across the Atlantic as a passenger and in 1932 completed a solo transatlantic flight. With co-pilot Frederick Noonan, she attempted a round-the-world flight in 1937, but somewhere over the Pacific their plane disappeared without trace. Clues found 1989 on Nikumaroro island, southeast of Kiribati's main island group, suggest that she and her co-pilot might have survived a crash only to die of thirst. Experts believe the plane simply ran out of fuel.

> In 1997, Linda Finch completed a round-the-world flight to duplicate and complete Amelia Earhart's last journey. She dropped a wreath on Howland Island in the central Pacific close to the area in which Earhart disappeared.

Edison, Thomas Alva (1847–1931)

A US scientist and inventor whose work in the fields of communications and electrical power greatly influenced the world. He is most remembered for the phonograph and electric light bulb. Edison was born in Milan, Ohio, and was self-educated. As a 19-year-old telegraph operator, he took out his first patent, for an electric vote recorder. By 1889, he had formed the Edison Light Company, which became the General Electric Company. With more than 1,000 patents, Edison produced his most important inventions in Menlo Park, New Jersey, from 1876 to 1887. They included:

- an electric transmitter system for the human voice, patented in 1876
- the practical incandescent light bulb on 19 October 1879
- the phonograph in 1877
- the kinetoscopic camera, an early cine camera and
- the first talking films in 1912.

When Edison died on 18 October 1931, all non-essential electric lights in the USA, including the torch on the Statue of Liberty, were turned off for one minute.

> 6 Genius is 1% inspiration and 99% perspiration. 9
>
> **Thomas Alva Edison**, newspaper interview mentioned in *Life*, 1932

Einstein, Albert (1879–1955)
The German-born US physicist whose theories of relativity revolutionized our understanding of matter, space, and time. Einstein was born in Ulm, Württemberg, and eventually settled in Switzerland. He emigrated to the USA in 1933 and became professor of mathematics and a permanent member of the Institute for Advanced Study at Princeton, New Jersey. His accomplishments include:

- establishing that light may have a particle nature and deducing the photoelectric law, for which he was awarded the Nobel Prize for Physics in 1921
- investigating Brownian motion (the random movement of fine particles that can be seen through a microscope) to confirm the existence of atoms
- devising the special theory of relativity that said if a system were to move at the velocity of light, to an observer carried with it, its length would be zero, time would be at a stop, and its mass would be infinite. These conclusions were later verified with observations of fast-moving atomic clocks and cosmic rays

- showing in 1907 that mass is related to energy by the famous equation $E=mc^2$
- devising the general theory of relativity in which the properties of space–time would be modified by the presence of a body with mass; and light rays should bend when they pass by a massive object. This was proven during observations of a solar eclipse in 1919 and made him world famous.

> 6 At any rate, I am convinced that He [God] does not play dice. 9
>
> **Albert Einstein**, letter to Max Born, 4 December 1926

Eisenhower, Dwight David (1890–1969)

The 34th president of the USA from 1953 to 1960, a Republican. His nickname was 'Ike'. A general in **World War II**, he commanded the Allied invasion of Europe, and from October 1944 all the Allied armies in the West. After the war he served as commander of the US Occupation Forces in Germany and became supreme commander of the Allied Powers in Europe in 1950, organizing the defence forces in **NATO**. He resigned from the army in 1952 to campaign for the presidency, being elected and re-elected by a wide margin in 1956. A popular president, Eisenhower held office during a period of domestic prosperity and growth but with international tension. Major problems during his administration included the ending of the **Korean War**, the **Cold War**, and the growing **civil rights movement** at home.

Eisenhower *US soldier and politician Dwight D Eisenhower. After commanding Allied forces in Europe during World War II, he became the 34th president of the USA in 1953.*

> ❝ Every gun that is made, every warship launched, every rocket fired signifies, in the final sense, a theft from those who hunger and are not fed, those who are cold and are not clothed. ❞
>
> **Dwight Eisenhower**, speech in Washington, DC, 16 April 1953

electoral college

The indirect system of voting for the president and vice-president of the USA. The people of each state officially vote not for the presidential candidate, but for a list of electors nominated by each party. The whole electoral-college vote of the state then goes to the winning party (and candidate). The system can lead to a presidential candidate being elected with a minority of the total vote over the whole country (as happened when Benjamin Harrison was elected over Grover Cleveland in 1888).

Ellis Island

An island in New York harbour that was once the reception centre for immigrants to America. Named after a Welshman, Samuel Ellis, who owned it in the late 18th century, the island handled the **immigration** waves between 1892 and 1943 (12 million people passed through it from 1892 to 1924. It was later used (until 1954) as a detention centre for non-residents without documentation or for those who were being deported. Ellis Island has been a national historic site since 1964 and, after a $170 million restoration, has contained the Museum of Immigration since 1989. **See also:** *immigration*.

The US **Supreme Court**, concluding a lengthy dispute, declared in 1998 that Ellis Island belonged to New Jersey and not to New York.

Emancipation Proclamation

The announcement by President Abraham **Lincoln** on 22 September 1862 during the **Civil War** that from the beginning of 1863 all slaves in states still engaged in rebellion against the federal government would be emancipated. Slaves in border states still remaining loyal to the Union were excluded. Lincoln had read a preliminary proclamation to his cabinet, who urged him to wait until a major Union victory before delivering it publicly. The proclamation followed the Union victory at **Antietam**.

Embargo Act

US legislation in 1807 forbidding any international trade with US ports. President Thomas **Jefferson** believed it would force Britain and France, then at war with each other, to drop their separate restrictions on neutral countries like America from trading with either. British warships pursued this policy by stopping and searching American ships, during which they often used **impressment** (seizure) of British citizens for the Royal Navy. The Embargo Act did not work, because it was difficult to enforce and American traders suffered, so the government repealed the act in 1810.

Equal Rights Amendment (ERA)

A proposed amendment to the **Constitution of the United States** that would have guaranteed women equal rights with men. Although **Congress** introduced the proposal in 1923, it did not approve it until 1972. To become a law, it required the approval of 38 of the 50 states. The deadline was extended to 1982, but the proposal failed by three states. Recent efforts have been underway to initiate a new proposal for a similar amendment.

> ❝ Equality of rights under the law shall not be denied or abridged by the United States or any state on account of sex. ❞
>
> **Equal Rights Amendment**, 1972

ERA See *Equal Rights Amendment.*

Erie Canal

A canal in New York state that connects Lake Erie north of Buffalo with the Hudson River at Albany and Troy; it passes through the cities of Utica, Syracuse, and Rochester. The canal was begun in 1817 and completed in 1825 at a cost of over $7 million. Its construction cost 1,000 lives. Now part of the New York State Barge Canal System that is 845 km/525 mi in length, the expanded Erie Canal is 45 m/148 ft wide and has an average depth of 3.6 m/12 ft.

Fair Deal

The policy of social improvement advocated from 1945 to 1948 by President Harry S **Truman**. The Fair Deal proposals, first voiced in 1945 after the end of **World War II**, aimed to extend the **New Deal** on health insurance, housing development, and laws to maintain farming prices. Although some bills became law - for example a Housing Act, a higher minimum wage, and wider social security benefits - the main proposals were blocked by a hostile **Congress**.

Fair Oaks, Battle of See *Seven Pines, Battle of.*

Farragut, David Glasgow (1801–1870)

A US admiral during the **Civil War**. He took New Orleans in 1862, after destroying the Confederate fleet there, and in 1864 effectively put an end to blockade-running with his victory at the battle of **Mobile Bay** in Alabama. The ranks of vice admiral (1864) and admiral (1866) were created for him by **Congress**. Although a Southerner, born near Knoxville, Tennessee, he remained loyal to the US government on the outbreak of the **Civil War** and in 1862 was appointed to the command of the West Gulf Blockading Squadron. After the war, Farragut commanded the European Squadron in 1867 and 1868.

FBI

The abbreviation for the Federal Bureau of Investigation, the US criminal organization that investigates and handles all violations of federal laws, unless they have been assigned to other agencies. It is in charge of counter-intelligence, such as cases involving espionage and sabotage. Located in **Washington, DC**, as part of the US Department of Justice, the FBI was established in 1908 as the Bureau of Investigation, changing its name in 1935. Much of its efforts have been against organized crime, and its '10 most wanted list' is well known. J Edgar Hoover directed it from 1924 until his death in 1972 and was criticized late in his career for illegally gathering information on ordinary Americans, especially activists in antiwar protests and the **civil rights movement**, such as Martin Luther **King**.

Federal Bureau of Investigation See *FBI*.

Federalist Papers
A series of 85 letters published in newspapers in the newly independent USA between October 1787 and July 1788, attempting to define the relation of the states to the nation, and making the case for a federal government. Their short-term objective was to win support in New York state for the proposed **Constitution of the United States**. The papers were signed 'Publius', the joint pseudonym of three leading political figures: Alexander **Hamilton**, John Jay, and James **Madison**. The papers were later published as a book titled *The Federalist*.

> ❢ Why has government been instituted at all?
> Because the passions of men will not conform to the
> dictates of reason and justice, without constraint. ❢
>
> **Alexander Hamilton**, *The Federalist*, No. 15, (1787–88)

Federalist Party
The first US political party, established in 1789 by Alexander **Hamilton** and supported by those who wanted a strong central government. George **Washington** was a Federalist president, and the only other was John **Adams**, who won the nation's first partisan presidential election. The party held power from 1794 to 1800 but became weakened when Hamilton and Adams began to disagree, losing voters to the **Democratic Republican Party**. It ended as a national party in 1816, continuing as a New England one until the 1820s.

Fifth Amendment
The amendment to the **Constitution of the United States** that protects a person from being a witness against himself or herself in court. It is part of the **Bill of Rights**. Some Americans believe that anyone who repeatedly 'takes the Fifth' in order to remain silent during a trial, must be guilty. It has been a popular plea with those protecting their civil rights, but also with communists and members of crime syndicates. This amendment also protects people from double jeopardy (being tried twice for the same crime) and says a person cannot be 'deprived of life, liberty of property without due process of law'.

First Amendment

The amendment to the **Constitution of the United States** that guarantees freedom of religion, of speech, of assembly, and of the press. It is part of the **Bill of Rights**. Journalists use it to print controversial articles and to protect their sources. Adopted in 1791, the First Amendment is often cited in the **Supreme Court** decisions, including recent rulings striking down Congressional censorship of the Internet.

Five Civilized Tribes

The term used to describe the Choctaw, **Creek**, Chickasaw, **Cherokee**, and **Seminole** peoples of the southeast USA. They were considered 'civilized' because they were farmers who lived in settled towns, had a democratic form of government, and had assimilated many US and European laws and customs, including European dress. After the Removal Act of 1830, they were forcibly relocated to **Indian Territory** from 1835 to 1843. In 1906 the Dawes Commission, in order to determine who was eligible for allotments of land, prepared the Final Rolls of the Five Civilized Tribes, listing individual members of each tribe. Today, membership of a group is dependent on being descended from someone listed on the Final Rolls.

Five Forks, Battle of

The last major battle of the **Civil War**, on 1 April 1865 at Five Forks about 16 km/10 mi southwest of Petersburg, Virginia. About 28,000 Union troops commanded by Maj-Gen Philip Sheridan and Brig-Gen Gouverneur Warren defeated 19,000 Confederates under Maj-Gen George A Pickett. At the time, the main Confederate force under Gen Robert E **Lee** was besieged in Richmond and Petersburg by Union forces led by Gen Ulysses S **Grant**. The defeat at Five Forks exposed Lee's flank, forcing him to abandon Richmond, and led to his surrender eight days later.

❦ Hold Five Forks at all hazards. ❧

Gen Robert E Lee, message to Maj-Gen George A Pickett, 31 March 1865

'Flying Tigers'

The nickname given to the American Volunteer Group in **World War II**, a group of US pilots recruited to fight in China by Maj-Gen Claire

L Chennault 1940–41. The group proved an effective force against the Japanese over southern China and Burma from 1941 to 1942, destroying some 300 enemy aircraft. In 1942, it was absorbed into the regular US air forces as the 14th Air Force with Chennault as its commander.

Ford, Gerald R(udolph) (1913–)

The 38th president of the USA from 1974 to 1977, a Republican. He was elected to the House of Representatives in 1948 and was nominated to the vice-presidency by Richard **Nixon** in 1973 on the resignation of Spiro Agnew. Ford then became president in 1974, when Nixon was forced to resign following the **Watergate** scandal. He granted Nixon a full pardon in September 1974. Ford's visit to Vladivostok in 1974 resulted in agreement with the USSR on strategic arms limitation. He was defeated by Jimmy **Carter** in the 1976 election by a narrow margin.

- Ford was an All-American football player at college

- as president, he survived two assassination attempts in September 1975

- he is the only US president never to have been elected as vice-president or president

- in August 1999 he was awarded the Presidential Medal of Freedom.

Ford, Henry (1863–1947)

The famous US automobile manufacturer. He built his first car in 1896 and founded the Ford Motor Company in 1903. His Model T (from 1908 to 1927) was the first car to be constructed solely by assembly-line methods and to be mass-marketed; 15 million of these cars were sold. Ford's inno-vative policies, such as a $5 daily minimum wage (at the time nearly double the average figure in Detroit) and a five-day working week, revolutionized employment practices, but he opposed the introduction of trade unions. In 1928 he launched the Model A, a stepped-up version of the Model T. In 1936 he founded, with his son Edsel Ford, the philanthropic Ford Foundation. He retired in 1945 from the Ford Motor Company, then valued at over $1 billion.

❜ People can have the Model T in any colour, so long as it's black. ❜

Henry Ford, 1909

Forrest, Nathan Bedford (1821–1877)

A Confederate cavalry general during the **Civil War**. At its outbreak, Forrest escaped from Union troops before the fall of Fort Donelson in Tennessee in 1862. After the Battle of **Shiloh** that year, he was promoted to the rank of brigadier general and led daring raids against Union forces throughout the South. Born in Chapel Hill, Tennessee, Forrest had little formal schooling but accumulated enough wealth through slave dealing to buy land in Mississippi and establish a cotton plantation. After the war, he founded the **Ku Klux Klan** in 1866 while working as a civilian railroad executive.

> ❝ Get there first with the most men. ❞
>
> **Nathan Bedford Forrest**, explaining his military successes, quoted by
> Basil Duke, *Reminiscences*, 1911

Fort Sumter

The fort that was bombarded by Confederates on 12 April 1861 to begin the **Civil War**. It is in the harbour of Charleston, South Carolina, 6.5 km/4 mi southeast of the city. The attack had been initiated when President Abraham **Lincoln** refused to evacuate the fort, sending reinforcements instead. The bombardment began after its commander, Maj Robert Anderson, refused the call to surrender made by the Confederate Brig-Gen Pierre Beauregard. (Anderson had been **Beauregard's** instructor at the US Military Academy.) A day later, the fort surrendered, and the South held it until the end of the war in 1865.

Nobody was killed during the bombardment of Fort Sumter, but a Union private died when a cannon exploded during a 100-gun salute to the US flag before the fort was turned over to the Confederates.

forty-niners

The people who travelled to California to become prospectors during the Gold Rush of 1849. About 89,000 men stampeded west, as many as 35,000 coming in their wagons from the Missouri towns of Independence and St Joseph. The gold also drew adventurers from as far away as Europe and China.

Many forty-niners hit it rich with only a pick, shovel, and tin pan. Most, however, ended up with disappointment and debts. **See also**: *gold rush*.

Founding Fathers
The name given to the American leaders who created the United States' form of government when they drafted and approved the **Constitution of the United States**. This occurred before and during the Federal Constitutional Convention in Philadelphia where the document was signed on 17 September 1787. Among the Founding Fathers were George **Washington**, Thomas **Jefferson**, Benjamin **Franklin**, John **Adams**, James **Madison**, and Alexander **Hamilton**.

Four Freedoms, the
The four kinds of liberty essential to human dignity, as defined by President Franklin D **Roosevelt** in his State of the Union message to **Congress** on 6 January 1941:

- freedom of speech and expression
- freedom of worship
- freedom from want
- freedom from fear.

Roosevelt was urging, before US entry into **World War II**, support of the democracies fighting to defend freedom. The Four Freedoms were the basis for the **Atlantic Charter** in 1941 that specified the Allied war aims.

Fourteen Points
The terms proposed by US president Woodrow **Wilson** in 1918 as a basis for the settlement of World War I. They were given in his address to **Congress** on 8 January of that year. The creation of the League of Nations was one of the points. The terms included:

- open diplomacy
- freedom of the seas
- removal of trade barriers
- international disarmament
- adjustment of colonial claims
- German evacuation of Russian, Belgian, French, and Balkan territories

- the restoration of Alsace-Lorraine to France
- autonomy for the various ethnic groups in Austria, Hungary, and the Ottoman Empire
- an independent Poland
- a general 'association of nations' (which was to become the League of Nations).

Wilson had to compromise on many of the points because of secret agreements concluded by several of the Allies.

Fourteenth Amendment

The amendment to the **Constitution of the United States** that permitted former slaves to become US citizens. Passed during **Reconstruction** after the **Civil War**, it also provided for all Americans equal protection under the law and due process of law. The amendment was passed by **Congress** in 1866 and was approved by the states in 1868. Southerners were able to evade the true meaning of the amendment for nearly a century by setting up a 'separate but equal' system of **segregation** which belied its name by being separate but not equal.

Franklin, Benjamin (1706–1790)

A US **Founding Father** who was a statesman, scientist, writer, printer, and publisher. As a Pennsylvania delegate to the **Continental Congress** from 1785 to 1788, he helped to draft the **Declaration of Independence** and the **Constitution of the United States**. He carried out famous experiments with kites to prove that lightning is a form of electricity, and he invented the lightning conductor. Franklin was born in Boston and self-educated. He was the 15th of 17 children and was apprenticed to a printer at the age of 12. In 1723, he left Boston for Philadelphia and in 1724 sailed for England, where he worked for 18 months in a printer's office. In 1737, he became deputy postmaster of Philadelphia, and from 1751 to 1764 was a member of the colony's legislative body. He then travelled to France to enlist help for the colonial cause in the **American Revolution** that followed. He was the first US ambassador to France from 1776 to 1785 and negotiated peace with Britain in 1783.

- Franklin started the *Pennsylvania Gazette* newspaper in 1730 but is better remembered for *Poor Richard's Almanack* begun in 1732, a collection of articles and advice on a huge range of topics, 'conveying instruction among the common people'.

- He founded the American Philosophical Society in 1743 and, in 1749, a college that later became the University of Pennsylvania.

- Franklin produced the first chart of the Gulf Stream following observations made in 1770, and he used a thermometer to aid navigation in the Gulf Stream in 1775.

> 6 We must indeed all hang together, or, most assuredly, we shall all hang separately. 9
>
> **Benjamin Franklin**, remark to John Hancock, at the signing of the Declaration of Independence, 4 July 1776

Fredericksburg, Battle of

A Confederate victory in the **Civil War**, fought from 11 to 15 December 1862 next to the Rapahannock River. The Union force, 125,000 troops under Maj-Gen Ambrose **Burnside**, was advancing south on Richmond, and Fredericksburg was the obvious place to cross the river. Gen Robert E **Lee** took up a position with 85,000 Confederate troops on Marye's Heights about two miles from the river. Burnside's troops threw pontoon bridges across the river and captured the town of Fredericksburg on 12 December and the next day advanced towards the Confederates, who poured fire into the ranks, with devestating results. About 9,000 Union troops fell on the slopes of the hills. A second assault met with a similar fate, and Burnside withdrew his forces back across the river. Union casualties were 13,000 dead and wounded; Confederate casualties 5,000.

> 6 A chicken could not live on that field when we open on it. 9
>
> **Col E Porter Alexander**, Confederate officer at the Battle of Fredericksburg, message to his commander, Lt-Gen James Longstreet, 12 December 1862

Freedom of Information Act

A federal law that requires documentary records of the US government to be made available to members of the public on request. This includes information kept on individuals and organizations, although certain categories of confidential information are exempt from disclosure. The Act was passed by **Congress** in 1966 and strengthened in 1974. A request for information must be made in writing, and government agencies must respond within ten working days. Many of the requests are made by journalists. The separate US states also have laws that grant freedom of information.

freedom rides

A series of bus rides taken in 1961 by civil rights groups, journeying from the Northern states into the South. The Congress of Racial Equality organized the first trips. The 'freedom riders' were protesting against bus companies that segregated passengers, requiring black people to sit in the back seats, and also against **segregation** in bus stations. The riders and their buses were confronted by angry crowds and sometimes attacked. In November of that year, the US Interstate Commerce Commission ordered all buses to be integrated. **See also:** *civil rights movement.*

Free Soil Party

An anti-slavery party formed in 1848. It nominated former US president Martin Van Buren for the presidency in 1848 and John P Hale in 1852, but both were defeated.

The party was really a combination of the political abolitionists, many of whom had been formerly identified with the more radical Liberty Party, with the Barnburners, and with the antislavery Whigs. It merged in 1854 with the **Republican Party**.

The Free Soil Party's slogan for the 1848 presidential election was 'Free Soil, Free Labour, Free Speech'.

Frémont, John Charles (1813–1890)

A US explorer and politician who travelled extensively throughout the western USA. He surveyed much of the territory between the Mississippi River and the coast of California with the aim of establishing an overland route across the continent. In 1842 he crossed the Rocky Mountains, climbing the peak that is named after him. In 1850 he was elected a senator of the newly created state of California and six years later he stood unsuccessfully as the first US presidential candidate of the new **Republican Party**. Between 1878 and 1883 he was governor of Arizona.

French and Indian War

A war over colonial possessions in North America from 1754 to 1763, won by Britain over France. It resulted from the conflict between the two countries over colonial supremacy during the Seven Years' War. Both sides had allies among **American Indian** groups. Gen James Wolfe won a major victory in 1759 when he captured Quebec. The Treaty of Paris in 1763 gave Britain all of Canada and much of the Louisiana Territory.

George **Washington** was a military leader for the British during the French and Indian War, and the conflict provided the American colonists with valuable military experience for the coming **American Revolution**.

frontier

Other countries had borders, but America had a frontier, always west and, for 250 years, constantly shifting. 'West' to the early colonists meant over the Appalachian Mountains. Indians were always forced to move west of its edge. Wherever it was, it represented the wilderness that the new Americans intended to conquer as their **manifest destiny**. By 1890, however, the US census report said that a frontier line of westward population movement was no longer discernible. Frontier characteristics beloved by Americans include individualism, independence, equality, a simple lifestyle, and the ability to overcome challenges. (It has also left a strong gun culture.)

> ❛We stand today on the edge of a new frontier...But the New Frontier of which I speak is not a set of promises – it is a set of challenges. ❜
>
> **John F Kennedy**, US president, speech in Los Angeles, 15 July 1960

fugitive slave acts

US laws from 1787 to 1864 concerning the treatment of slaves who had escaped from their owners. Before the **Constitution of the United States** there were no fugitive slave laws, and it was left to the good will of the states or colonies to surrender slaves who had escaped from service. In 1787 the slave-holding states inserted provisions in their constitutions regulating the surrender of fugitive slaves, and in 1793 a Federal Fugitive Slave Law was enacted. In 1850 **Congress** passed a new fugitive slave bill as part of the **Compromise of 1850**. It was repealed in 1864, and slavery was abolished by the 13th Amendment of 1865.

G

Gadsden Purchase

The purchase on 30 December 1853 by the USA of approximately 77,700 sq km/30,000 sq mi of Mexican territory along the southern borders of what is now New Mexico and Arizona. The land was bought from Mexico for $10 million in a treaty negotiated by the US minister to Mexico, James Gadsden, a railway president from South Carolina. The land was partly bought to construct a transcontinental railroad route, the Southern Pacific, which was completed in the 1880s.

Gates, Horatio (c. 1727–1806)

A British-born American military leader during the **American Revolution**. Born in Maldon, Essex, Gates joined the British army, serving in Nova Scotia, Canada, and seeing action in the **French and Indian War** from 1754 to 1763. After returning to England, he emigrated to America in 1772. Gen George **Washington** appointed him brigadier general in the Continental Army in 1775 at the outbreak of the war. Gates won a tide-turning victory at the Battle of **Saratoga** on 17 October 1777. Falling out of favour with Washington, he was dispatched to the South, where he was defeated at the Battle of Camden in 1780.

Geronimo (1829–1909)

The chief of the Chiricahua **Apache** Indians and their war leader. From 1875 to 1885, he fought US federal troops, as well as settlers encroaching on tribal reservations in the Southwest. After surrendering to Maj-Gen George Crook in March 1886 and agreeing to go to Florida, Geronimo and his followers escaped. Captured again in August 1886, they were eventually taken to Fort Sill, Oklahoma, where Geronimo became a farmer. He later appeared as a celebrity at the St Louis World's Fair in 1904, and dictated

Since World War II, US paratroopers have yelled 'Geronimo' to give them courage when leaping from their aircraft. This 'battle cry' is also sometimes used by people who jump from a high place.

Geronimo's *Story of His Life* (1906). He also earned money by selling brass buttons from his coat and photographs of himself.

gerrymandering

The political device of rearranging voting boundaries to give an unfair advantage to the ruling party. The term derives from US politician Elbridge Gerry (1744–1814), who in 1812, while governor of Massachusetts, reorganized the electoral districts to assure a legislative majority for his Republican party. An editor, Benjamin Russell, noted that one of the new districts was shaped like a salamander, and he coined the term 'gerrymander'.

Gettysburg Address, the

The name later given to a short speech made by President Abraham **Lincoln** on 19 November 1863 to dedicate the military cemetery at Gettysburg, Pennsylvania, four months after the Battle of **Gettysburg**. His speech, which took less than three minutes to deliver, was listed as 'Dedicatory Remarks' in the programme and followed a two-hour speech by Edward Everett, the former US secretary of state. Lincoln thought his contribution was a failure, and the Chicago Times called it 'silly, flat, and dishwatery utterances'. The Gettysburg Address has since been recognized as one of the greatest speeches in American history.

❛ Forescore and seven years ago our fathers brought forth on this continent a new nation, conceived in liberty and dedicated to the proposition that all men are created equal. ❜

Abraham Lincoln, Gettysburg Address, 19 November 1863

Gettysburg, Battle of

The crucial battle won by Union forces during the **Civil War** on 3 July 1863 at Gettysburg, Pennsylvania. It began on 1 July and was the largest and bloodiest battle ever fought on American soil. The opposing sides were led by Union major general George Meade with 93,500 men and Confederate general Robert E **Lee** with 77,000, on a daring march into the North. Confederate forces made suicide attacks on the Union lines at Cemetery Ridge, the most disastrous being **Pickett's charge**. The next day, both armies were too battered to advance, and Lee withdrew. The South had lost about 28,000 men (3,500 of them killed) and the North about 23,000 (3,155 killed).

- The Battle of Gettysburg began by accident, when Southern troops went into the town to buy shoes at a factory and encountered the 8th Illinois Cavalry.

- Maj-Gen George Meade was known to his men as the 'snapping turtle' because of his sharp tongue and fierce temper.

- A 70-year-old resident of Gettysburg, John L Burns, became so angry when Confederates drove off his cows, he grabbed a rifle and fought with the Union army. He was captured, nearly hanged, but then released.

Ghost Dance
A religious movement that spread through the Plains Indians, especially the Sioux, in the 1890s. In 1889, a Paiute **American Indian** named Wovoka had a vision that the old ways would be restored, the bison herds would return, white people would disappear, and the American Indians would be reunited with friends and relatives in the ghost world. This vision became the nucleus for the Ghost Dance, in which Indians engaged in frenzied trance-inducing dancing accompanied by ghost songs. The movement spread rapidly and caused fear among white settlers, ultimately leading to the massacre at **Wounded Knee** on 29 December 1990 when soldiers went to quell the movement.

ghost town
Many deserted or near-deserted towns that are scattered across the US West. The towns, located near gold or silver mines, flourished in the 19th century and then died as the mines played out. Arizona alone has about 50 ghost towns. Examples include Elizabethtown, New Mexico's first incorporated town, built by gold prospectors. The mines closed in 1871 and the town was unoccupied by 1903. Bullionville in northeast Utah boomed after copper was discovered in 1880, and Butch Cassidy's gang once hid there. After $3 million in copper was removed, however, everyone deserted the town.

GI Bill of Rights
US legislation signed on 22 June 1944 to provide money for **World War II** veterans. The benefits paid for four years of college (including living expenses) and assisted them in buying homes and businesses. The law was officially named the Serviceman's Readjustment Act. By 1947, about 4

million people had received the benefits, and the GI Bill of Rights was also available to veterans of the Korean and Vietnam wars.

gold rush

The main gold rush in the USA occurred in 1848 and 1849 when about 40,000 people, later called the **forty-niners**, descended on Calfornia after gold was discovered in Sutter's Mill. Other large gold rushes were to Colorado from 1858–64, Idaho from 1861–64, Montana from 1862–64, South Dakota from 1876–78, Cripple Creek, Colorado, in 1891, and the Klondike Gold Rush in 1897 of mostly US residents to Canada's Yukon Territory. Many gold-rush prospectors went broke, finding little gold while paying inflated prices in mining camps, where a jar of pickles could cost $8.

'Pike's Peak or bust' was the cry of prospectors in 1859 heading for gold fields discovered in the Rocky Mountains.

Goldwater, Barry (Morris) (1909–1998)

A US Republican politician who was the party's presidential candidate in the 1964 election, when he was overwhelmingly defeated by Lyndon **Johnson**. Democrats portrayed him as a frightening militarist who would be willing to use nuclear weapons. As senator for Arizona from 1953 to 1965 and from 1969 to 1987, he voiced the views of his party's right-wing faction. Many of Goldwater's conservative ideas were later adopted by the Republican right, especially the administration of Ronald **Reagan**.

Good Neighbour Policy

The efforts of US administrations between the two world wars to improve relations with Latin American and Caribbean states. The phrase was first used by President Franklin D **Roosevelt** in his 1933 inaugural speech to describe the foreign policy of his **New Deal**. Roosevelt withdrew US forces from Nicaragua and Haiti, renouncing any right to intervene, and concluding a treaty in 1934 that gave Cuba full independence. The good will

> 6 In the field of world policy, I would dedicate this Nation to the policy of the good neighbour. 9
>
> **Franklin D Roosevelt**, inaugural address, 4 March 1933

engendered was to be significant in maintaining the unity of the western hemisphere during World War II.

Gore, Al (Albert Arnold, Jnr) (1948–)

The 45th US vice-president, from 1993 under President Bill **Clinton**. A Democrat, Gore served in the House of Representatives from 1977 to 1985 and the Senate from 1985 to 1993 and became noted for his concern for the environment. As vice-president, he was extremely active in foreign affairs, putting forward proposals for 'reinventing government' by cutting red tape and improving efficiency. His father, Al Gore, Snr, was a prominent senator from Tennessee, and Gore was born in **Washington, DC**. He was an unsuccessful candidate for the Democrats' presidential nomination in 1988 but their strongest candidate for 2000. He officially started his presidential campaign in Carthage, Tennessee, in June 1999.

Granger Movement

A farmers' protest movement in the 1880s in the South and Midwest states against economic hardship and exploitation, especially by the railways that fixed high prices. This led eventually to government laws regulating transport. The movement grew out of a network of local farming organizations formed in 1867 and popularly known as 'The Grange.'

Grant, Ulysses S(impson) (1822–1885)

The commander in chief of the Union army during the **Civil War** and the 18th president of the USA from 1869 to 1877, a Republican. He was born Hiram Ulysses Grant, the son of an Ohio farmer. On the outbreak of the Civil War, he received a commission on the Mississippi front. He took command

Grant *General Ulysses S Grant at City Point, near Hopewell, Virginia, June 1864. Respected as a war hero, Grant was nominated as the Republican Party's presidential candidate in 1868. He was elected and served two terms, marred by poor administration, financial scandals, and official corruption.*

there in 1862, and by his successful Siege of **Vicksburg** in 1863 brought the whole Mississippi front under Northern control. In 1864 he was made commander in chief. He slowly wore down the resistance of Confederate general Robert E **Lee**, receiving his surrender in 1865 at **Appomattox Court House**. Grant was elected president in 1868 and re-elected in 1872. As president, he reformed the civil service and ratified the **Treaty of Washington** with Britain in 1871. Grant, however, failed to suppress political corruption within his own party and cabinet.

> ❝ England and the United States are natural allies, and should be the best of friends. They speak one language, and are related by blood and other ties. We together, or even either separately, are better qualified than any other people to establish commerce between all the nationalities of the world. ❞
>
> **Ulysses Grant**, *Personal Memoirs of U. S. Grant*, 1885

Great Depression

The world economic crisis precipitated by the Wall Street crash of 29 October 1929, when millions of dollars were wiped off US stock values by panic selling in a matter of hours. This forced the closure of many US banks whose reserves were involved in stock speculation and led to the recall of US overseas investments. This loss of US credit had serious repercussions on the European economy, especially that of Germany (still recovering from **World War I**), and led to a steep fall in the levels of international trade as countries attempted to protect their own economies. Despite unprecedented federal government intervention under the **New Deal** of President Franklin D **Roosevelt**, the economy began a real recovery only after the rearmament programs of the late 1930s and 1940s boosted employment and output.

Great Migration

The movement of black Americans from the South to the North in the 20th century. This shift of about 6 million people from 1910 and 1970 was mainly caused by Southern **segregation** and the job opportunities in Northern factories. The migration created large ghettos in such cities as New York, Chicago, and Detroit. Conditions of employment and discrimination often seemed no better, and eventually led to Northern urban riots in the 1960s. The migration route has recently been reversed, with many blacks returning to better economic and social conditions in the South.

Great Society

The political slogan coined in 1964 by President Lyndon B **Johnson** to describe the ideal society to be created by his administration (1963–68), and to which all other nations would aspire. The programme included extensive social welfare legislation, most of which was subsequently passed by **Congress**. As part of the Great Society, his administration passed the Voting Rights Act of 1965 and also created:

- Medicare and Medicaid, medical programmes for the poor and elderly
- Head Start, an educational programme for deprived children
- the US Department of Housing and Urban Development.

> 6 In your time we have the opportunity to move not only toward the rich society and the powerful society, but upward to the Great Society. 9
>
> **Lyndon B Johnson**, speech at the University of Michigan, 22 May 1964

'Great White Fleet'

The popular name for a fleet of 16 US warships that President Theodore **Roosevelt** sent on a 14-month worldwide tour from 16 December 1907 to 22 February 1909. This was a series of good-will visits, but the cruise was mainly to demonstrate to other nations, especially Japan, that America's navy had arrived as a world power. The fleet of white ships covered 74,000 km/46,000 mi, sailing round the tip of South America, up the US West Coast, to Australia and New Zealand, then to Japan, through the Suez Canal and the Mediterranean, and home to Hampton Roads, Virginia.

Greeley, Horace (1811–1872)

A US editor, publisher, and politician. He founded the *New York Tribune* in 1841 and, as a strong supporter of the **Whig Party**, advocated many reforms in his newspaper, such as feminism and

When Horace Greeley advised 'Go west, young man, go west', he was actually repeating the words in an editorial in the *Terre Haute Express* that were written by John L Soule.

abolitionism. He was an advocate of American westward expansion, and is remembered for his advice 'Go west, young man, go west'. One of the founders of the **Republican Party** in 1854, Greeley was the unsuccessful presidential candidate of the breakaway Liberal Republicans in 1872.

Green Mountain Boys
Irregular troops who fought to protect the Vermont part of what was then New Hampshire colony from land claims made by neighbouring New York. During the **American Revolution** they captured Fort Ticonderoga from the British. Their leader was Ethan **Allen** who was later captured by the British. Vermont declared itself an independent republic, refusing to join the Union until 1791. It is popularly known as the Green Mountain State.

Grenada invasion
The invasion on 5 October 1983 of the Caribbean island of Grenada by 3,000 US Marines and a small force from six Caribbean countries. This followed the assassination of Grenada's prime minister Maurice Bishop and a military coup. The US government of President Ronald **Reagan** said it had been asked to intervene by the Organization of East Caribbean States. The US forces left after two months and the following year, Grenada elected a new government. Because Grenada is part of the British Commonwealth, many people protested the US military action.

Guadalcanal, Battle of
In **World War II**, an important US operation from 1942 to 1943 on the largest of the Solomon Islands in the southwestern part of the Pacific Ocean. The battle for control of the area began when the US landed marines to take the site on 7 August 1942. The Japanese sent reinforcements by sea and a series of bitter engagements took place on land, for control of the airfield, and at sea. Both sides lost large numbers of ships and aircraft. The Japanese concluded that such heavy naval losses could not be justified by one island and evacuated on 9 February 1943. US casualties came to 1,600 killed and 2,400 wounded; Japanese losses were 14,000 killed, 9,000 dead from disease or starvation, and 1,000 captured.

Guantanamo Bay
The location of a US Navy base in Cuba, located on Guantanamo Bay on the island's eastern end. It was established in 1903 under an agreement that pulled out US troops who had occupied Cuba since they had helped end Spanish control in 1898.

'Gitmo' is the nickname given by American sailors to their Guantanamo Bay base.

Cuba's communist president Fidel Castro has tried unsuccessfully to close the base, once briefly cutting off electricity and water. The base has been used as a sanctuary for fleeing Cuban and Haitian refugees.

Gulf War

A war from 16 January to 28 February 1991 between Iraq and a coalition of 28 nations led by the USA. It was known to the Americans as 'Desert Storm' and to the British as 'Operation Granby'. The invasion and annexation of Kuwait by Iraq on 2 August 1990 provoked a build-up of US troops in Saudi Arabia, eventually totalling over 500,000. The UK subsequently deployed 42,000 troops, France 15,000, Egypt 20,000, and other nations smaller contingents. An air offensive lasted six weeks, in which 'smart' weapons came of age. A 100-hour ground war followed on 24 February that effectively destroyed the remnants of the 500,000-strong Iraqi army in the area. Kuwait was once more independent, but the Iraqi leader Saddam Hussein was allowed to stay in place.

- The war was the first large-scale demonstration of modern technological warfare, such as guided missiles and 'smart' bombs. About 90,000 tonnes/99,225 tons of ordnance were dropped by US planes and 3,000 tonnes/3,308 tons by British planes.

- Estimates of Iraqi casualties are from 80,000 to 150,000 troops and from 100,000 to 200,000 civilians.

- Of the 148 US service personnel killed during the war, 35 died as a result of 'friendly fire' by US or allied forces.

Gun Control

Although US gun laws are in force both at a federal and state level, the right to bear arms is considered a constitutional right, and pressure groups such as the National Rifle Association (NRA) wield considerable power. It is estimated that half of all American households own at least one gun. In 1994 the Brady Bill, named after former White House press secretary James Brady who was seriously hurt in the 1981 attempted assassination of President Ronald **Reagan**, became effective. This law enforced a five-day waiting period for people buying handguns. Other gun-control strategies exist, and in 1997 homicides by guns dropped by 9.2% (but still accounted for 60% of all deaths).

The USA has experienced recent gun-related tragedies by teenagers, including the massacre of 14 students and 1 teacher at Columbine High School in Denver, Colorado, in April 1999.

Hale, Nathan (1755–1776)

A colonial hero of the **American Revolution**, hanged by the British as a spy on 22 September 1776. Born in Coventry, Connecticut, Hale graduated from Yale in 1773 and became a schoolteacher. He fought with the Connecticut militia in the American Revolution. He crossed British lines disguised as a teacher and told George **Washington** that he wished 'to be useful.' He was sent behind enemy lines on Long Island to gather information about the British army. Captured, he was hanged. Reputedly, his final words were 'I only regret that I have but one life to lose for my country'.

Nathan Hale's famous words were actually first used by the British writer Joseph Addison in his play, *Cato*. (1713)

Halsey, William Frederick (1882–1959)

A US admiral during **World War II**. His nickname was 'Bull'. A highly skilled naval air tactician, his handling of carrier fleets in the war played a significant role in the eventual defeat of Japan. He was appointed commander of US Task Force 16 in the Pacific in 1942 and almost immediately launched the Doolittle raid on Tokyo. He took part in operations throughout the Far East, including Santa Cruz, **Guadalcanal**, Bougainville, and the Battle of Leyte Gulf. He was promoted to fleet admiral in 1945 and retired in 1947.

Hamilton, Alexander (1757–1804)

A US politician who influenced the adoption of a constitution with a strong central government and was the first secretary of the Treasury from 1789 to 1795. During the **American Revolution**, he served as a captain and was secretary and aide-de-camp to George **Washington**. He was a member of the **Continental Congress** and wrote some of the **Federalist Papers**, influencing public opinion in favour of the ratification of the **Constitution of the United States**. As the first secretary of the treasury, he advocated a national bank.

Hamilton publicly supported the wealthy urban sector of American life and encouraged renewed ties with Britain, remaining distrustful of revolutionary France. He led the **Federalist Party** and incurred the bitter hatred of Aaron Burr when he voted against Burr and in favour of Thomas **Jefferson** for the presidency in 1801. Challenged to a duel by Burr, Hamilton was wounded and died the next day.

Hampton Roads, Battle of
The first battle between armoured warships, known as ironclads. The inconclusive naval engagement in the **Civil War** was on 8 March 1862 off the southeast coast of Virginia, between the Confederate *Virginia* (the recently renamed *Merrimack*) and the Union battleship *Monitor*. Each captain watched their shots bounce off the other vessel, and although they circled and bombarded for some hours, no decision was reached. *Monitor* ran out of ammunition, and *Virginia* withdrew to make some minor repairs. They never encountered each other again.

Hancock, John (1737–1793)
A US politician and a leader of the **American Revolution**. As president of the **Continental Congress** from 1775 to 1777, he was the first to sign the **Declaration of Independence** in 1776. In popular belief, his signature on document was written large so that it would be big enough for British king George III to see. Hancock had coveted command of the Continental Army, deeply resenting the selection of George **Washington**. He was governor of Massachusetts from 1780 to 1785 and from 1787 to 1793. In 1788 he presided at his state convention to ratify the **Constitution of the United States**.

Because John Hancock signed the Declaration of Independence in a large, bold hand, his name became a nickname for a signature in the USA, such as: 'Put your John Hancock on this'.

Harvard
The oldest educational institution in the USA and usually considered the best. It is especially famous for its business, law, and medical schools. It was founded in 1636 at New Towne (later Cambridge), Massachusetts, with a grant from the Massachusetts Bay Colony. Two years later it was named Harvard College after John Harvard (1607–1638), a British-born Puritan minister, who bequeathed half his estate and his library to it. Harvard was

organized as a university in 1869. Women were first admitted 1969, and the women's college is Radcliffe College.

Hearst, William Randolph (1863–1951)

A US editor and publisher who controlled a vast communications empire and wielded great political power in the first half of the 20th century. He bought the *New York Journal* in 1895 and began a famous newspaper battle with Joseph Pulitzer's *New York World*. Hearst was accused of helping incite the **Spanish–American War** to help his paper's circulation. His holdings eventually included newspapers in most major cities, magazines such as *Good Housekeeping* and *Cosmopolitan*, the Hearst News Service, several radio stations and two film companies. He served as a Congressman from New York from 1903 to 1907

William Randolph Hearst's life was the basis of Orson Welles's film *Citizen Kane* (1941), which Hearst tried to suppress.

Henry, Patrick (1736–1799)

A US patriot who in 1775 supported the arming of the Virginia militia against the British by a speech ending, 'Give me liberty or give me death!' Henry was born in Studley, Virginia, and became a very successful lawyer. In 1765 he became a member of the Virginian House of Burgesses, and in the same year declared the **Stamp Act** illegal. He was governor of Virginia from 1776 to 1779 and from 1784 to 1786. Henry assisted in the creation of the **Continental Congress**, of which he was a member. He opposed ratification of the **Constitution of the United States** on the grounds that it jeopardized states' rights. His influence, however, helped to ensure the passage of ten amendments to it that constitute the **Bill of Rights**.

> ❝ I know not what course others may take; but as for me, give me liberty, or give me death! ❞
>
> **Patrick Henry**, speech in the Virginia Convention, 23 March 1775

Hickok, 'Wild Bill' (1837–1876)

The nickname of James Butler Hickok, a US pioneer and law enforcer who was a legendary figure in the **Wild West**. In the **Civil War** he was a sharpshooter and scout for the Union army. He then served as marshal in Kansas, killing as many as 27 people. From 1872 to 1874, he was a performer in Buffalo Bill's Wild West Show and was rumoured to be the lover of **Calamity Jane**. Hickok was a prodigious gambler and was fatally shot from behind while playing poker in Deadwood, South Dakota.

In American poker, a hand consisting of two aces, two eights, and another card, is called the 'dead man's hand', because that was what 'Wild Bill' Hickok was holding when he was killed.

Hiroshima

The Japanese industrial city that, on 6 August 1945, was the first to be destroyed by a US atomic bomb dropped by the *Enola Gay*. It is located on the south coast of Honshu island. More than 10 sq km/4 sq mi of Hiroshima were obliterated. Casualties totalled at least 137,000 out of a population of 343,000: 78,150 were found dead, others died later. By 1995 the death toll, which included individuals who had died from radiation-related diseases in recent years, had climbed to 192,000. An annual commemorative ceremony is held on 6 August.

Hiss, Alger (1904–1996)

A US diplomat and former state department official imprisoned in 1950 for perjury when he denied having been a Soviet spy. Hiss, a liberal Democrat, was accused in 1948 by a former Soviet agent, Whittaker Chambers, of having passed information to the USSR from 1926 to 1937. He was convicted of perjury before the **House Committee on Un-American Activities** and served four years in prison. He spent the remainder of his life attempting to clear his name and was still living when the official Soviet commission on KGB archives reported in 1992 that he had never been a spy.

Hollywood

A district in the city of Los Angeles, California, that has been the centre of the US film industry since 1911. The 'Golden Age' of Hollywood is said to have been from 1930 to 1949 when the industry was ruled by large studios. It is still the home of film studios such as Twentieth Century Fox, MGM, Paramount, Columbia Pictures, United Artists, Disney, and Warner Bros. The Hollywood film industry seemed in jeopardy in the 1950s from television and in the 1960s and 1970s from productions moving to cheaper European locations, especially Italy. It then rebounded and has re-established its international dominance, spreading American culture and ideals via its cinema and television productions. This virtual monopoly on commercial films has caused concern in other countries, particularly in France.

The American film industry was established on the East Coast and then began to move to the tiny community of Hollywood in 1908 to take advantage of the sunshine, cheap labour and land, and the beautiful nearby scenery.

Homestead Act

An act of **Congress** in 1862 to encourage settlement of land in the West by offering 65-hectare/160-acre plots cheaply or even free to those willing to cultivate and improve the land for five years. By 1900 about 32 million hectares/80 million acres had been distributed to 'homesteaders'. US homestead lands are available to this day. **See also:** *Sooners.*

Hooker, Joseph (1871–1879)

A Union brigadier general in the **Civil War**, known as 'Fighting Joe' Hooker.

He became the commander of the Army of the Potomac on 26 January 1863 but was relieved of that position five months later after losing the Battle of **Chancellorsville** to Gen Robert E **Lee**. He also fought in the battles

Brig-Gen Joseph Hooker was known for his drinking and gambling, and prostitutes in Washington, DC, were humorously called 'Hooker's Army'.

of **Antietam, Fredericksburg** and Chattanooga, where he led the formidable charge up Lookout Mountain to secure the victory.

Hoover, Herbert (Clark) (1874–1964)

The 31st president of the USA from 1929 to 1933, a Republican. Hoover lost public confidence after the stock-market crash of 1929, when he opposed direct government aid for the unemployed in the **Great Depression** that followed. Shantytowns, or **Hoovervilles**, of the homeless sprang up around large cities. In 1933 he was succeeded by Franklin D **Roosevelt**. Hoover was born in West Branch, Iowa. He became a mining engineer, and travelled widely before **World War I**. After the war he organized relief work in occupied Europe. President Woodrow **Wilson** made him a member of the War Trade Council, and he took part in Paris in the negotiation of the Versailles Treaty. Before becoming president, he was secretary of commerce from 1921 to 1928.

> 6 When there is a lack of honour in government, the morals of the whole people are poisoned. 9
>
> **Herbert Hoover**, quoted in the *New York Times*, 9 August 1964

hotline
The direct telephone link established on 13 August 1963 between US president John F Kennedy and Soviet premier Nikita Khrushchev. The object of the special instant communications system was to avoid misunderstandings that could lead to nuclear war. The need for such a system was realized the previous year during the **Cuban missile crisis**. The hotline has remained a vital connection between the White House and Kremlin.

House Committee on Un-American Activities (HUAC)
A Congressional committee established in 1938 as the Special Committee to Investigate Un-American Activities under the chairmanship of Martin Dies. Noted for its public investigation of alleged subversion, it achieved its greatest notoriety during the late 1940s and the 1950s through its hearings on communism in the film industry, sending 10 producers, directors, and screenwriters (known as the 'Hollywood Ten') to prison for about a year. Known from 1969 as the House Committee on Internal Security, it was abolished in 1975. **See also:** *McCarthy, Joseph.*

Houston, Sam (Samuel) (1793–1863)
The US general who led the **Texas Revolution** in 1836 and was president of the Republic of Texas from 1836 to 1845. His troops won the crucial Battle

> 6 I tell you that, while I believe with you in the doctrine of States' Rights, the North is determined to preserve this Union. They are not a fiery, impulsive people as you are, for they live in colder climates. But when they begin to move in a given direction...they move with a steady momentum and perseverance of a mighty avalanche. 9
>
> **Sam Houston**, speaking to Texans in Austin, 1861

of San Jacinto in 1836 over Mexican general Santa Anna. The city of Houston, Texas, is named after him. In his earlier life he was governor of Tennessee from 1827 to 1829. After Texas joined the Union in 1845, Houston was a US senator from Texas from 1846–59 and the state's governor from 1859–61, giving up that position because he opposed Texas leaving the Union to join the **Confederate States of America**.

HUAC See *House Committee on Un-American Activities.*

Hudson, Henry (*c.* 1565–1611)
An English explorer of America. Under the auspices of the Muscovy Company in 1607 and 1608, he made two unsuccessful attempts to find the Northeast Passage to China. In September 1609, commissioned by the Dutch East India Company, he reached New York Bay and sailed 240 km/150 mi up the river that now bears his name, establishing Dutch claims to the area. In 1610 he sailed from London in the *Discovery* and entered what is now the Hudson Strait. After an icebound winter, he was turned adrift by a mutinous crew in what is now Hudson Bay and was never seen again.

immigration

The USA was created by waves of immigrants fleeing their native lands for various political, religious, and economic reasons. More than 15 million immigrants arrived, mostly from north Europe, between 1820 and 1890, and then more than 18 million, mostly from southern and eastern Europe, between 1891 and 1920. These massive numbers led to the establishment of national quotas in 1921, which were ended in 1965. A more recent problem has been illegal immigration from such southern neighbours as Mexico, Cuba, and Haiti. The Immigration Act of 1990 established a total for all immigrant admissions at 700,000 and built in preferences for skilled workers, a move expected to increase immigration from Europe. The USA still receives more immigrants into its population each year than any other nation. **See also:** *Ellis Island.*

❝ There is no part of our nation that has not been touched by our immigrant background. Everywhere immigrants have enriched and strengthened the fabric of American life. ❞

President John F Kennedy, *A Nation of Immigrants*,
1964 (published posthumously)

---

impeachment

The judicial procedure used in the USA by which government officials are accused of 'high crimes and misdemeanours' and brought to trial by **Congress**. The House of Representatives may impeach offenders to be tried before the Senate. Convictions require a two-thirds majority of senators. Only two presidents have been impeached, Andrew **Johnson** in 1868 and Bill **Clinton** in 1999. Both were found not guilty of acting illegally. Richard Nixon resigned the US presidency in 1974 when threatened by impeachment.

> ❝ I welcome this kind of examination because people have got to know whether or not their president is a crook. Well, I'm not a crook. ❞
>
> **President Richard Nixon**, press conference concerning the Watergate scandal, 17 November 1973

impressment

The impressment, or seizure, of seamen to force them to serve in the British Royal Navy was one of the main causes of the US **Embargo Act** and of the **War of 1812**. British warships were stopping American vessels and boarding them to remove both British deserters and American citizens. At the Treaty of Ghent in 1814 ending the War of 1812, the British agreed to give up the practice. In 1841 when Britain asserted the right to board US ships to search for slaves being transported, the US also refused.

income tax

The first US income tax (of 3%) was introduced on 5 August 1861 during the **Civil War** to help finance that conflict, but **Congress** repealed it in 1870. The US **Supreme Court** ruled in 1895 that a federal income tax was unconstitutional, but a permanent US income tax came into effect in 1913 with the passage of the 16th Amendment to the **Constitution of the United States**. Today, every citizen (with certain exemptions on the grounds of age or income level) must file an annual income-tax report to the Internal Revenue Service. A state income tax has also levied in many states since 1919. In a few cases, such as New York City, there is a city income tax as well.

Independence Day

A public holiday in the USA on 4 July, commemorating the adoption of the **Declaration of Independence** on that date in 1776. It is popularly called 'the Fourth of July'. The holiday is celebrated with parades, picnics, fireworks, speeches, and by flying the Stars and Stripes.

John Adams and Thomas Jefferson both died on Independence Day in 1826, the 50th anniversary of the Declaration of Independence. Adams's last words were, 'Thomas Jefferson still surv....'

Independence Hall

The building in Philadelphia, Pennsylvania, where the **Continental Congress** wrote and signed the **Declaration of Independence** in 1776 and also where the Federal Constitution Convention wrote and approved the **Constitution of the United States** in 1787. The **Liberty Bell** is also displayed outside the hall. The building was designed by Andrew Hamilton as the Pennsylvania State House (capitol) and constructed in 1732. Located in Independence National Historical Park, it is now a historical museum and in 1979 became a World Heritage Site.

Indians See *American Indians*.

Indian Territory

A territory set aside by the US government for **American Indian** peoples. It was initially most of the land west of the Mississippi River, but after 1834 the term was restricted to the present state of Oklahoma. After the Indian Relocation Act of 1830, most of the American Indians east of the Mississippi were relocated to Indian Territory, some forcibly, including the **Five Civilized Tribes** from 1835 to 1843. Indian Territory became the Territory of Oklahoma in 1890.

> 'Oklahoma' means 'red people' in the Choctaw language.

Indian Wars

A term used for the battles between **American Indians** and the new white settlers, from colonial times until 1890. The colonial conflicts included the Pequot War of 1637 in Connecticut and the large King Philip's War in 1675 and 1676 involving many American Indian people and all the New England colonies. Major Indian Wars of the 19th century included the **Creek** War of 1813 and 1814, the **Seminole** War from 1835 to 1842, the **Apache** revolts from 1876 to 1886, the Nez Percé War involving Chief **Joseph** in 1877, and the US suppression of the **Ghost Dance** in 1890, the last Indian War.

INF Treaty

The abbreviation and common name for the Intermediate Nuclear Forces Treaty signed on 8 December 1987 in **Washington, DC**, by US president Ronald **Reagan** and Soviet leader Mikhail Gorbachev. The USA and the USSR agreed to eliminate all ground-based nuclear missiles in Europe that were capable of hitting only European targets (including European Russia).

The treaty reduced the countries' nuclear arsenals by some 2,000 (4% of the total) and included provisions for each country to inspect the other's bases.

Intermediate Nuclear Forces Treaty See *INF Treaty*.

Intolerable Acts

The colonists' name for acts passed by the British Parliament in 1774 to punish the American colonists in Massachusetts who had defied British laws. They also called them the Coercive Acts. The five acts were:

- The Boston Port Act, closing Boston Harbour in retaliation for the **Boston Tea Party**
- The Massachusetts Bay Regulating Act, withdrawing many general rights
- The Impartial Administration of Justice Act, requiring accused British officials to be tried in other colonies or Britain
- The Quartering Act, requiring colonists to provide shelter and food for British soldiers
- The Quebec Act, moving Quebec's border south to the Ohio River.

The Intolerable Acts enraged most Americans and led them to organize the First **Continental Congress** on 5 September 1774.

Iran-Contra Affair

A US political scandal in 1987 involving senior members of the **Reagan** administration. It was also called Irangate. Congressional hearings in 1986 and 1887 revealed that the US government had secretly sold weapons to Iran in 1985 and traded them for hostages held in Lebanon by pro-Iranian militias, and used the profits to arm right-wing Contra guerrillas in Nicaragua. The negotiator in the field was Lt-Col Oliver **North**. The Congressional Joint Investigative Committee reported in November 1987 that it found no firm evidence that President Reagan had been aware of the Contra diversion. In December 1993, however, the independent prosecutor Lawrence Walsh reported that Reagan and Vice-President George **Bush** were fully aware of the arms sales to Iran.

The total cost of the Iran-Contra enquiries came to $35 million.

Irangate See *Iran-Contra Affair*.

Iran hostage crisis

A long crisis from 4 November 1979 until 19 January 1981 when Iranian militant students held 90 US embassy personnel, including 66 Americans, as hostages in their embassy in Teheran for 444 days. The students demanded without success that the US turn over the former Shah of Iran. The event placed President Jimmy **Carter** under pressure, and on 24 April 1980 he finally authorized a military rescue mission that failed. The crisis helped defeat him in the 1980 election, and the Iranians released all of the hostages on the day Ronald **Reagan** was inaugurated as president.

isolationism

Isolationism in the USA was first called for by President George **Washington** in his farewell address, advising his country not to become involved in European affairs. More recently, it has usually been associated with the **Republican Party**, especially politicians of the Midwest. Intervention in **World War I** was initially resisted, and the Neutrality Acts from 1935 to 1939 aimed to keep the nation out of **World War II**. In the 1960s some Republicans even demanded the removal of the **United Nations** from American soil. America's commitment to world affairs, however, has kept isolationists in the minority.

Iwo Jima, Battle of

Intense fighting between US and Japanese forces from 19 February to 17 March 1945 during **World War II**. In February 1945, US marines landed on the island of Iwo Jima, a Japanese air base, intending to use it to prepare for a planned final assault on mainland Japan. The 22,000 Japanese troops put up a fanatical resistance, but the island was finally secured on 16 March. US casualties came to 6,891 killed and 18,700 wounded, while only 212 of the Japanese garrison survived.

A famous photograph was taken of the marines raising the Stars and Stripes on Mount Suribachi at Iwo Jima. The picture became a symbol for America's victory in the Pacific War.

Iwo Jima *The Iwo Jima monument in Washington showing marines raising the Stars and Stripes on Mount Suribachi.*

Jackson, Andrew (1767–1845)

The 7th president of the USA from 1829 to 1837, a Democrat. A major general in the **War of 1812**, he defeated a British force at New Orleans in 1815 (not knowing the war had officially ended in 1814) and was involved in the war that led to the purchase of Florida in 1819. The political organization he built as president was the basis for the modern **Democratic Party**. He created the first 'Kitchen Cabinet' of personal advisers, and his administration is particularly associated with the **spoils system**. Jackson was born in South Carolina and spent his early life in poverty. Despite his youth, he fought in the **American Revolution**. He became the first Congressman from Tennessee in 1796 and 1797, then a senator from that state in 1797 and 1798. He was a famed Indian fighter, defeating the **Creek** at the Battle of Horseshoe Bend on 27 March 1814 and campaigning against the **Seminole** in Florida in 1817 and 1818.

Americans gave Andrew Jackson the nickname of 'Old Hickory' because of his rugged style and tough leadership.

Jackson, 'Stonewall' (Thomas Jonathan) (1824–1863)

A US Confederate lieutenant general in the **Civil War**. He acquired his nickname and his reputation at the first Battle of **Bull Run** in 1861, from the firmness with which his brigade resisted the Northern attack. In 1862 he organized the Shenandoah Valley campaign and assisted Gen Robert E **Lee** in his invasion of Maryland. Jackson helped to defeat Gen Joseph E Hooker's Union army at the Battle of **Chancellorsville**, but was fatally wounded by one of his own soldiers in the confusion of battle.

- 'Stonewall' Jackson was deeply religious and was constantly seen raising his arm in prayer during a battle.
- He had many odd habits, such as refusing to eat pepper, sucking lemons, and going into battle wearing his cap from the Mexican War. Once under a furious artillery fire, his soldiers saw him astride his horse, pouring molasses over his meal of one cracker.

- Told that Jackson's arm had been amputated, Robert E Lee said of his best general, 'He has lost his left arm, but I have lost my right'.

Jackson, Jesse Louis (1941–)

An African-American Democratic politician who is a cleric and campaigner for minority rights. He contested his party's 1984 and 1988 presidential nominations in an effort to increase voter registration and to put black issues on the national agenda. He sought to construct a 'Rainbow Coalition' of ethnic-minority and socially deprived groups. Jackson is an eloquent public speaker, and in 1998 emerged as a spiritual adviser to President Bill **Clinton**. Jackson first worked with the civil-rights leader Martin Luther **King** Jr, then on building the political machine that gave Chicago a black mayor in 1983.

> 6 We've removed the ceiling above our dreams.
> There are no more impossible dreams. 9
>
> **Jesse Jackson**, quoted in the *Independent*, 9 June 1988

James, Jesse Woodson (1847–1882)

An infamous US bank and train robber in Missouri. He and his brother Frank (1843–1915) rode with the Quantrill raiders, a ruthless Confederate guerrilla band in the **Civil War**. After the war, they led their 'James Gang' from 1866 to 1879, conducting robberies as far as Texas. Jesse later settled down and was killed by Bob Ford, his 19-year-old cousin and accomplice, who shot him in the back to collect the $10,000 reward on his life. Frank was never convicted and became a farmer.

Jamestown

The first permanent British settlement in North America, established by Captain John **Smith** in 1607. It was capital of Virginia from 1624 to 1699. The colony initiated the first representative government in North America; it also brought the first slaves and built the first Anglican church there. Subject to a

Today in the nearby Jamestown Festival Park there is a replica of the original Fort James, and models of the ships (*Discovery*, *Godspeed*, and *Constant*) that carried the 105 pioneers.

high mortality rate, the population remained small, and the settlement was the victim of fire in 1608. It was about to be abandoned when Lord De La Warr arrived with new supplies.

Japanese-American internments

The forced removal in 1942 of about 110,000 Japanese-Americans to internment camps during **World War II**. Most lived on the West Coast and, although loyal Americans, were considered to be security risks during the war. They were held for three years at War Relocation Camps in the country's interior. In 1983, the US government paid $20,000 in compensation to those who had been interned.

Jayhawkers

Union guerrilla forces along the Missouri border during the **Civil War** who attacked slave owners in Missouri, killing them and burning their homes and towns. The most infamous Jayhawer was a former US senator from Kansas, James H Lane. Confederate guerrillas known as Bushwrackers responded in an equally bloody fashion, the worst example being **Quantrill's Raiders**.

Jay's Treaty

An agreement in 1794 between the USA and Britain that changed the two nations' trade agreements and ended the British occupation of forts in the US northwest territory. It was negotiated by John Jay, a diplomat and the first chief justice of the US **Supreme Court**. The treaty was unpopular with Americans because it restricted US trade with the West Indies and did not address the problem of the **impressment** of American sailors by British naval ships.

Jefferson, Thomas (1743–1826)

The 3rd president of the USA from 1801 to 1809, and the founder of the **Democratic Republican Party**. As a member of the **Continental Congress**, he was largely responsible for the drafting of the **Declaration of Independence**. He was then governor of Virginia from 1779–81, ambassador to Paris from 1785–89, US secretary of state from 1789–93, and US vice-president from 1797 to 1801. Notable achievements of his presidency include the public land system, the **Bill of Rights**, and the **Louisiana Purchase**. He once described the presidency as 'splendid misery'. Jefferson was born in Virginia into a wealthy family, educated at William and Mary

Jefferson was instrumental in the establishment of the US capital (now Washington, DC) on the banks of the Potomac River, and he was the first president inaugurated there.

College, and became a lawyer. His interests included music, painting, architecture, and the natural sciences; he was very much a product of the 18th-century Enlightenment. He designed the state capitol at Richmond, Virginia, and the University of Virginia in Charlottesville. His political philosophy of 'agrarian democracy' placed responsibility for upholding a virtuous American republic mainly upon a citizenry of independent yeoman farmers. He carried on a battle with Alexander **Hamilton**, who held views directly opposed to his own agrarian, democratic inclinations. Ironically, his two terms as president saw the adoption of some of the ideas of his political opponents, the Federalists.

Jefferson *The 3rd US president and great liberal statesman, Thomas Jefferson. He was the first president to be inaugurated in Washington (a city that he helped to plan). Among the important events of his presidency were the Louisiana Purchase in 1803 of the French territories in the Mississippi Basin, and the abolition of the slave trade in 1808.*

❝ A little rebellion now and then is a good thing, ❞

Thomas Jefferson, letter to James Madison, 30 January 1787

Jehovah's Witnesses

A religious organization originating in the USA in 1872 under Charles Taze Russell (1852–1916). Jehovah's Witnesses attach great importance to Christ's second coming, which Russell predicted would occur in 1914, and which Witnesses still believe is imminent. There are no clergy, and all

Witnesses are expected to take part in house-to-house preaching. Witnesses believe that after the second coming the earth will continue to exist as the home of humanity, apart from 144,000 chosen believers who will reign with Christ in heaven. In 1998, there were nearly 976,000 Jehovah's Witnesses in the USA and 10,671 churches.

Johnson, Andrew (1808–1875)
The 17th president of the USA from 1865 to 1869, a Democrat. He succeeded to the presidency on the assassination of Abraham **Lincoln**. His conciliatory policy to the defeated South during **Reconstruction** after the **Civil War** involved him in a feud with the Radical Republicans, causing his **impeachment** in 1868 before the Senate, which failed to convict him by one vote. Among his achievements as president was the purchase of Alaska from Russia in 1867. Johnson was a congressman from Tennessee from 1843 to 1853, governor of Tennessee from 1853 to 1857, a US Senator from 1857 to 1862, and became vice-president in 1865.

> 6 An insolent drunken brute, in comparison with
> whom Califula's horse was respectable. 9
>
> **Anonymous**, on Andrew Johnson, quoted in the *New York World*, 1875

Johnson, Lyndon Baines (1908–1973)
The 36th president of the USA from 1963 to 1969, a Democrat. He was popularly known as 'LBJ'. Johnson became president on the assassination of John F **Kennedy** and successfully won congressional support for many of Kennedy's **New Frontier** proposals, especially civil rights. He declared a **War on Poverty** supported by his **Great Society** legislation. His foreign policy met with considerably less success. He increased US involvement in the Vietnam War, but after violent antiwar protests he declined to run for reelection in 1968. Johnson was born in Stonewall, Texas, and served as a

> 6 I am a free man, an American, a United States
> senator, and a Democrat, in that order. 9
>
> **Lyndon Baines Johnson**, quoted in *Texas Quarterly*, Winter 1958

Congressman from 1937 to 1949 and as a senator from 1949 to 1960, becoming minority leader in 1953 and majority leader the following year. He was noted for his persuasive skills in bringing about political agreements. **See also:** *Tonkin Gulf Resolution.*

Jones, John Paul (1747–1792)
A Scottish-born American naval officer in the **American Revolution**. He was born John Paul and adopted the Jones name. Heading a small French-sponsored squadron in the *Bonhomme Richard*, he raided British ships in the English Channel, capturing the warship *Serapis* in a bloody battle off Scarborough, Yorkshire, in 1799.

Jones was originally a trader and slaver but became a privateer in 1775, and then a commodore. After the war, he joined the Russian navy as a rear admiral in 1788, fighting against Turkey, but lost the Empress Catherine's favour and died in France.

John Paul Jones named his ship *Bonhomme Richard* in honour of Benjamin Franklin's Poor Richard in his *Poor Richard's Almanack.*

❝ I have not yet begun to fight. ❞

John Paul Jones, on being asked to surrender as his ship was sinking during the battle with the British ship *Serapis*.

Joseph, Chief (c. 1840–1904)
An American Indian chief of the Nez Percé people. Born in the Wallowa Valley of Oregon, Joseph became chief in 1873 and was originally an advocate of passive resistance. After initially agreeing to leave tribal lands in 1877, he later led his people in armed resistance. He killed 20 whites and ordered a mass retreat to Canada, marching more than 1,600 km/1,000 mi, but the Nez Percé were caught by the troops of Gen Nelson Miles only 48 km/30 mi from the Canadian border. They were sent in 1885 to the Colville Reservation in the state of Washington.

Kansas–Nebraska Act

Legislation passed by Congress in 1854, regulating the territories of Kansas and Nebraska. By allowing the settlers there to decide for themselves whether or not to permit slavery, the act upset the political balance between North and South established in 1820 by the **Missouri Compromise**. The Kansas-Nebraska Act helped to start the **Civil War** and caused the rise of the **Republican Party**.

Kellogg–Briand Pact

An agreement negotiated in 1927 between the USA and France to renounce war and seek settlement of disputes by peaceful means. It took its name from the US secretary of state Frank B Kellogg and the French foreign minister Aristide Briand. Most other nations subsequently signed. Some successes were achieved in settling South American disputes, but the pact made no provision for measures against aggressors and became ineffective in the 1930s, with Japan in Manchuria, Italy in Ethiopia, and Hitler in central Europe.

Kennedy, Edward Moore (1932–)

A US liberal Democratic politician. His nicknames are 'Ted' and 'Teddy'. He aided his brothers John **Kennedy** and Robert **Kennedy** in their presidential campaigns of 1960 and 1968, respectively, and entered politics as a senator for Massachusetts in 1962. He is known for his support of healthcare reform, civil rights, welfare, and the environment. He failed to gain the presidential nomination in 1980, largely because of questions about his delay in reporting a car crash in 1969 at Chappaquiddick Island, near Cape Cod, Massachusetts, in which his passenger, Mary Jo Kopechne, was drowned.

Kennedy, John F(itzgerald) (1917–1963)

The 35th president of the USA from 1961 to 1963, a Democrat. He was the first Roman Catholic, and the youngest person, to be elected president. His popular nickname was 'Jack'. The son of financier Joseph Kennedy, he was born in Brookline, Massachusetts, educated at **Harvard** and briefly at the London School of Economics. He served in the navy during **World War II**, winning the **Purple Heart**. After the war, he was

In the 30 years following his assassination, more than 2,000 books were published about John Kennedy's death and a number of conspiracy theories put forward, mostly involving the KGB, FBI, or CIA.

elected from Massachusetts to the House of Representatives in 1946 and the Senate in 1952. As president, Kennedy approved the unsuccessful **Bay of Pigs** invasion of Cuba in 1961, and a year later secured the withdrawal of

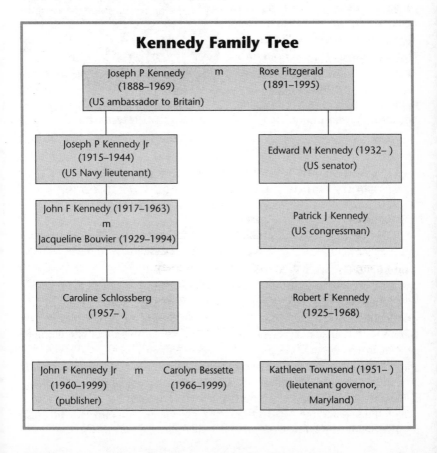

Kennedy Family Tree

Joseph P Kennedy (1888–1969) (US ambassador to Britain) m Rose Fitzgerald (1891–1995)

Joseph P Kennedy Jr (1915–1944) (US Navy lieutenant)

Edward M Kennedy (1932–) (US senator)

John F Kennedy (1917–1963) m Jacqueline Bouvier (1929–1994)

Patrick J Kennedy (US congressman)

Caroline Schlossberg (1957–)

Robert F Kennedy (1925–1968)

John F Kennedy Jr (1960–1999) (publisher) m Carolyn Bessette (1966–1999)

Kathleen Townsend (1951–) (lieutenant governor, Maryland)

Soviet missiles from the island after the **Cuban Missile Crisis**. With the aid of his brother Robert **Kennedy**, who was attorney general, he used National Guard troops to force Southern schools to accept black students. Kennedy also created the **Peace Corps** of volunteers to developing nations. His programme for reforms at home, called the **New Frontier**, was later pushed through by Lyndon **Johnson**. Kennedy was assassinated while on a visit to Dallas, Texas, on 22 November 1963. Lee Harvey Oswald, a communist activist, who was shot dead by Jack Ruby, was within a few days named by police as the assassin. **See also***: Warren Commission.*

Kennedy *J F Kennedy, the 35th president of the USA.*

> ❝ And so, my fellow Americans: ask not what your country can do for you — ask what you can do for your country. ❞
>
> **John F Kennedy**, inaugural address, 20 January 1962

Kennedy, Robert Francis (1925–1968)

The US attorney general from 1961 to 1964, and a key aid to his brother, President John F **Kennedy**. His popular nickname was 'Bobby'. He was the chief counsel of the Senate Select Committee on Improper Activities in the Labour and Management Field from 1957 to 1961. Appointed US attorney general by his brother, he pursued a racket-busting policy and worked to enforce federal law in support of civil rights. When President Lyndon **Johnson** preferred Hubert H Humphrey for the 1964 vice-presidential nomination, Kennedy resigned as attorney general and was elected senator from New York. When running for the 1968 Democratic presidential nomination, he was assassinated by Sirhan Bissara Sirhan in California after a campaign speech.

❝ We have always believed it possible for men and women who start at the bottom to rise as far as their talent and energy allow. Neither race nor creed nor place of birth should affect their chances. ❞

Robert Kennedy, introduction to John F Kennedy's book,
A Nation of Immigrants, 1963

Khe Sanh siege

During the **Vietnam War** in 1968, the siege of about 5,000 US Marines and South Vietnamese troops at their Khe Sanh base in northwestern South Vietnam. The siege by 15,000 communist soldiers lasted from 21 January to 14 April and was part of their **Tet Offensive**. US warplanes constantly bombed around the base, and the siege was broken by 'Operation Pegasus', led by the US 1st Air Cavalry Division and a South Vietnamese airborne company.

King, Martin Luther, Jr
(1929–1968)
A US civil-rights campaigner, black leader, and Baptist minister. He first came to national attention when he organized the Montgomery, Alabama, bus boycott in 1955. He was one of the organizers of the march of 200,000 people on **Washington, DC**, in 1963 to demand racial equality, during which he gave his famous 'I have a dream' speech. An advocate of non-violence, he was awarded the Nobel Peace Prize in 1964. The son of a Baptist minister, King was born in Atlanta, Georgia, and ordained to the ministry in 1947. He was a founder of the Southern Christian Leadership Conference in 1957, but

King *Martin Luther King, the US Baptist minister and civil rights campaigner who won the Nobel Peace Prize in 1964.*

in the mid-1960s his moderate approach was criticized by black militants. On 4 April 1968 he was assassinated in Memphis, Tennessee, by James Earl Ray. King's birthday (15 January) is observed on the third Monday in January as a public holiday in the USA.

> ❛I may not get there with you, but I want you to know tonight that we as a people will get to the promised land.❜
>
> **Martin Luther King**, addressing a rally on 3 April 1968, the night before he was assassinated

Kissinger, Henry (Alfred) (1923–)

A German-born US diplomat famous for his 'shuttle diplomacy'. After a brilliant academic career as professor of government at **Harvard** from 1962 to 1969, he was appointed national security adviser in 1969 by President Richard **Nixon** and was secretary of state from 1973 to 1977. His missions to the USSR and China improved US relations with both countries, and he took part in negotiating US withdrawal from Vietnam in 1973. Kissinger received the Nobel Peace Prize in 1973.

> ❛There cannot be a crisis next week. My schedule is already full.❜
>
> **Henry Kissinger**, quoted in the *New York Times* Magazine, 1 June 1969

KKK See *Ku Klux Klan*.

Know-Nothing Party

A US political party that flourished in the early 1850s. It was so called because 'I know nothing' was the initial response of its members when asked what they stood for. Its policies were conservative, opposed to immigration and Catholics. It became known as the American Party in 1854 and Millard Fillmore was its unsuccessful presidential candidate in the election of 1856.

Korean War

A war from 1950 to 1953 between North Korea (supported by China) and South Korea, aided by the United Nations, (although the troops were mainly US). North Korean forces invaded South Korea on 25 June 1950, and the Security Council of the United Nations, owing to a walkout by the USSR, voted to oppose them. The North Koreans held most of the South when US reinforcements arrived in September 1950, to fight their way through to the North Korean border with China. The Chinese retaliated, pushing them back to

> The US government insisted on calling the war the Korean Conflict, saying it was not an official war.

the original boundary on the 38th parallel by October 1950. The UN troops were led by Gen Douglas **MacArthur**, but President Harry S **Truman** relieved him of duty in 1951 when MacArthur wanted to expand the war into China. Truce negotiations began in 1951, although the war did not end until 1953.

Ku Klux Klan (KKK)

A secret US society dedicated to white supremacy. It was founded in 1866 to oppose **Reconstruction** in the Southern states after the **Civil War** and to deny political rights to the black population. It was founded by former Confederate general Nathan Bedford **Forrest**. Members wore hooded white robes to hide their identity, and burned crosses at their night-time meetings. In the late 20th century the Klan evolved into a paramilitary extremist group and forged loose ties with other white supremacist groups.

Ku Klux Klan *The Ku Klux Klan attempted, at times successfully, to become an accepted part of mainstream politics – here they are seen parading through Washington, DC. However, internal rivalries, a series of scandals, and a greater public awareness of their racism and violence meant that they achieved only local influence.*

In the 1990s, the Ku Klux Klan began actively recruiting and organizing in the UK, with membership coming primarily from existing extreme-right groupings.

Lafayette, Marquis de (1757–1834)

A French soldier and politician who fought with the colonists in the **American Revolution**. His full name was Marie Joseph Paul Yves Roch Gilbert de Motier. Lafayette joined the staff of Gen George **Washington** as a major general and took part in battles from 1777 to 1778 and returned to France in 1779 to persuade King Louis XVI to support the colonists with troops and a fleet. He was at the **Yorktown surrender** in 1781. During the French Revolution, Lafayette sat in the National Assembly as a constitutional royalist and in 1789 presented the Declaration of the Rights of Man.

> Lafayette was a popular hero in the USA, and several towns and cities are named after him, such as those in Louisiana, Indiana, and Alabama.

Lafitte, Jean (c. 1780–1825)

A pirate in America, reportedly born in France. He settled in New Orleans, where he became a smuggler and privateer. Gathering a band of followers around him, he set up headquarters in nearby Barataria Bay and spent several years raiding Spanish shipping in the Gulf of Mexico. Suspected of complicity with the British, he was attacked by American forces soon after the outbreak of the **War of 1812**. He proved his loyalty to Gen Andrew **Jackson** by his heroic participation in the Battle of New Orleans in 1815. After the war, Lafitte established headquarters in Galveston Bay, Texas, returning to piracy. When the US Navy pursued him, Lafitte sailed away and was never heard of again.

Lee, Robert E(ward) (1807–1870)

The general who commanded the Confederate forces during the **Civil War**. As commander of the Army of Northern Virginia, Lee was mostly defending against Union marches on the Confederate capital of Richmond. Born in Virginia, he graduated from West Point military academy and served in the **Mexican War**. In 1859 he suppressed the raid by John **Brown** on Harpers Ferry. On the outbreak of the Civil War in 1861 he turned down an offer by

During the war, the US government siezed Arlington House, Robert E Lee's home across the Potomac River from Washington, DC, and used the land to create Arlington National Cemetery.

President Abraham **Lincoln** to command the Union forces because he would not fight against his own state. Commanding the Confederate army, he was known for his brilliant manoeuvres over the larger forces of the North, winning such major battles as the **Seven Days, Fredericksburg**, and **Chancellors-**

Lee *Gen Robert E Lee*

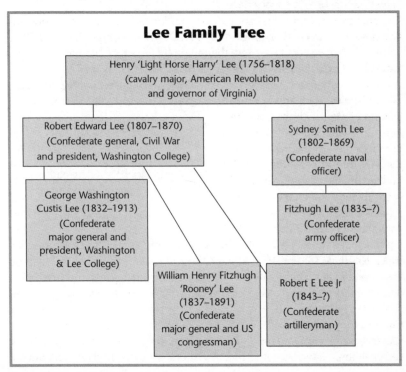

Lee Family Tree

Henry 'Light Horse Harry' Lee (1756–1818)
(cavalry major, American Revolution and governor of Virginia)

Robert Edward Lee (1807–1870)
(Confederate general, Civil War and president, Washington College)

Sydney Smith Lee (1802–1869)
(Confederate naval officer)

George Washington Custis Lee (1832–1913)
(Confederate major general and president, Washington & Lee College)

Fitzhugh Lee (1835–?)
(Confederate army officer)

William Henry Fitzhugh 'Rooney' Lee (1837–1891)
(Confederate major general and US congressman)

Robert E Lee Jr (1843–?)
(Confederate artilleryman)

ville, but losing the critical Battle of **Gettysburg**. Besieged finally in Peterburg with a starving and ill-quipped army, Lee surrendered to Gen Ulysses S **Grant** on 9 April 1865 at **Appomattox Court House**. After the war, he became president of Washington College in Virginia, now named Washington and Lee University.

Lend-Lease Agreement

A policy followed by the USA after President Franklin D **Roosevelt** signed an act in 11 March 1941 that gave him power to order 'any defence article for the government of any country whose defence the president deemed vital to the defence of the USA'. During **World War II**, the USA negotiated many such agreements, notably with Britain and the Soviet Union. Lend-lease was officially stopped in August 1945, by which time goods and services to the value of $42 billion had been supplied in this way, of which the British Empire had received 65% and the Soviet Union 23%.

Lewis and Clark Expedition

The exploration from 1804 to 1806 of the United States' new **Louisiana Purchase** by Meriwether Lewis (1774–1809) and William Clark (1770–1838). Commissioned to explore the region by President Thomas **Jefferson**, they led an expedition of 23 men. The party left St Louis on 14 May 1804 and proceeded up the Missouri River, halting for the winter at Fort Mandan (near today's Bismarck, North Dakota). There they became friends with a 17-year-old Shoshoni girl, Sacagawea, who guided them over the north Rockies to the Oregon Country, reaching the Pacific Ocean at the mouth of the Columbia River on 7 November 1805. Their return

> Meriwether Lewis died mysteriously in 1809 after being shot in a Tennessee cabin while travelling to Washington, DC. Authorities believed he had committed suicide or was murdered.

trip reached St Louis on 23 September 1806, completing their total journey of 11,263 km/7,000 mi. Lewis and Clark's success was hailed throughout the country, and their detailed descriptions of the West increased the American desire to expand to the Pacific.

Lexington, Battle of

The first major engagement of the **American Revolution**, on 19 April 1775 at Lexington, Massachusetts. The first shots were fired when 700 British

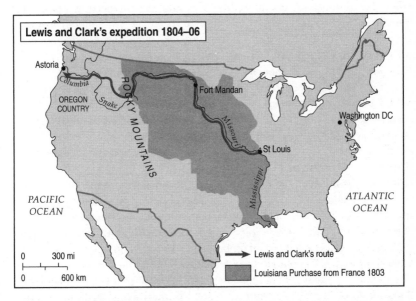

Lewis and Clark's expedition 1804–06

Astoria

Columbia

Snake

OREGON COUNTRY

Fort Mandan

ROCKY MOUNTAINS

Missouri

St Louis

Mississippi

Washington DC

PACIFIC OCEAN

ATLANTIC OCEAN

0   300 mi
0   600 km

→ Lewis and Clark's route

Louisiana Purchase from France 1803

troops under Gen Thomas Gage were marching to nearby Concord to seize illegal military stores and arrest rebel leaders John **Hancock** and Samuel **Adams**. An advance party encountered about 50 Minutemen on Lexington Common. The colonials refused to disperse when ordered to do so, and the British opened fire, killing eight of the **Minutemen**. They then continued on their mission and later became engaged in the larger Battle of **Concord**.

Liberty Bell

The bell that was rung in 1776 on the occasion of the adoption of the **Declaration of Independence** by the **Continental Congress**. It was cast in London in 1752, with the motto 'Proclaim liberty throughout the land unto all the inhabitants thereof'. The bell had cracked the first time it was rung in Philadelphia in 1752 and again in 1835 and 1846. It is now preserved under glass outside **Independence Hall** in Philadelphia, Pennsylvania.

Liberty Bonds

The popular name for US government Liberty Loan Bonds sold during **World War I** to raise money for the war effort. More than $18 billion were sold, with appeals made at huge bond rallies by such **Hollywood** stars as Charlie Chaplin, Mary Pickford, and Douglas Fairbanks. The bonds had been put in circulation by the Liberty Loan Act of 24 April 1917 that immediately created a $5 billion national debt, $3 billion of which could be loaned to the Allies.

Library of Congress

The national US library that was established by and for **Congress** in 1800 in **Washington, DC**. Since 1807, it has had the right to receive two copies of all US copyrighted material. It now contains more than 80 million items in 470 languages. James H Billington has been the librarian of Congress since his appointment by President Ronald **Reagan** in 1987.

Lincoln, Abraham (1809–1865)

The 16th president of the USA from 1861 to 1865 during the **Civil War**, a Republican. He was born in a log cabin in Kentucky and was self-educated. He practised law from 1837 in Springfield, Illinois, and served in **Congress** from 1847 to 1849. Lincoln joined the new **Republican Party** in 1856 and two years later opposed the incumbent US senator Stephen **Douglas**, losing after the famous **Lincoln-Douglas Debates**. In 1860 he was chosen by the Republicans as their presidential candidate, defeating Douglas. In his inau-

gural address in 1861, he said he would not interfere with slavery that already existed, but declared that no state had the right to secede. In 1862, Lincoln's **Emancipation Proclamation** proclaimed the freedom of all slaves in the Confederacy. In his **Gettysburg Address** in 1863, he declared the aims of preserving a 'nation conceived in liberty, and dedicated to the proposition that all men are created equal'. He was re-elected in 1864 on a National Union ticket, advocating a reconciliatory policy towards the South. Five days after the surrender of Gen Robert E **Lee**, Lincoln was shot in a theatre audience by an actor and Confederate sympathizer, John Wilkes Booth.

Lincoln *Abraham Lincoln*

> ❧ That we here highly resolve that the dead shall not have died in vain, that this nation, under God, shall have a new birth of freedom; and that government of the people, by the people, and for the people, shall not perish from the earth. ❧
>
> **Abraham Lincoln**, Gettysburg address, 19 November 1863

Lincoln-Douglas Debates

A famous series of debates from 21 August to 15 October 1858 between Abraham Lincoln and US senator Stephen **Douglas** when they were contesting his seat. Lincoln lost the election but gained the reputation as an impressive orator. During the debates, Douglas accused Lincoln of being a great supporter of **abolitionism**, and Lincoln painted Douglas as being indifferent to the problem of slavery.

Lindbergh, Charles A(ugustus) (1902–1974)

The US aviator who became a national hero after making the first solo non-stop flight across the Atlantic. This was done in 1927 in 33.5 hours from Roosevelt Field, Long Island, New York, to Le Bourget airport, Paris, France. He flew in the *Spirit of St Louis*, a Ryan monoplane designed by him. Lindbergh was a barnstorming pilot, performing in air shows, who took up the challenge after hearing that a prize of £25,000 had been offered to the person who first made a non-stop air flight between New York and Paris. After he had become famous, his young son Charles Jr was kidnapped and killed, an incident that led to legislation against kidnapping called the Lindbergh Act. Lindberg later flew 50 combat missions in the Pacific theatre in **World War II**.

> ❧ I have seen the science I worshipped, and the aircraft I loved, destroying the civilization I expected them to serve. ❧
>
> **Charles A Lindbergh**, quoted in *Time* magazine, 26 May 1967

Little Bighorn, Battle of

The engagement on 25 June 1876 in Montana in which Lt-Col George **Custer** and all 259 of his men of the Seventh Cavalry were killed by **Sioux** and **Cheyenne** Indians led by **Crazy Horse** and **Sitting Bull**. The battle is also known as 'Custer's last stand'. It was preceded by the discovery of gold in the Black Hills and the subsequent violations of the 1868 treaty with the Sioux, which had granted them 'sole use' of the area. Custer ignored scouting reports of an overwhelming Indian force and led a column of soldiers into a ravine where thousands of Indian warriors lay in wait. After the massacre, US reprisals against the Indians followed, driving them from the area.

log cabin

A type of small house built in colonial America and on the frontier. It became an early symbol of simplicity, decency, and hard work. The walls were constructed of logs placed horizontally and connected at the corners by notches but no nails. Clay and mud were used to fill the spaces between the logs. Abraham **Lincoln** was born in a Kentucky log cabin, and many later US politicians claimed such a humble house as their birthplace.

> The log cabin was introduced to America by Swedish and Finnish immigrants.

Long, Huey Pierce (1893–1935)

US Democratic politician who became legendary for his crude dictatorial power as the governor of Louisiana from 1928 to 1932. He then became a senator from Louisiana from 1932 to 1935. He was popular with poor white voters for his programme of social and economic reform, which he called the 'Share Our Wealth' programme. It called for high inheritance taxes and for taxes on high incomes. His slogan was 'Every man a king, but no man wears a crown'. Long's own extravagance, including the bronze and

> ❝ It didn't surprise me when they shot him. These demagogues, the ones that live by demagoguery. They all end up the same way. ❞
>
> **Harry S Truman**, US president, on Huey Long's assassination, quote in Merle *Miller's Plain Speaking*, 1973

marble state capitol building at Baton Rouge, brought him wide criticism, and he was nicknamed 'the Kingfish'. He was assassinated on his capitol's steps, one month after announcing his intention to run for the presidency.

Long Island, Battle of
An early colonial defeat in the **American Revolution** from 27 to 29 August 1776 on Long Island, New York. The British under Gen William Howe landed and forced Gen George **Washington** and his troops back to Brooklyn Heights where the Americans escaped over the East River at night to Manhattan. The colonials had lost about 2,000 men (with three generals taken prisoner), and the British less than 400.

Lookout Mountain, Battle of
An amazing Union victory in the **Civil War** on 24 and 25 November 1863 on Lookout Mountain near Chattanooga, Tennessee, during the Battle of Chattanooga. Confederate troops of Gen Braxton Bragg commanded the top. Union general Ulysses S **Grant** sent Brig-Gen Joseph **Hooker** to attack Lookout Mountain on 24 November, and they forced the rebels higher to Missionary Ridge. The next day, Grant ordered an attack halfway to the top and was dismayed to see his troops storm the entire way to the steep ridge. The charge, however, routed the surprised Confederates. Grant's men later explained that it was safer to keep moving than to pause under the enemy's fire.

Lost Colony, the
The name later given to the first English colony in North America, established in 1585 at Fort Raleigh on Roanoke Island (now off North Carolina) by the English adventurer Walter **Raleigh**. When supplies began to run out for the 117 settlers, their leader, John White, sailed to England for stocks. When he returned in 1590, he found that the entire colony had disappeared without a trace, and their fate has remained a mystery.

Since 1937 a symphonic drama entitled *The Lost Colony* has been performed each summer at the outdoors Waterside Theatre. A reconstruction of the fort, Fort Raleigh National Historic Site, was erected in 1941.

Louisiana Purchase
The purchase by the USA from France in 1803 of an area covering about 2,144,000 sq km/828,000 sq mi, including the present-day states of

Louisiana, Missouri, Arkansas, Iowa, Nebraska, North Dakota, South Dakota, and Oklahoma. The purchase, which doubled the size of the USA, marked the end of Napoleon's plans for a colonial empire and ensured free navigation on the Mississippi River. The **Lewis and Clark Expedition** was sent out a year after the purchase to explore and record the new land.

Loyalist

An American colonist who remained loyal to Britain before and during the **American Revolution**. Such a person was also called a Tory. Approximately 30% of the US population remained loyal, many moving to eastern Ontario, Canada, after the war. Most were crown officials, Anglican clergy, and economically advantaged, although they were represented in every segment of colonial society.

Lusitania

A British ocean liner sunk by a German submarine off Ireland on 7 May 1915 with the loss of 1,200 lives, including 128 Americans. The Cunard passenger ship had also been carrying a store of military supplies, and the week before the sinking the German government had warned Americans not to travel on it. The tragedy helped to bring the USA into **World War I**.

MacArthur, Douglas (1880–1964)

A US general in **World War II**, commander of the US forces in the Far East and, from March 1942, of the Allied forces in the southwestern Pacific. He was responsible for the reconquest of New Guinea and of the Philippines. After the surrender of Japan, he commanded the Allied occupation forces there. During 1950 he commanded the UN forces in Korea, but in April 1951, after threatening to bomb China, he was relieved of all his commands by President Harry S **Truman** but received a hero's welcome on his return to the USA. Born in Arkansas, Macarthur graduated from West Point military academy in 1903, distinguished himself in **World War I**, and rose to become Chief of Staff in 1930.

> ❝ Old soldiers never die, they just fade away. ❞
>
> **Douglas MacArthur**, quoting a British soldiers' song from World War I in his farewell speech to Congress, 19 April 1955

Madison, Dolley (1768–1849)

The wife of US president James **Madison**. Extremely popular as first lady, she was a great asset to Madison's political career. During the **War of 1812** she saved the original **Declaration of Independence** and many state papers along with a portrait of George **Washington** from the British soldiers advancing in 1814. In later life she retained a place in Washington society and was granted a life-long seat on the floor of the House of Representatives.

Dolley Madison was 1.75 m/ 5 ft 9 in tall, and her husband only 1.6m/5 ft 4 in.

Madison, James (1751–1836)

The 4th president of the USA from 1809 to 1817, a Democratic Republican. He was born in Port Conway, Virginia, graduated from the

College of New Jersey (now Princeton) in 1771, and afterwards studied law. He was one of the three writers of the **Federalist Papers**. In 1787 he became a member of the Constitutional Convention and took a leading part in drawing up the **Constitution of the United States**, bringing him the title of 'Father of the Constitution'. He determined that the government was to be composed of three divisions: legislative, executive, and judicial. He also helped draft the **Bill of Rights**. As secretary of state in Jefferson's government from 1801 to 1809, Madison completed the **Louisiana Purchase** negotiated by James **Monroe**. During his presidential administration, the **War of 1812** took place and there were threats of secession by New England states. Although the war ended in stalemate, Madison's fortunes rose with the national expansion that followed. See also *Madison, Dolley*.

> 6 The people, not the government, possess the absolute sovereignty. 9

James Madison, report to the Virginia House of Delegates, December 1799

Mafia

The Mafia in the USA became organized in the late 19th century and grew during **Prohibition**. It is also known as La Cosa Nostra ('our affair') or the Mob. Several of its infamous leaders have been arrested: Al **Capone** was sentenced for federal tax evasion in 1931 and Lucky Luciano was deported in 1946. Recent cases of the US government versus the Mafia implicated Sicilian-based operators in the drug traffic that plagues much of the Western world (the 'pizza connection'). In 1992 John Gotti, reputedly head of the Gambino 'family' of the Mafia, was convicted.

The Mafia features frequently in fiction, as in the 1960s television series *The Untouchables* and in the *Godfather* films of 1972, 1974, and 1990, based on the novel by Mario Puzo.

Maine

The US battleship that was mysteriously blown up in Havana Harbour, Cuba, on 15 February 1898, with the loss of 260 men. It had been sent there to protect American lives and property, and it was suspected that the

Spanish had sunk it. The tragedy helped initiate the **Spanish–American War** with the cry being 'Remember the *Maine*'.

---

6 DESTRUCTION OF THE WAR SHIP *MAINE* WAS THE WORK OF AN ENEMY 9

New York Journal, headline, 15 February 1898

Malcolm X (1926–1965)

The adopted name of Malcolm Little, a US black nationalist leader. Convicted of burglary in 1946, he spent seven years in prison, becoming a follower of the **Black Muslims** leader Elijah Muhammad and converting to Islam. On his release he campaigned for black separatism, condoning violence in self-defence. In 1964, he modified his views and publicly broke with the Black Muslims to found the Organization of Afro-American Unity, preaching racial solidarity. A year later he was assassinated by Nation of Islam opponents while addressing a rally in Harlem, New York.

---

6 You can't separate peace from freedom because no one can be at peace unless he has freedom. 9

Malcolm X, speech in New York City, 7 January 1965

Manhattan Project

The code name for the development of the atom bomb in the USA in **World War II**. The team included the physicists J Robert Oppenheimer, who led the team, and Enrico Fermi. The project began in 1942, first in Oak Ridge, Tennessee, and then Los Alamos, New Mexico. The first bomb was detonated as a test on 16 July 1945 in New Mexico.

manifest destiny

The belief that Americans had a providential mission to extend both their territory and their democratic processes westwards across the continent. This philosophy was expounded by the Democratic followers of President Andrew **Jackson**. The phrase was coined by journalist John L O'Sullivan in

1845. Reflecting this belief, Texas and California were shortly afterwards annexed by the USA.

March on Washington

The largest civil-right gathering that had ever been seen in the USA, held in **Washington, DC**, on 28 August 1963 by more than 200,000 people. The non-violent march and rally at the foot of the Lincoln Memorial heard Martin Luther **King** deliver his famous 'I have a dream' speech. The leaders of the march also visited President John **Kennedy**. Many famous black people participated, and white performers at the event included the folksingers Bob Dylan, Joan Baez, and Peter, Paul, and Mary.

> ❝I have a dream that one day this nation will rise up and live out the true meaning of its creed: 'We hold these truths to be self-evident, that all men are created equal'❞
>
> **Martin Luther King**, addressing the crowd at the Lincoln Memorial, 28 August 1963

Marianas, Battle of the

The World War II battle in 1944 between the US and Japanese navies to control the Mariana Islands in the western Pacific Ocean between Japan and the Philippines. Some 50,000 Japanese soldiers were killed. The most important battle was for the American island of Guam, taken by the Japanese on 13 December 1941 six days after **Pearl Harbor** was attacked. US Marines landed and defeated the Japanese on 10 August 1944 after a 20-day battle, leading to 17,000 Japanese casualties and 1,214 American ones. The US then used the island as a base to bomb Japan.

Marshall Plan

A programme of US economic aid to Europe, set up at the end of **World War II**, totalling $13,000 billion between 1948 and 1952. Officially known as the European Recovery Programme, it was announced by secretary of state George C Marshall in a speech at Harvard on 5 June 1947, but it was in fact the work of a state department group led by Dean Acheson. The perceived danger of a communist take-over in post-war Europe was the main reason for the aid effort.

> 6 Our policy is directed not against any country or doctrine, but against hunger, poverty, desperation and chaos. 9

George C Marshall, speech at Harvard, 5 June 1947

Mason–Dixon Line

The boundary line in the USA that is popularly seen as dividing the North from the South. It is between Maryland and Pennsylvania, named after Charles Mason and Jeremiah Dixon, English astronomers and surveyors who surveyed it from 1763 to 1767. The two colonies had argued for almost a century and even fought some armed skirmishes over the boundary. In 1760, the two agreed to allow Mason and Dixon to delineate the line. Some believe that the name **Dixie** was derived from the line's name.

Massachusetts Bay Company

A self-governing British joint stock company and trading company established in 1629 by royal charter. The members bought up all the stocks and elected John **Winthrop** as their first governor. The following year, the company took more than 1,000 Puritan emigrants to Massachusetts. The Massachusetts Bay Colony became restricted to Puritan freemen (voters) rather than stockholders, and it began to coin its own money. This independence let to the charter being revoked in 1684, turning Massachusetts into a royal colony.

> 6 We must consider that we shall be a city upon a hill. 9

John Winthrop, in a sermon aboard the *Arbella* taking the Massachusetts Bay Company members to America, 1630

mass production

Henry **Ford** began industrial mass production in the USA in 1913 by installing an assembly line at his automobile plant in Detroit, Michigan. The 75-m/250-ft line cut the time needed to produce a Model T car from 13 to

6 hours. A type of mass production had actually begun in 1798 when Eli **Whitney** introduced his 'uniformity system' at his Hartford, Connecticut, musket factory, making guns with interchangeable parts, with one worker handling only one particular part.

Masterson, Bat (William Barclay) (1853–1921)

A US marshal in the **Wild West**. Born in Iroquois County, Illinois, and raised in Kansas, Masterson worked in his early adult years as a buffalo hunter and scout before becoming a deputy marshal in Dodge City in 1876. He briefly served with Wyatt **Earp** in 1880 before moving to Kansas City. He moved to New York in 1902, where he became a sportswriter for the *Morning Telegraph*. He became a great friend of President Theodore Roosevelt.

Bat Masterson was blue-eyed, carried a Colt 45 pistol, and always dressed in fancy clothes. He once rescued a friend from an angry crowd in Ogallala, Nebraska, by starting a fight in a dance hall just as a train arrived; they both left on it.

Mayflower Compact

An agreement signed aboard the *Mayflower* on 21 November 1620 by the **Pilgrim Fathers** the day they landed in Massachusetts. It was largely created by William Bradford, who became the colony's governor in 1621 and served 30 years. The Compact, signed by the 41 heads of their households, established a 'civil body politie' to keep the group together and to 'frame just and equal laws' based on church covenants. This evolved into the government of the Plymouth colony.

McCarthy, Joe (Joseph Raymond) (1908–1957)

A right-wing Republican senator from Wisconsin whose unsubstantiated claim in 1950 that the State Department had been infiltrated by 200 communists started a wave of anticommunist hysteria. McCarthy's witch-hunting campaign included members of the administration of President Harry S **Truman**. McCarthy's tactics were denounced by President Dwight **Eisenhower**, and he was censured in 1954 by the Senate for misconduct. By this time, however, many people had been blacklisted as suspected communists or 'fellow travellers' (communist sympathizers). 'McCarthism' came to represent the practice of using unsubstantiated accusations against political adversaries.

McClellan, George Brinton (1826–1885)
A Union general during the **Civil War**. He was general in chief of the Union forces in 1861 and 1862 but was dismissed by President Abraham **Lincoln** when he delayed five weeks in following up his victory at the Battle of **Antietam**. Lincoln had also replaced him earlier in the war for various delays in attacking the enemy. McClellan was born in Philadelphia, graduated from West Point military academy, and served in the **Mexican War**. During the Civil War, in 1864, he was the unsuccessful Democratic presidential candidate against Lincoln. After the war he served as governor of New Jersey from 1878 to 1881.

McNamara, Robert Strange (1916–)
The US secretary of defence from 1961 to 1968 during the **Cold War**. He advised President John F **Kennedy** during two Cuban crises, the **Bay of Pigs** disaster in 1961, when a Cuban invasion failed, and the **Cuban missile crisis** in 1962 when the Russians were forced to remove their missiles from the island. After Kennedy's assassination, McNamara held his office under President Lyndon **Johnson** when his administration was increasing US involvement in the **Vietnam War**. He then left in 1968 to become the president of the International Bank for Reconstruction and Development.

Medal of Honor
The highest US military decoration, sometimes called the Congressional Medal of Honor. It was established in 1862 and is given by Congress to those in combat who courageously risk their lives above and beyond the call of duty. The number of medals given during major wars have been:

- World War I: 125
- World War II: 433
- Korean War: 131
- Vietnam War: 239

In 1997, President Bill **Clinton** belatedly awarded the Medal of Honor to seven black servicemen (six deceased) who served in World War II, the first blacks from that war to receive the decoration. **See also:** *Purple Heart.*

melting pot
The description of America as a melting pot that merges different races and cultures, was first used in 1909 by the British writer Israel Zangwill in his play, *The Melting Pot*, about Jewish immigrants in the USA. The metaphor

was weakened from the late 20th century by American ethnic groups wishing to retain their own identity and culture.

> 6 America is God's Crucible, the great Melting-Pot where all the races of Europe are melting and re-forming! 9
>
> **Israel Zangwill**, *The Melting Pot*, 1909

Mexican War

The war between the USA and Mexico from 1846 to 1848, begun in territory disputed between Mexico and Texas (annexed by the USA in 1845 but claimed by Mexico). President James Polk was determined to pursue his notion of **manifest destiny** for the USA and dispatched Gen Zachary **Taylor** to add the disputed territories, by force if necessary. Taylor invaded New Mexico after efforts to purchase what are now California and New Mexico failed. Mexico City was taken 1847, and under the Treaty of Guadaloupe Hidalgo that ended the war, the USA acquired New Mexico and California, as well as clear title to Texas in exchange for $15 million.

Midway, Battle of

In **World War II**, a decisive US naval victory over Japan from 3 to 6 June 1942 off Midway Island, northwest of Hawaii. The Midway victory was one of the most important battles of the Pacific War, with Japanese naval air superiority destroyed, putting an end to Japanese expansion and placing them on the defensive thereafter. The Americans sank one Japanese carrier and so damaged another two that

The wreck of the USS *Yorktown* was found in 1998 three miles down on the floor of the Pacific Ocean.

they were abandoned. The remaining Japanese carrier managed to launch a strike that sank the USS *Yorktown* on 7 June but was later in the day so damaged by another US strike it had to be scuttled. With no aircraft carriers or aircraft left, the Japanese abandoned their attack and retreated.

Minutemen

Volunteer colonial militia during the **American Revolution**. They adopted the name because they were prepared to take up arms at a minute's notice.

The colonies of Massachusetts, Maryland, Connecticut, and New Hampshire had Minutemen. They fought at the war's first battles at **Lexington** and **Concord** and were of great importance before the regular colonial army was established.

Missouri Compromise

The solution by **Congress** of a sectional crisis caused by the 1819 request from Missouri for admission to the Union as a slave state, despite its proximity to existing non-slave states. The Compromise, mostly devised by Henry **Clay**, consisted of several laws passed in 1820 and 1821. Its solution was the simultaneous admission of Maine as a non-slave state to keep the same ratio. In addition, slavery was forbidden in the **Louisiana Purchase** north of latitude 36° 30′ N with the exception of Missouri. Missouri was then admitted as a slave state on 10 August 1821.

Mobile Bay, Battle of

A Union naval victory on 5 August 1864 in the **Civil War**. It was won by the Union fleet commanded by Admiral David **Farragut** over the Confederate fleet under Admiral Franklin Buchanan. The Union forces were much greater, with 3,000 naval personnel against 470 Confederates. Mobile Bay is a deep inlet in the coast of southwestern Alabama and was the Confederacy's last open port on the Gulf of Mexico east of Texas. Farragut's ships had to manoeuvre pass 'torpedoes' (floating mines) and two forts guarding the entrance to the bay. The admiral had himself tied to the mast of his ship, the USS *Hartford*, in order to direct his forces better.

> ❝ Damn the torpedoes! Full speed ahead. ❞
>
> **David Farragut**, during the battle of Mobile Bay, 5 August 1864

Molly Maguires, the

A secret Irish-American coalminers' organization in the USA in the 1870s that staged strikes and used violence against coal-company officials and property in the anthracite fields of Pennsylvania, beginning a long period of turbulence in industrial relations. The movement was infiltrated by Pinkerton agents (detectives), and in 1876 trials led to convictions and executions.

'Monkey Trial'

A highly publicized trial held in Dayton, Tennessee, in 1925. John T Scopes, a science teacher at the high school, was accused of teaching, contrary to a state law, Charles Darwin's theory of evolution. The defence counsel, arranged by **American Civil Liberties Union**, was Clarence Darrow and the prosecutor was William Jennings Bryan. Scopes was convicted and fined $100, but this was waived on a technical point. Tennessee did not change the law until 1967.

Monmouth, Battle of

During the **American Revolution**, an engagement on 28 June 1778 at Monmouth Court House (now Freehold), New Jersey, by American soldiers under Gen George Washington and the British under Gen Sir Henry Clinton. It was a stand-off, with American general Charles Lee infuriating **Washington** by ordering a retreat. (Lee was later court-martialled and dismissed from the army.)

'Molly Pitcher' was the nickname given to Mary Ludwig after she became an American heroine in this battle. She carried water to the colonial soldiers and supposedly fired on the British with her husband's gun after he fell.

Monroe Doctrine

The declaration by US president James **Monroe** in 1823 that any further European colonial ambitions in the western hemisphere would be regarded as threats to US peace and security. It was made in response to proposed European intervention against newly independent former Spanish colonies in South America. In return for the quietening of such European ambitions, the USA would not interfere in European affairs. The doctrine, subsequently broadened, has been a recurrent theme in US foreign policy, although it has no basis in US or international law.

Monroe, James (1758–1831)

The 5th president of the USA from 1817 to 1825, a Democratic Republican. He served in the **American Revolution**, was minister to France from 1794 to 1796, and in 1803 negotiated the **Louisiana Purchase**. He was secretary of state from 1811 to 1814 and from 1815 to 1817. As president, he presided over the so-called 'Era of Good Feeling', a period of domestic tranquillity. He obtained Florida from Spain and settled Canadian border disputes with Britain. He is mostly remembered for the **Monroe Doctrine** opposing European intervention in the Americas. Monroe was born in Westmoreland County, Virginia, and represented Virginia in the **Continental Congress** from 1783 to 1886. He initially opposed ratification of the **Constitution of the United States**, fearing a central government with excessive power. He was a member of the US Senate from 1790 to 1794 and governor of Virginia from 1799 to 1802

❝ National honour is national property of the highest value. ❞

James Monroe, first inaugural address, 4 March 1817

Moral Majority

A US right-wing evangelical Christian pressure group, which promotes traditional family values and has opposed abortion, gay rights, single parenthood, feminism, the **Equal Rights Amendment**, 'welfare dependency', and pornography. The movement, which is close to the **Republican Party**, was led from the 1970s by the Rev. Jerry Falwell of Virginia. It formed the cutting edge for what became known as the New Right, attaining political power with the election of Ronald Reagan as president in 1980. The Rev. Pat Robertson, a Baptist television preacher who challenged for the Republican presidential nomination in 1988, has been the most vocal proponent of its values in recent years, but the movement's influence has weakened.

Mormons

The common name for a Christian sect, the Church of Jesus Christ of Latter-Day Saints, founded in the USA in 1830. Mormons advocate a strict sexual morality, large families, and respect for authority. Polygamy was officially practised until 1890. In 1997 the church claimed a worldwide membership of 10 million, with 56,000 missionaries in 161 countries. Joseph Smith established the sect in Manchester, New York, after he said an angel gave him sacred records written on golden plates by the North American prophet Mormon. In 1831, the Mormons began a 16-year movement westwards, their route became known as the Mormon Trail. In 1843 Smith claimed to have received a revelation about 'plural marriages'. The next year he and his brother, Hyrum Smith, were imprisoned and then shot by a mob. Brigham Young succeeded as head of the church and in July 1846 led the Mormons to the Great Salt Lake Valley in the Utah Territory, declaring it the

Promised Land and establishing Salt Lake City and a new temple that today remains the Mormon headquarters.

Muckrakers

A derogatory name for the US journalists and writers from about 1880 to 1914 who aimed to expose political, commercial, and corporate corruption. President Theodore **Roosevelt** pinned the name on them in 1906, saying they were only interested in bad news. The muckrakers were closely associated with **progressivism**. Major figures include the journalist Ida M Tarbell, whose 1904 exposé of the Standard Oil Company led to its successful prosecution, and the novelist Upton Sinclair, whose 1906 novel, *The Jungle*, about Chicago meat-packers, led to the US Pure Food and Drug Act.

> ❝ The men with the muck-racks are often indispensable to the well-being of society, but only if they know when to stop raking the muck. ❞
>
> **Theodore Roosevelt**, US president, speech in Washington, DC, 14 April 1906

mugwump

A nickname name for the reform Republicans who voted in the 1884 presidential election for Grover Cleveland, the Democratic candidate, rather than for their own Republican nominee James G Blaine. Blaine was accused of financial improprieties, and the reform-minded mugwumps were partly responsible for his defeat. The term has come to mean a politician who remains neutral on divisive issues.

'Mugwump' means 'chief' in the language of the American Indian people, the Algonquin.

Murfreesboro, Battle of See
Stones River, Battle of.

My Lai massacre

The killing of 109 civilians in My Lai, a village in South Vietnam, by US troops on 16 March 1968 during the **Vietnam War**. News of the massacre shocked Americans and contributed to domestic pressure for the USA to end its involvement in Vietnam. An investigation in 1969 produced enough evidence to charge 30 soldiers with war crimes, but the only soldier convicted was Lt William Calley, commander of the platoon. Sentenced to life imprisonment in 1971, Calley was released less than five months later on parole.

NAACP

The abbreviation for the National Association for the Advancement of Colored People, a US civil-rights organization dedicated to ending inequality and segregation for black Americans through non-violent protest. Founded in 1910, its first aim was to eradicate lynching. The NAACP campaigned to end segregation in state schools and funded test cases that eventually led to the **Supreme Court** decision, in 1954, outlawing school segregation. Its chairman from 1998 is Julian Bond, an early civil-rights leader.

The NAACP initiated a campaign in August 1999 to increase its membership of about 500,000. 'Knock Across America' was an appeal for each member to sign up at least 10 neighbours of any race.

NAFTA

The abbreviation and common name for the North American Free Trade Agreement between the USA, Canada, and Mexico, agreed in August 1992 and effective from January 1994. The first trade pact of its kind to link two highly industrialized countries to a developing one, it created a free market of 375 million people, with a total GDP of $6.8 trillion (equivalent to 30% of the world's GDP).

NASA

An acronym for the National Aeronautics and Space Administration, the US government agency for space-flight and aeronautical research, founded in 1958 by the National Aeronautics and Space Act. Its headquarters are in **Washington, DC**, and its main installation is at the Kennedy Space Center in Florida. NASA's early planetary and lunar programmes included Pioneer spacecraft from 1958, which gathered data for the later crewed missions, the most famous of which took the first people to the moon in *Apollo 11* in 1969. In the early 1990s, NASA moved towards lower-budget 'Discovery Missions', which should not exceed a budget of $150 million (excluding launch costs), nor a development period of three years.

Nashville, Battle of

During the **Civil War**, a Union victory over the Confederate army, fought on 15 and 16 December 1864 at Nashville, Tennessee. After Atlanta fell to Union troops, a Confederate army of some 55,000 under Gen John B Hood marched west towards Tennessee. Nashville was held by Union troops under Maj-Gen George H Thomas. Hood fought a fierce battle against the advance guard, losing about 4,500 troops, and the Union soldiers retired to Nashville. Hood pursued, took up a position on the hills around the town and waited for Thomas to make the next move. On 15 December, he unleashed an attack that forced the Confederates back across the Tennessee River, leaving behind about 2,000 dead and 5,500 prisoners.

National Aeronautics and Space Administration See *NASA*.

National Association for the Advancement of Colored People See *NAACP*.

National Guard

An armed force of volunteers maintained by each US state. They are used for civil unrest, such as the 1965 Watts riots in Los Angeles that were suppressed by 12,000 Guard members. They also help communities damaged by natural disasters. The US government can transfer Guard members to federal control to support regular troops, as happened in the **Gulf War** in 1991. When Alabama governor George **Wallace** brought

> In 1970, four students at Kent State University in Ohio were shot and killed by nervous members of the Ohio National Guard as they demonstrated against the Vietnam War.

in his Alabama National Guard to keep black students from entering the University of Alabama, President John F **Kennedy** turned the force into national troops who then forced Wallace to admit the students.

National Recovery Administration See *NRA*.

National Republican Party

A US political party established in the 1820s as the **Democratic Republican Party** was splitting up. Its leaders included John Quincy **Adams** and Daniel **Webster**. The party advocated taking an active role in the economy. It lost two elections to Andrew **Jackson**, losing in 1828 with Adams as its candidate and in 1832 with Henry **Clay**. In 1836, the party merged with others to form the **Whig Party**.

National Road
A historic US highway running west from Cumberland, Maryland, and eventually extending to St Louis, Missouri. Authorized in 1806, it was the main route for migration over the Appalachians in the early 19th century. Its first section, the Cumberland Road, was completed in 1818. This followed the route of 'Nemacolin's Path', a trail blazed by a Delaware chief from 1749 to 1750. The National Road played a major role in the settlement of the Great Plains, but declined in importance after the advent of the railways in the 1850s. Nowadays, highway US 40 roughly follows the route.

Nation, Carry Amelia (1846–1911)
A US campaigner for temperance in the late 19th century who gained fame by entering saloons and smashing up bottles and barrels with a hatchet. The attacks were effective because Nation was a large, strong woman. Born in Kentucky, she moved to Kansas (where liquor was officially illegal) after her first husband died from alcoholism. She soon began her rampage through saloons, and was arrested some 30 times in the 1890s.

- Carry Nation also attacked paintings of naked women when she spied them in saloons
- She paid her jail fines by selling souvenir hatchets
- In her spare time, she lectured against alcohol, tobacco, and foreign food
- Nation expanded her influence by publishing her own newspaper, *Smasher's Mail*.

Native Americans See *American Indians*.

NATO
The abbreviation and common name for the North Atlantic Treaty Organization, established on 24 August 1949 by 12 nations to counter the military threat of the USSR. They agreed that an attack on one member country would be considered an attack on all. The members in 1998 were the USA, Britain, Canada, Belgium, Denmark, France, Germany, Greece, Iceland, Italy, Luxembourg, Netherlands, Norway, Portugal, Spain, and Turkey. The break-up

of the USSR has encouraged former communist nations to apply for NATO membership, and in 1998 the US **Congress** ratified the expansion of the organization to include Poland, Hungary, and the Czech Rebublic. In 1999 NATO conducted its first military bombing campaign to subdue Serbian forces in Kosovo and return the refugees who had fled that land.

Navaho or Navajo

A member of the second-largest group of American Indian people, numbering about 220,000 (1990) and living in Arizona, New Mexico, and Utah. They were traditionally cultivators, although many now herd sheep. They are renowned for their painted pottery, woven rugs and blankets, and silver and turquoise jewellery. Their persistent raiding of white settlers in the southwest resulted in their being attacked by Kit **Carson** and US troops in 1863. They were rounded up and imprisoned until 1868 when a reservation was created for

The name 'Navahu' in their language means 'large planted field'. The Navajo refer to themselves as Dineh ('people').

them, the largest in the USA, mainly in northeastern Arizona but extending into northwest New Mexico and southeast Utah. Some uranium and natural gas is extracted on their land, and this provides a large income for them.

Navigation Acts

A series of acts of passed by the British Parliament to protect English shipping from foreign competition and to ensure monopoly trading between Britain and its colonies. The Navigation Acts helped to establish Britain as a major sea power, although they led to higher prices. Their strict enforcement was a major cause of the **American Revolution**. The acts and restrictions included:

- **1650** Foreign ships were forbidden to trade in English colonies
- **1651** Goods could only be imported in English vessels or in vessels of the country of origin of the goods
- **1660** All colonial produce was required to be exported in English vessels
- **1663** Colonies were prohibited from receiving goods in foreign (rather than English) vessels.

Neutrality Acts

Three acts passed in the 1930s by **Congress** to prevent the USA from being drawn into the growing European conflicts that eventually led to **World War II**. The acts' years and prohibitions were:

- **1935** Imposed a temporary embargo on arms shipments to any belligerent nation
- **1936** banned loans or credits to belligerents
- **1937** prohibited munition shipments to both sides fighting the Spanish Civil War.

The Neutrality Acts were modified in 1939 and eventually replaced by the **Lend-Lease Agreement** of 1941 allowing the USA to aid the Allies without fighting.

New Amsterdam

The original name of New York City. In Dutch, it was 'Nieuw Amsterdam'. The Dutch West India Company bought Manhattan Island from **American Indians** for 60 guilders, paying in goods. The Dutch town was

In 1658, the burgomasters of New Amsterdam banned the sport of 'kolven' (an early form of golf).

a commercial settlement, established in 1624 as capital of the their colony of New Netherlands. After its capture by the British in 1664, it was renamed New York.

New Deal

The programme introduced by President Franklin D **Roosevelt** in 1933 to tackle the **Great Depression**. The centrepiece of the New Deal was the Social Security Act of 1935, which introduced a comprehensive federal system of insurance for the elderly and unemployed. Several administrative agencies were formed to handle the programme, and these included:

- The Public Works Administration, given $3.3 billion to spend on roads, public buildings, and similar developments
- The Agricultural Adjustment Administration, to raise agriculture prices by restricting output
- The Works Progress Administration (**WPA**), to manage public works, including federal theatre, and writers' and arts projects.

The New Deal encouraged the growth of trade-union membership, brought previously unregulated areas of the US economy under federal control, and revitalized cultural life and community spirit.

New England Confederation

An agreement from 1643 to 1684 between the American colonies of Massachusetts, Plymouth, Connecticut, and New Haven to establish a confederation. Officially titled the United Colonies of New England, it was primarily needed to settle boundary disputes and to deal with **American Indians**, conducting wars against them if needed. Competition among the colonies made the alliance less effective by 1664, but it continued in existence for another two decades.

New Frontier

The vigorous social reform programme proposed by President John F **Kennedy** in 1960 in his speech accepting the nomination of the **Democratic Party**. The domestic programme included measures to reduce unemployment, increase education funding, improve housing, offer medical care to the elderly, reduce taxes, and protect civil rights. Congressional opposition prevented the enactment of many New Frontier proposals. Kennedy experienced greater success with his foreign-policy initiatives, improving relations with Latin America, making agreements on atomic test bans, and establishing the **Peace Corps**. After Kennedy's assassination, President Lyndon B **Johnson** worked to ensure the passage and execution of New Frontier policies.

New Netherland

A Dutch colony in America established by the Dutch West India Company in the Hudson River valley of today's New York State. They established Fort Orange (now Albany) in 1617 and **New Amsterdam** (New York City) in 1624. The colony also included parts of what are now New Jersey, Delaware, and Connecticut. The colony was taken by the British in 1664 and renamed New York.

New Orleans, Battle of

In the **War of 1812**, a battle between British and American forces from December 1814 to January 1815, at New Orleans. The city was held by a garrison of about 6,000 troops under Gen Andrew **Jackson**. A British fleet overpowered the American warships in the Mississippi River on 13 December and landed a force of about 6,000 British troops. Gen Sir Edward Pakenham launched a determined attack on the city's defences on 1 January 1815. This failed, largely due to mismanagement and argument between the

The war was already over by the time the battle of New Orleans was fought, but neither of the two forces in the area had received the news.

various commanders. They made another unsuccessful attack on 8 January (dispersing their forces across the battle front) so the expedition withdrew. The British lost 1,500 troops and Gen Pakenham was killed.

Nimitz, Chester William (1885–1966)
A US admiral in **World War II**, commander in chief of the US Pacific fleet. He re-conquered the Solomon Islands in 1942 and 1943, the Gilbert Islands in 1943, and the Mariana Islands and the Marshall Islands in 1944. He signed the Japanese surrender in 1945 as the US representative. Born at Fredericksburg, Texas, Nimitz graduated from the US Naval Academy in 1905. He was chief of the Bureau of Navigation in the Navy Department from 1939 to 1941. After the war, in 1949, he headed the United Nations mediation commission over the Kashmir dispute.

Nixon, Richard M(ilhous) (1912–1994)
The 37th president of the USA from 1969 to 1974, a Republican. He is the only president to ever resign. As president he was responsible for US withdrawal from Vietnam, and the normalization of relations with communist China, but at home his cover-up of the **Watergate** scandal led him to resign in 1974 when threatened with **impeachment**. Nixon was born in Yorba Linda, California, and practised law from 1937 to 1942, then served in the navy during **World War II**, rising to the rank of lieutenant commander. He was vice-president to Dwight **Eisenhower** from 1953 to 1961 and narrowly lost the 1960 presidential election to John F **Kennedy**. He won the 1968 election and was re-elected in 1972 in a landslide victory, but immediately faced allegations about Watergate. Unlike his closest aides, Nixon escaped imprisonment, being pardoned in 1974 by President Gerald Ford.

> **6** There can be no whitewash at the White House. **9**
>
> **Richard Nixon**, on Watergate, television speech, 30 August 1973

North American Free Trade Agreement See NAFTA.
North Atlantic Treaty Organization See NATO.
North, Oliver (1943–)
The US Marine lieutenant colonel at the centre of the **Iran-Contra Affair**. In 1981 he joined the staff of the National Security Council, where he super-

vised the arms-for-hostages deal with Iran in 1985. When this was uncovered in 1986, North was convicted on felony charges of obstructing **Congress**, mutilating government documents, and taking an illegal payment. In September 1991, all charges against him were dropped because his evidence before Congressional committees had been televised, making a fair trial impossible. He was unsuccessful as Virginia's Republican candidate for the US Senate in 1994.

Northwest Territory

The first territory established by the USA. The area now comprises the states of Ohio, Indiana, Illinois, Michigan, Wisconsin, and (part of) Minnesota, all located on the Great Lakes. The French explored the territory in the 17th century. The British ceded it to the USA after losing the **American Revolution**. People living in New England wanted to establish a colony there, so the Northwest Ordinance of 1787 drew up the type of government (also followed by later US territories) with a territorial governor. It also banned slavery. Most of the Northwest Territory's **American Indians** were moved west after the Treaty of Greenville in 1795.

NRA

The abbreviation and popular name for the National Recovery Administration, the main agency formed under the **New Deal** of President Franklin D **Roosevelt**. It set up codes of conduct for fair competitive business practices and also created jobs and raised wages. Many people criticized it for having too many codes that were difficult to administer. The NRA was established by the National Industrial Recovery Act of 1933 but two years later the US **Supreme Court** ruled it unconstitutional and the agency was abolished. It did make significant progress with working conditions, setting the 40-hour week as a standard and abolishing all child labour.

Oakley, Annie (1860–1926)

The stage name of Phoebe Anne Oakley Mozee, a sharpshooter who toured with Buffalo Bull's Wild West Show in the late 1880s, along with her husband, Frank Butler, also a marksman. They were married in 1880 after she defeated him in a shooting match. Oakley was known as 'Little Sure Shot', being less than 153 cm/5 ft tall. The 1946 **Broadway** musical 'Annie Get Your Gun' (1950) and its 1950 film version were based on her life.

A free ticket to an event in the USA is called an 'Annie Oakley' because it is punched like the playing cards she would riddle with bullets.

OAS See *Organization of American States*.

Okinawa, Battle of

An American victory during **World War II** in 1945 on Okinawa Island in the western Pacific about halfway between Japan and the Philippines. US Marines landed on 1 April and were met by fierce resistance that was not overcome until 21 June. Japan launched suicidal kamikaze plane attacks on the supporting US fleet, killing about 5,000 navy-men. About 110,000

Rather than surrendering, many Japanese soldiers committed suicide by leaping from Okinawa's high cliffs.

Japanese soldiers died in the land battle, and the Americans suffered 80,000 killed and wounded. In 1972, the USA officially returned Okinawa to Japan.

'Old Ironsides'

The nickname of the USS *Constitution*, a famous warship used in the **War of 1812**. Its popular name evolved because the ship's oak timbers were put into place by bending (rather than the usual steaming) to keep them harder. The 1,429-tonne/1,576-ton frigate, which cost $302,718, was launched on 21 October 1797 in Boston, Massachusetts. Commanded by Captain Isaac Hull, it used its 55 guns to defeat the British frigate, the *Guerriere*, on 19 August 1812. The *Constitution*, stationed in Boston, has been open to the public since 1934.

On its 200th birthday in 1997, 'Old Ironsides' was sailed around Boston waters on its first voyage in 116 years.

Old Spanish Trail

A 19th-century trail used for trade and immigration from 1829 to 1850 between Santa Fe, New Mexico, and Los Angeles, California. It ran north from Santa Fe, New Mexico, through what is now Colorado and Utah, then southwest through Las Vegas, Nevada, to California. There were alternate branches near the eastern end and also in the west at the Mojave Desert. Parts of the trail had been used in the 18th century by Spanish expeditions moving goods and Indian slaves west. The territory was controlled during the next century by the Mexicans until 1848, and they carried goods west to sell in Los Angeles, returning with mules and horses (often stolen). The first immigrants to use the trail were led by John Rowland and William Workman in 1841, but many followed from New Mexico and more eastern regions.

Open Door Policy

An economic philosophy of equal access by all nations to another nation's markets.

The term was suggested by US secretary of state John Hay in 6 September 1899 to allow all nations free access to trade with China. This would reject any sphere-of-influence agreement for Chinese trade which excluded US and British interests.

Oregon Trail

A 3,218-km/2,000-mi route used mostly in the 1840s by about 10,000 settlers moving to the Northwest. It was the longest trail taken by pioneers, whose journey in covered wagons lasted about six months. The Oregon Trail went from Independence, Missouri, along the River Platte in Nebraska to Fort Laramie, Wyoming, then through the South Pass of the Rocky Mountains and along the Snake and Columbia rivers into the Willamette Valley in the Oregon Territory. In 1842 John

The hoof marks and deep ruts made by wagon wheels along the Oregon Trail can still be seen today.

Frémont mapped the trail beyond the South Pass. In 1978, the route was officially made the Oregon National Historic Trail.

Organization of American States (OAS)

An association founded in on 30 April 1948 at Bogotá, Colombia, by a charter signed by representatives of North, Central, and South American states. It evolved out of the Pan-American Union that existed from 1910 to 1948. The OAS aims to maintain peace and solidarity within the hemisphere, and is also concerned with the social and economic development of Latin America. The headquarters are in Washington, DC, and it had 35 member countries in 1997. Cuba was suspended from membership in 1962.

Osceola (c. 1800–1838)

A **Seminole** leader, born in Georgia. Although not a chief, he took the lead in opposing all efforts to remove his people from their Florida homeland. His warriors' killing of a US agent in 1835 touched off the second Seminole War, and he led his people in actively resisting the Federal forces. US troops seized Osceola under a flag of truce and imprisoned him in Fort Moultrie, South Carolina, where he died.

Overland Trail

The name of various routes taken from the late 1850s to the 1870s between the Midwest and West by settlers and stagecoach companies. It was sometimes called an 'overland route'. An important Overland Trail led to the gold fields of California, running from Fort Bridger in the Utah Territory to Sutter's Fort, California. Another went to Oregon as a southern alternative of the **Oregon Trail**, running through Nebraska and used in 1860 and 1861 by the **Pony Express**. The 'Butterfield Trail', used from 1858 to 1861 by carriers for the Butterfield Stage Company, began at Tipton, Missouri, crossed the Mojave Desert to Los Angeles and then turned northwest to San Francisco.

Paine, Thomas (1737–1809)

An English left-wing political writer whose pamphlet *Common Sense* (1776) ignited passions in the **American Revolution**. His later writings include *The Rights of Man* (1791) and *The Age of Reason* (1793). He advocated republicanism, deism, the abolition of slavery, and the emancipation of women. Paine, born in Thetford, Norfolk, was a friend of Benjamin **Franklin** and went to America in 1774, where he published several republican pamphlets and fought for the colonists in the war. In 1787 he returned to Britain where, in 1792, he was indicted for treason and escaped to France to sit in the National Convention. Narrowly escaping the guillotine, Paine returned to the USA in 1802 and died in New York.

❝ Even the distance at which the Almighty has placed England and America is a strong and natural proof that the authority of the one over the other was never the design of Heaven. ❞

Thomas Paine, *Plain Arguments for Independence*, January 1776

Panama Canal

The canal built by the USA from 1904 to 1914 across the Panama isthmus in Central America, connecting the Pacific and Atlantic oceans. The canal runs southeast from Cristóbal on the Atlantic to Balboa on the Pacific. Its length is 80 km/50 mi, with 12 locks; the average width is 150 m/492 ft. The French had first attempted the construction and failed. The Panama Canal Zone was acquired 'in perpetuity' by the USA in 1903, comprising land extending about 5 km/3 mi on either side of the canal. Nationalist feeling in Panama led to anti-US riots in 1964, and the zone was given to Panama in 1979. Control of the canal itself was ceded to Panama in January 1990.

Pan-American Union See *Organization of American States.*

Patton, George Smith (1885–1945)

A US general in **World War II**, known as 'Old Blood and Guts'. He was known for his strict discipline and tough attitude that inspired both fear and admiration in his soldiers. During **World War I**, he formed the first US tank force and led it in action in 1918.

He was appointed to command the 2nd Armored Division in 1940 and became commanding general of the First Armored Corps the following year. In 1942 he led the Western Task Force

The actor George Scott played the general in the 1970 film *Patton*, which won three Academy Awards.

that landed at Casablanca, Morocco. After commanding the 7th Army in the invasion of Sicily, he led the 3rd Army across France and into Germany, and in 1945 took over the 15th Army.

Peace Corps

The US organization that provides skilled volunteer workers for Third World countries. It was established by President John F **Kennedy** in 1961. Men and women work in the countries for a period of two years, especially in the fields of teaching, agriculture, and health. Living among the country's inhabitants, workers are paid only a small allowance to cover their basic needs and maintain health. The organization provides around 6,500 volunteers in 94 countries each year, and by 1995 over 140,000 people had been involved. The Peace Corps was inspired by the British programme Voluntary Service Overseas.

Pearl Harbor

The US Pacific naval base in Oahu, Hawaii, that was attacked by Japanese aircraft on 7 December 1941, bringing the USA into **World War II**. The attack took place while Japanese envoys were holding so-called peace talks in Washington. It was carried out by a large Japanese naval force that included six carriers and over 300 aircraft. Four US battleships were sunk, three severely damaged, and almost 200 aircraft were destroyed on the ground. Combined US service casualties were 3,303 killed or missing and 1,272 wounded. The attack galvanized public opinion and raised anti-Japanese sentiment to fever pitch. 'Remember Pearl Harbor' became a patriotic cry. Today Pearl Harbor is a submarine base, supply centre, and naval shipyard.

> ❝ Yesterday, December 7, 1941, a day which will
> live in infamy, the United States of America was
> suddenly and deliberately attacked by naval and air
> forces of the Empire of Japan. ❞
>
> **President Franklin D Roosevelt**, emergency address to Congress,
> 8 December 1941

Peninsula Campaign

A Union campaign in the **Civil War** from April to July 1862 to take
Richmond, Virginia, the capital of the **Confederate States of America**. The
thrust, led by Maj-Gen George B **McClellan**, was along the peninsula
between the James and York rivers. The campaign failed when Confederate
troops under Gen Robert E **Lee** defeated the invaders in the Battles of the
Seven Days.

Pennsylvania Dutch

The popular name given to German immigrants who settled into areas of
eastern Pennsylvania. This influx of settlers began in 1683, and reached its
peak in the early and mid-18th century. They included persecuted sects
such as the Moravians, Mennonites (including the **Amish**), Dunkards (members of the Church of the Brethren), Schwenkfelders, and others. The
designation 'Dutch' is a corruption of 'Deutsch', and their language is a
form of German. For religious reasons, members of the groups still wear
simple black clothes and will not use machines, travelling by horse and
buggy rather than by car.

- The Pennsylvania Dutch groups were attracted by the religious tolerance
  proclaimed in William Penn's colony.
- They set up home in the rich farmland around Philadelphia. A ring of
  their settlements surrounds the city at a distance of some 80 km/50 mi.
- The major cities are Allentown, Bethlehem, Reading, and Lancaster.
- Their names, arts and crafts, building styles, farming techniques, and
  local dialect all still strongly reflect a German heritage.

Penn, William (1644–1718)

An English Quaker who established the colony of Pennsylvania as a refuge
for persecuted Quakers. Born in London, he joined the Society of Friends

(Quakers) in 1667 and obtained (in settlement of a debt owed by the king to his father) a grant of American land in 1681 on which he founded the colony. Penn made religious tolerance a cornerstone of his administration. He maintained good relations with neighbouring colonies and with the American Indians in the area, but his utopian ideals were not successful for the most part. In 1697 he presented a plan, never acted upon, for a union among the colonies. In 1701 he established, with his Charter of Privileges, a bicameral legislature as the government for Pennsylvania.

> ❪ Let the people think they govern
> and they will be governed. ❫
>
> **William Penn**, *Some Fruits of Solitude*, 1693

Pentagon Papers

A top-secret US Defence Department report on the history of US involvement in the **Vietnam War** that was leaked to the *New York Times* by Defence Department employee Daniel Ellsberg in June 1971. It contained information about the war that had been withheld from the public and even lied about. President Richard **Nixon** tried to stop publication, but the **Supreme Court** ruled in favour of the press. The first instalment was published on 13 June of that year by the newspaper and fuelled the antiwar movement.

Perry, Matthew Calbraith (1794–1858)

A US naval officer who commanded the expedition of 1853 that reopened communication between Japan and the outside world after 250 years' isolation. By a show of military superiority and the use of steamships (thought by the Japanese to be floating volcanoes), he was able to negotiate the Treaty of Kanagawa on 31 March 1854, granting the US trading rights with Japan.

Pershing, John Joseph (1860–1948)

The US general who commanded the **American Expeditionary Force** sent to France in **World War I**. During the war, he stuck to the principle of using US forces as a coherent formation and refused to attach regiments or brigades to British or French divisions. Pershing had served in the **Spanish–American War** in 1898, then in the Philippines from 1899

Gen Pershing's nickname was 'Black Jack' because of his stern look and strict discipline.

to 1903 and in Mexico from 1916 to 1917. He was made a full general in 1919, a rank that had been previously held by only four people, including George **Washington**. In 1921 Pershing became the army Chief of Staff.

Petersburg, Siege of

In the **Civil War**, the Union capture of Petersburg, Virginia, after a prolonged siege from June 1864 to March 1865. Lying south of Richmond, Virginia, Petersburg commanded the main Confederate supply routes. On 17 and 18 June the Union had made a fierce attack on the town which was successfully repulsed, at a cost of over 10,000 Union casualties. From then on, the siege became a drawn-out affair. Gen Robert E **Lee** was finally forced to abandon Petersburg and Richmond on 2 April 1865 and surrendered a week later.

During the siege, on 30 July 1864, the Union forces exploded four tons of gunpowder beneath the Confederate line, leaving an enormous crater for an attack. The Union troops rushing into the crater were rapidly shot by Confederates and sustained 3,798 casualties, including many black soldiers, killed while trying to surrender.

Pickett's charge

During the **Civil War**, the gallant but nearly suicidal charge by Confederate troops on 3 July 1863 during the Battle of **Gettysburg**. The charge was directed by Maj-Gen George E Pickett who sent 13,000 soldiers across 1.6 km/1 mi of open field against Union artillery fire and lost 6,500 of them. Breaking through the Union line on Cemetery Ridge had been the last hope of victory. Gen Robert E **Lee** had issued the order, and Pickett remained bitter after the war, saying 'That old man had my division massacred'. The charge lost the battle, and the battle virtually lost the war.

Pikes Peak

A mountain in the Rocky Mountains of southern Colorado whose sighting was eagerly awaited by prospectors arriving in 1859 to hunt for gold and by settlers on their way to California. It inspired the cry of 'Pikes Peak or bust!' The reddish granite peak is 4,300 m/14,110 ft high and is near the city of Colorado Springs.

- Pikes Peak was explored in 1806 by an expedition led by Zebulon Pike and first scaled in 1820 by James Long

- To the Ute Indians, Pikes Peak was the place where the Great Spirit created living things
- The US poet Katherine Lee Bates, on visiting it in 1893, wrote 'America the Beautiful'
- Today the peak is accessible by cog railway and road.

Pilgrim Fathers

The general name for the 102 Pilgrims who landed at **Plymouth Rock** and founded the **Plymouth Colony**. They had intended to go to Virginia but stormy weather forced them into the safe harbour of Massachusetts. Among their group were 35 English Puritan Separatists from the Netherlands. The Pilgrim Fathers had crossed the Atlantic on the *Mayflower* in which they signed the **Mayflower Compact**. They had a harvest festival after their first bumper crop in 1621, and this evolved into the American holiday of **Thanksgiving**.

Britain presented *Mayflower II*, a full-sized replica of the *Mayflower*, to the USA in 1957, now moored next to **Plymouth Rock** on the Massachusetts coast.

Pilgrim Fathers *The Pilgrim Fathers advancing into America after crossing from Europe in the Mayflower.*

Pledge of Allegiance

A patriotic pledge to the Stars and Stripes made by Americans in schools and during special public gatherings. Both children and adults face the flag and place their right hands over their hearts when making the pledge. It was written by Francis Bellamy, a journalist, and first published in *Youth's Companion* magazine on 8 September 1892. The original version said 'my flag' instead of 'the flag of the United States of America'. Congress added the words 'under God' to the pledge in 1954.

THE PLEDGE OF ALLEGIANCE

I pledge allegiance to the flag of the United States of America and to the republic for which it stands, one nation under God, indivisible, with liberty and justice for all.

Plymouth Colony

The colony established by the **Pilgrim Fathers** in 1620 after they landed at **Plymouth Rock**. Its government was drawn up in the **Mayflower Compact** signed the day they landed. About half of the 102 colonists died during the first winter, but the survivors became efficient farmers after being taught how to grow maize by the Indian Squanto. The Council for New England granted the colony a land patent in 1621, and its population grew to nearly 7,000 before it became part of Massachusetts in 1691.

Plymouth Rock

The impressive granite boulder on the Massachusetts coast where the **Pilgrim Fathers** landed in 1620 aboard the *Mayflower*. The rock split in 1774 when it was being pulled into Plymouth to serve as a symbol of independence. It was soon returned to its original site, and in 1920 a protective Greek-type temple was built over it by the Society of Colonial Dames.

Pilgrim records never actually mentioned Plymouth Rock. It was identified by a church elder in 1741 as their landing place.

Pocahontas (*c.* 1595–1617)

An American Indian woman alleged to have saved the life of English colonist John **Smith** when he was captured by her father, Powhatan. Pocahontas was kidnapped in 1613 by an Englishman, Samuel Argall, and she later married colonist John Rolfe and was entertained as a princess at the English Court. Her marriage and conversion to Christianity (changing her name to Rebecca) brought about a period of peaceful relations between Indians and settlers, but she fell ill and died whilst on her return to Virginia.

Ponce de León, Juan (*c.* 1460–1521)

A Spanish explorer who discovered Florida. He sailed on Columbus's second voyage to the Americas in 1493 and settled in the colony on Hispaniola, later conquering Puerto Rico from 1508 to 1509 and becoming its governor. In 1513, while searching for the legendary 'fountain of youth' he discovered Florida, exploring much of its east coast and part of the west coast. Ponce de León returned to Florida in 1521 and was wounded in a battle with Indians. He died soon after in Cuba.

Pony Express

A system of mail-carrying by relays of horse riders that operated from April 1860 and October 1861 between St Joseph, Missouri, and Sacramento, California, a distance of about 2,900 km/1,800 mi. The trip could be made in about 11 days, and one of the most famous riders was William **Cody** ('Buffalo Bill'). The Pony Express was put out of business by the telegraph. In 1992, the Pony Express National Historic Trail was established.

Pony Express advertisements seeking riders asked for 'skinny, expert riders willing to risk death daily'.

Potsdam Conference

A conference held in Potsdam, Germany, from 17 July to 2 August 1945, between representatives of the USA, Britain, and the USSR. They established the political and economic principles governing the treatment of Germany in the initial period of Allied control at the end of **World War II**. An ultimatum was also sent to Japan demanding unconditional surrender on pain of utter destruction.

Princeton, Battle of

A colonial victory in the **American Revolution** on 3 January 1777 in Princeton, New Jersey. Gen George **Washington** devised a surprise attack on the troops of British general Charles Cornwallis. His men moved quietly through the night, wrapping rags around the cannon wheels, and about 400 soldiers were left in camp to make noises to fool the enemy. The battle turned into a rout. Colonial casualties were 44, but the Americans killed about 100 Redcoats and captured some 300, driving most of the rest towards New Brunswick.

❝ It's a fine fox chase, my boys! ❞

Gen George Washington, to his troops pursuing the British, 3 January 1777

progressivism

A US reform movement especially strong in the two decades before **World War I**. Mainly middle-class and urban-based, progressives secured legislation at national, state, and local levels to improve the democratic system, working conditions, and welfare provision. Three political parties in US history have taken the name of the Progressive Party and all failed to elect their presidential candidates. They were:

- 1912 Also known as the **'Bull Moose' Party** (Theodore Roosevelt)
- 1924 Formed by agriculture and trade-union leaders (Robert M La Follette)
- 1948 Composed of left-wing Democrats (Henry A Wallace).

Prohibition

The period from 1920 to 1933 when alcohol was illegal in the USA. This led to bootlegging (the illegal distribution of liquor, often illicitly distilled), to the financial advantage of organized crime. The 18th Amendment to the **Constitution of the United States** prohibited the 'manufacturing, sale, or transportation' of alcohol. The Volstead Act of 1919 enforced the amendment. Prohibition represented the culmination of a long campaign by church and women's organizations, Populists, progressives, temperance societies, and the Anti-Saloon League. The result was widespread disdain for the law; 'speakeasies' for illicit drinking sprang up, and organized crime activity increased, especially in Chicago and towns near the Canadian border. Public opinion insisted on repeal in 1933 (the 21st Amendment).

> 💬 Great! When does it begin? 💬
>
> **Prince of Wales**, after being asked, on a New York visit in 1933, what he thought of Prohibition

Pueblo

A member of one of the **American Indian** groups who now live in Arizona and New Mexico in villages called pueblos. There were more than 50,000 Pueblos in 1990, and they include the Hopi and Zuni peoples. They are farmers who are renowned for their baskets, weaving, and pottery. The Pueblos' ancestors had a pre-Columbian civilization, living in multi-storied cliff houses. Their great era was from 1050 until the end of the 13th century. Peaceful and religious, they were not involved in the **Indian Wars** during the westward expansion of the USA.

Pulitzer Prize

The name of some 30 awards presented every May, mostly for US journalism, literature, and music. They were established in 1917 through a foundation created by the will of Joseph Pulitzer, who had owned the *New York World*. In 1998, each winner received $5,000. Novelists who have won a Pulitzer include John Steinbeck for *The Grapes of Wrath* (1940), Harper Lee for *To Kill a Mockingbird* (1961), and Philip Roth for *American Pastoral* (1998).

Puritans

The Puritan immigrants who settled in New England in the 17th century, most of them Congregationalists and Presbyterians. The first group went to Plymouth, Massachusetts (supposedly landing on Plymouth Rock), in 1620 from England via Holland. Puritans had a profound, formative influence on American culture, political institutions, education, and church democracy. The Puritans were characterized by a strong conviction of human sinfulness and the wrath of God and by a devotion to plain living and hard work.

Purple Heart

A US medal awarded to members of the armed forces who are wounded in battle. Gen George **Washington** established it on 7 August 1782 as the Badge of Military Merit. The medal had an image of Washington set on a purple heart, so the new name quickly took over. **See also:** *Medal of Honor.*

Quantrill's Raiders

A ruthless guerrilla band of Confederate soldiers under Captain William C Quantrill that operated on the Missouri-Kansas border during the **Civil War**.

They were among the Bushwacker groups who fought with the loyalist **Jayhawkers**. Their members included Frank and Jesse **James** and the murderous 'Bloody Bill'. On 21 August 1863, the gang rode into Lawrence, Kansas, and killed over 150 men and boys in front of their families. Quantrill, who

Quantrill was born in the North in Ohio and fought for the Jayhawkers before switching sides. He began his career as a respected schoolteacher and ended up being called 'the bloodiest man in the Annals of America.'

sometimes used the alias of Charlie Hart, was shot in 1865 by Union soldiers and died in a US prison infirmary.

Raleigh or Ralagh, Walter (c. 1552–1618)

An English adventurer, writer, and courtier to Queen Elizabeth I who organized unsuccessful expeditions to colonize North America from 1584 to 1587. One of these was the **Lost Colony** of 117 settlers who had mysteriously disappeared by 1590. Raleigh also made exploratory voyages to South America in 1595 and 1616. He

> Walter Raleigh is traditionally credited with introducing the potato to Europe and popularizing the use of tobacco.

was imprisoned for treason from 1603 to 1616 and later executed on his return from an unsuccessful final expedition to South America.

Reagan, Ronald (Wilson) (1911–)

The 40th president of the USA from 1981 to 1989, a Republican. He was wounded in an assassination attempt in 1981. Reagan was born in Tampico, Illinois, and became a Hollywood actor in 1937, appearing in 50 films. He entered politics and was governor of California from 1966 to 1974. Reagan was a popular and hawkish president, increasing military spending (sending the national budget deficit to record levels). He adopted an aggressive policy in Central America, ordering the **Grenada invasion** in 1983. His Strategic Defence

> As an actor, Ronald Reagan's most famous line was in the film *Knute Rockne, All American* (1940), when he said 'Win one for the Gipper'. He later used it as a slogan in his presidential campaigns.

Initiative (**SDI**), popularly known as 'Star Wars', announced in 1983, proved costly and unfeasible. In 1987 he and Soviet leader Mikhail Gorbachev agreed a 4 per cent reduction in nuclear weapons. In the **Iran-Contra scandal** in 1987, Reagan admitted that US negotiations with Iran had become an 'arms for hostages deal', but denied knowledge of funds being illegally sent to the Contra guerrillas in Nicaragua.

Reconstruction

The period from 1865 to 1877 after the **Civil War** during which US troops occupied the South after the defeat of the **Confederate States of America**. The economy of the South began to recover but most former slaves remained land-less labourers. Reconstruction saw an influx of Northern profiteers known as **carpetbaggers**. The outside military authority and the equality given former slaves (including the election of some to state legislatures) made Southerners bitterly resentful. They were also required to take a loyalty oath to regain their US citizenship. When President Andrew **Johnson** first refused to agree to the punitive measures against the South demanded by Radical Republicans, they sought to remove him by impeachment, but failed by one vote.

Republican Party

One of the two main political parties of the USA, formed in 1854. It is more right-wing than the Democratic Party, favouring capital and big business. The party was founded by a coalition of slavery opponents, who elected their first president, Abraham Lincoln in 1860. Former general Ulysses S **Grant** was elected to the presidency in 1868 and 1872. The party became divided during attempts by Theodore **Roosevelt** to regulate and control big business. It remained in eclipse until the election of Dwight D **Eisenhower** in 1952 and then Richard **Nixon** who was forced to resign during the Watergate scandal. The party enjoyed landslide victories for Ronald **Reagan** and George **Bush** but then lost the presidency to the Democrat Bill **Clinton** who was re-elected in 1996, although the Republicans retained control of **Congress** and had governors in 32 of the 50 states.

Revere, Paul (1735–1818)

The American revolutionary, a Boston silversmith, who carried the news of the approach of British troops to Lexington and Concord on the night of 18 April 1775. The next morning the first shots of the **American Revolution** were fired at Lexington. (H W Longfellow's poem '*The Midnight Ride of Paul Revere*' commemorates the event.) Revere, who took part in the **Boston Tea Party**, was a courier for the **Continental Congress** and the **Committees of Correspondence**, often riding from Boston to Philadelphia.

Paul Revere's silver *Sons of Liberty* punchbowl of 1768 (Museum of Fine Arts, Boston) is a notable piece. He also printed the first continental money in 1775 and produced propaganda prints exposing British atrocities in the war.

Ridgway, Matthew B(unker) (1895–1993)

A US general who commanded troops in **World War II** and the **Korean War**. In the former, he led the first-ever major airborne assault by the US Army during the invasion of Sicily in 1943 and a year later parachuted with his men into Normandy. He replaced Gen Douglas **MacArthur** in 1951 in Korea and then replaced Gen Dwight **Eisenhower** in 1952 at **NATO** as supreme allied commander of Europe. The following year he became Army Chief of Staff until 1955. He received the Presidential Medal of Freedom in 1986.

'robber barons'

The term applied to wealthy and unscrupulous American businessmen in the late 19th century. The derogatory name was first pinned on railway barons like Jay Gould and Jim Fisk of the Erie Railroad and Cornelius **Vanderbilt** of the New York Central Railroad. It was then extended to industrial leaders like Andrew Carnegie of the United States Steel Corporation and John D **Rockefeller** of the Standard Oil Company.

Rockefeller, John D(avison) (1839–1937)

The founder of the Standard Oil Company in 1870, becoming a well-known millionaire. He also established the philanthropic Rockefeller Foundation in 1913, to which his son John D Rockefeller Jr devoted his life. Standard Oil had achieved control of 90% of US refineries by 1882, and the activities of the Standard Oil Trust led to an outcry against monopolies and to the passing of the Sherman Antitrust Act of 1890. Rockefeller was branded one of the '**robber barons**'.

> John D Rockefeller's grandson, Nelson A Rockefeller, was the 41st US vice-president.

'rolling thunder'

The popular name during the **Vietnam War** for the US bombing offensive against North Vietnam from 2 March 1965 to 31 October 1968. This included industrial sites around the capital of Hanoi. The range of American warplanes included F-4B Phantom jets and B-52 Stratofortresses. 'Rolling thunder' failed to hinder communist attacks, however, in part because of the restraints placed on the military by the administration of President Lyndon B **Johnson**.

Roosevelt, (Anna) Eleanor (1884–1962)

A US social worker, lecturer, and the first lady to President Franklin D

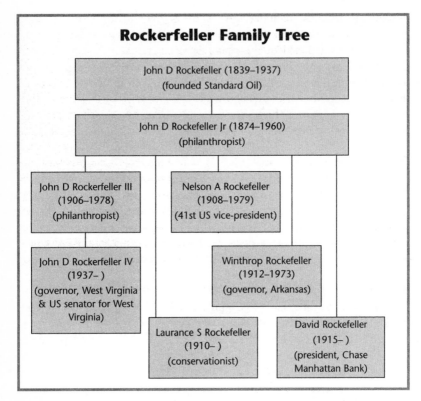

Rockerfeller Family Tree

John D Rockefeller (1839–1937)
(founded Standard Oil)

John D Rockefeller Jr (1874–1960)
(philanthropist)

John D Rockerfeller III
(1906–1978)
(philanthropist)

Nelson A Rockefeller
(1908–1979)
(41st US vice-president)

John D Rockefeller IV
(1937–)
(governor, West Virginia
& US senator for West
Virginia)

Winthrop Rockefeller
(1912–1973)
(governor, Arkansas)

Laurance S Rockefeller
(1910–)
(conservationist)

David Rockefeller
(1915–)
(president, Chase
Manhattan Bank)

Roosevelt. She was his cousin and the niece of Theodore Roosevelt. She influenced **New Deal** policies, especially concerning desegregation, making her unpopular in the South. She was a delegate to the United Nations General Assembly and chair of the UN commission on human rights from 1946 to 1951, helping to draw up the UN's Declaration of Human Rights in 1945. After her husband's death in 1945, Mrs Roosevelt continued to work for civil rights in the USA and for human rights worldwide.

Roosevelt, Franklin D(elano) (1882–1945)
The 32nd president of the USA from 1933 to 1945, a Democrat. He served during two of the 20th century's greatest crises, the **Great Depression** and **World War II**. He was the cousin of President Theodore **Roosevelt**. Born in Hyde Park, New York, of a wealthy family, Roosevelt was educated in Europe and at **Harvard** and Columbia universities. He was the assistant secretary of the navy from 1913 to 1921. He suffered from polio from 1921 but

returned to politics, winning the governorship of New York State in 1929. Becoming president during the Great Depression, he launched the **New Deal** economic and social reform programme. He inculcated a new spirit of hope by his skilful 'fireside chats' on the radio. After the outbreak of World War II he introduced the **Lend-Lease** programme to supply war materials to the Allies and drew up the **Atlantic Charter** of solidarity. Roosevelt was eager for US entry into the war

Roosevelt *Franklin D Roosevelt, the 32nd president of the USA.*

but was restrained by **Congress** until the Japanese attack on **Pearl Harbor** in 1941. He became ill towards the end of the war and died in 1945, having been re-elected for an unprecedented fourth term a few months before.

> ❝ Let me assert my firm belief that the only thing we have to fear is fear itself nameless, unreasoning, unjustified terror which paralyses needed efforts to convert retreat into advance. ❞
>
> **Franklin D Roosevelt**, inaugural address, 4 March 1933

Roosevelt, Theodore (1858–1919)

The 26th president of the USA from 1901 to 1909, a Republican. Nicknamed 'Teddy', he was a cousin of President Franklin D **Roosevelt**. Born in New York City, he graduated from **Harvard** in 1880 and was elected to the state legislature in 1881. He was the assistant secretary of the navy in 1897 and 1898. During the **Spanish–American War** in 1898, he commanded a volunteer force of **Rough Riders**. After serving as governor of New York from 1898 to 1900, he became vice-president to William McKinley, whom he succeeded as president on McKinley's assassination in 1901. As president,

A big-game hunter (on one safari he killed over 3,000 animals), Roosevelt refused in 1902 to shoot a bear cub, which led to **teddy bears** being named after him.

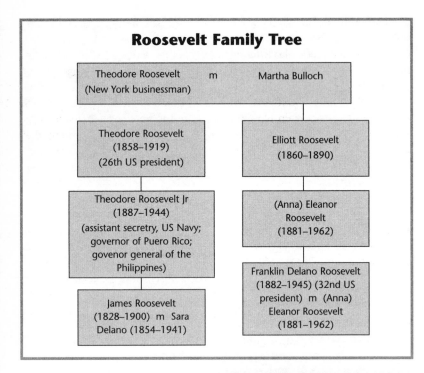

Roosevelt Family Tree

Theodore Roosevelt (New York businessman) m Martha Bulloch

Theodore Roosevelt (1858–1919) (26th US president)

Elliott Roosevelt (1860–1890)

Theodore Roosevelt Jr (1887–1944) (assistant secretry, US Navy; governor of Puero Rico; govenor general of the Philippines)

(Anna) Eleanor Roosevelt (1881–1962)

Franklin Delano Roosevelt (1882–1945) (32nd US president) m (Anna) Eleanor Roosevelt (1881–1962)

James Roosevelt (1828–1900) m Sara Delano (1854–1941)

Roosevelt tackled business monopolies, initiated measures for the conservation of national resources, and introduced the Pure Food and Drug Act. One of his favourite sayings was to 'speak softly and carry a big stick'. He won the Nobel Peace Prize in 1906 for his part in ending the Russo-Japanese war. A feature of his presidency was the Hay-Pauncefote Treaty, which made possible the **Panama Canal**. Roosevelt later formed the Progressive Party, known as the '**Bull Moose**' Party, and unsuccessfully ran for the presidency in 1912. **See also:** *progressivism.*

Roosevelt *Theodore Roosevelt, the 26th president of the USA.*

Rosenberg, Julius (1918–1953) and **Ethel Greenglass** (1915–1953)
A US married couple who have been the only Americans executed for spying during peacetime. They were convicted of being leaders of an atomic-espionage ring passing information from Ethel's brother via courier to the USSR. They were executed after much public controversy. The Rosenbergs were born in New York City, and Julius was a member of the Communist Party. Despite an offer of clemency from the government, they both maintained their innocence right up to their executions. Recently published journals kept by the Soviet leader Nikita Khrushchev further implicate the Rosenbergs.

Ross, Betsy (1752–1836)
The American said to have made the first US flag. According to popular legend, she was approached in 1776 by a family acquaintance, George **Washington**, to create an official flag for the new nation. Despite little historical substantiation, it is believed by many that the familiar red and white stripes with white stars on a field of blue was Ross's original concept. She was born in Philadelphia and married upholsterer John Ross 1773. When he died in 1776, she took over his business. Becoming famous after the war, she continued the business until her retirement in 1827.

Rough Riders
The nickname for the First Volunteer Cavalry during the **Spanish–American War** in 1898. The unit, made up mostly of **cowboys** and ranchers, were commanded by Col Leonard Wood and Lt-Col Theodore **Roosevelt**. The Rough Riders and Roosevelt became famous during the Battle of San Juan Hill in Cuba on 1 July 1898, but actually arrived after the Spaniards had fled.

❝I want to say here plainly that the behaviour of these Rough Riders while marching through the woods shook me with terror as I have never before been shaken.❞

Kennett Harris, war correspondent, describing the troops laughing and making noise in enemy territory, *New York World*, 7 July 1898.

St Augustine

The oldest continuously settled city in the USA, located in northeast Florida. It was founded in 1565 on the site of an **American Indian** village by Spanish explorer Pedro Menéndez de Avilés, near the 1513 landing place of Ponce de León. Twice burned by English buccaneers, it passed to England in 1763 and was a **Loyalist** refuge during the **American Revolution**. It reverted to Spain in 1783, and was ceded to the USA in 1821. Many historic buildings remain, including the city's massive Castillo de San Marcos (1672), the oldest masonry fort in the USA.

St Valentine's Day Massacre

The murder in Chicago of seven unarmed members of the 'Bugs' Moran gang on 14 February 1929 by members of Al **Capone's** gang disguised as police. The victims were machine-gunned in the Windy City beer warehouse. The killings, which eliminated the Capone rival, testified to the intensity of gangland warfare for the control of the trade in illicit liquor during **Prohibition**.

Salem witch trials

Several trials held in Salem in colonial Massachusetts in 1692, that resulted in 19 people being hanged as witches. They were accused after young girls in the town said they were possessed and began to behave wildly. Neighbours began to accuse one another without true evidence, and Salem's citizens were carried along in the hysteria. One of the trial judges, Samuel Sewall, apologized in 1697, saying he believed the victims had not been witches.

The Salem trials were dramatized by Arthur Miller in his famous play, *The Crucible* (1953).

SALT

The abbreviation and common name for Strategic Arms Limitation Talks, a series of US-Soviet discussions from 1969 to 1979 aimed at reducing the rate of nuclear-arms build-up (as opposed to disarmament, as discussed in the **START** negotiations). The SALT talks began in 1969 between US president Lyndon **Johnson** and the Soviet leader Leonid Brezhnev. Neither the SALT I accord (effective from 1972 to 1977) nor SALT II called for reductions in nuclear weaponry, merely a limit on their expansion. SALT II, signed by President Jimmy Carter and Brezhnev in Vienna, Austria, on 18 June 1979, was never fully ratified because of the Soviet occupation of Afghanistan. SALT talks were then superseded by the START negotiations.

Sand Creek Massacre

A massacre of about 500 **Cheyenne** and Arapaho Indians (men, women, and children) by US soldiers on 29 November 1864 at Sand Creek near Fort Lyon, Colorado. The Indians had camped there to have peace talks and await US surrender terms. The Colorado volunteers, led by Col John M Chivington, attacked for no reason, ignoring the white flag and US flag the Indians were flying. Some of the Cheyenne bodies were mutilated by the soldiers.

San Francisco earthquake

An earthquake that killed more than 1,000 people and badly damaged San Francisco, California, on 18 April 1906. Nearly 250,000 residents were made homeless. The earthquake hit at 5:16 a.m., shaking for 47 seconds and setting off wind-blown fires that burned for three days and caused the most damage, destroying over 28,000 buildings on several hundred city blocks. The estimated damage was $250 million.

San Franciscans rebuilt so quickly, no evidence of the earthquake could be seen nine years later when the city hosted the Panama-Pacific International Exposition.

Santa Fe Trail

The oldest US trade route to the West, extensively used from 1821 to 1880. It ran about 1,255 km/780 mi from Independence, Missouri, along the Cimarron River to Santa Fe, New Mexico. An infamous town that grew up along it was Dodge City, Kansas. The trail had been carved out by the merchant William Beckness, with factory goods

In 1831, one caravan of 100 wagons made the trip over the Santa Fe Trail carrying more than $200,000 worth of goods.

later transported west and furs and gold sent east. The trail became disused when the Sante Fe Railroad began operating in 1880. It was designated the Sante Fe National Historic Trail in 1987.

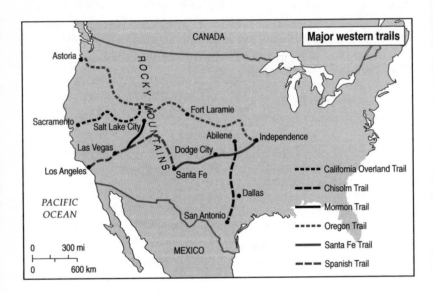

Saratoga, Battles of

Two engagements of the **American Revolution** near Saratoga Springs in New York State, resulting in an American victory on 7 October 1777. British general John **Burgoyne** was marching about 4,000 troops from Canada to join Gen Sir William Howe. They met a 3,000-strong American force under Gen Horatio **Gates** near Saratoga on 19 September. After two hours of hard fighting, the result was inconclusive, though both sides suffered severe casualties. Burgoyne launched another attack on 7 October, but the Americans, led by Benedict **Arnold**, met him and forced the British to retreat. On 17 October, Burgoyne surrendered to Gates, who by now had some 5,000 troops.

Scalawag

A derogatory term for a white Southerner who, after the **Civil War**, supported the **Republican Party** and cooperated with Northern forces during **Reconstruction**. They also were in favour of giving the vote to former slaves. A Scalawag was more despised in the South than a **carpetbagger**. One of the most infamous to Southern minds was the former Confederate lieutenant general James Longstreet.

> 6 Miss Scarlett, the country's gone plumb to hell, if you'll pardon me. Those Carpetbaggers and Scalawags can vote and most of us Democrats can't. 9
>
> **Will Benteen**, character in *Gone With the Wind* (1936)

SDI
The abbreviation and common name for the Strategic Defence Initiative, an attempt by the USA to develop a defence system against incoming nuclear missiles, based in part outside the Earth's atmosphere. It was announced by President Ronald **Reagan** in March 1983, and the research had, by 1990, cost over $16.5 billion. In 1988, the Joint Chiefs of Staff announced that they expected to be able to intercept no more than 30 per cent of incoming missiles, and SDI was scaled down in 1991.

SEATO
The abbreviation and common name for the Southeast Asia Treaty Organization, a former collective military system established by the USA, UK, Australia, France, New Zealand, Pakistan, the Philippines, and Thailand. It existed from 1954 to 1977 to halt the spread of communism and was invoked by the USA for the **Vietnam War**. Its nonmilitary aspects were assumed by the Association of Southeast Asian Nations (ASEAN).

secession
The right of American states to secede from the Union was argued from the ratification of the **Constitution of the United States** in 1789 to the end of the **Civil War** in 1865. The New England states considered the possibility of leaving in 1809 and 1814, and the Southern states developed the doctrine of 'nullification' saying each state could refuse to obey a federal law that worked against its interest. It took the **Civil War** to close the debate and convince all states that they were in a permanent union. **See also:** *states' rights*.

segregation

The practice of segregation (separation) of the races lasted in the Southern states from the end of the **Civil War** until the 1960s. It meant that black Americans had to attend their own schools and sit in the back of buses, in the balconies of cinemas, and even use different drinking fountains and lifts. They could not eat at restaurants, stay at hotels, or enjoy recreation areas reserved for whites. This doctrine of 'separate but equal' was overturned for schools by the US **Supreme Court** in 1954, but it took **busing** and the **civil rights movement** to remove the final remains of segregation.

> 6 Segregation now, segregation tomorrow and segregation forever! 9
>
> **George Wallace**, Alabama governor, inaugural speech, January 1963

Seminole

A member of an **American Indian** people living in Florida and Oklahoma and numbering about 14,000 (1990). They were one of the **Five Civilized Tribes**. Originally part of the **Creek** nation, they moved in the late 18th century from Georgia to Florida where they were joined by runaway slaves. Gen Andrew **Jackson** invaded their territory in 1817 and 1818 (the First Seminole War) and US troops fought them again in the Second Seminole War between 1835 and 1842 in the most expensive of the **Indian Wars**, costing the US government almost $40 million. Most Seminole eventually surrendered and nearly 5,000 were forcibly moved to reservations in **Indian Territory** between 1836 and 1842. Today, about 1,200 live on three reservations in Florida.

separation of powers

The concept of limiting the powers of government by separating the functions into the executive, legislative, and judiciary branches, has its fullest practical expression in the **Constitution of the United States**. Executive powers were given to the US president, legislative ones to **Congress**, and judiciary ones to the **Supreme Court**. The three branches operate on a 'checks and balances' system, each serving as a 'watchdog' on the other two.

Sequoya or Sequoyah (c. 1770–1843)

A **Cherokee** Indian who in 1826 invented an 85-character alphabet for the Cherokee language. It was used to teach thousands of his people to read and write. The Cherokee also then established a press, the *Cherokee Phoenix* newspaper in 1828, and a written constitution. Born in Tennessee, Sequoya was probably the son of an Englishman and Cherokee mother. He was a silversmith who sometimes used the name George Guess.

> The giant sequoia tree is named after Sequoya, whose name is therefore perpetuated in California's Sequoia National Park.

Seven Days, Battles of the

During the **Civil War**, a successful Confederate campaign from 25 June to 2 July 1862 to drive back Union forces threatening Richmond, Virginia. The series of battles ended Union major general George McClellan's **Peninsula Campaign**. The Confederate success was largely due to the tactical initiatives of Gen Robert E **Lee**. Two Union armies of over 100,000 men were advancing on Richmond, one under McClellan and the second under Maj-Gen Irwin McDowell. Lee, who had about 85,000 troops, ordered Maj-Gen Thomas 'Stonewall' **Jackson** to start activity keeping McDowell busy, and then attacked McClellan who withdrew his forces, fighting a series of rearguard actions until he extricated most of his army.

Seven Pines, Battle of

An indecisive battle of the **Civil War** from May 31 to June 1, 1862, at the intersection of two roads about 10 miles from the Confederate capital of Richmond, Virginia. It was also called the Battle of Fair Oaks, named for a nearby railway station. It began when Confederate major general Daniel H Hill sent his troops charging at Union forces entrenched at Seven Pines, driving them back after fierce fighting. He was supported by units of Gen Joseph E Johnston, but the endangered Union soldiers were saved by reinforcements who had to cross a dangerous, rickety bridge over the flooded Chickahominy River.

> Confederate general Joseph E Johnston was badly wounded during the battle of Seven Pines and was replaced by Gen Robert E Lee who became one of the war's most brilliant commanders.

'Seward's Folly'

The nickname for Alaska after secretary of state William H Seward purchased it from Russia in 1867. Many Americans thought it was ridiculous to pay $7.2 million for a frozen wasteland, even though the price came to two cents an acre. They also called Alaska 'Seward's Icebox', 'Icebergia', and 'Walrussia'. It turned out to be a valuable region of natural resources yielding fish and furs, then later gold (and oil in the late 20th century).

William Seward survived an assassination attempt by the same conspiracy that killed President Abraham Lincoln.

Shakers

The popular name for the Christian sect of the **United Society of Believers in Christ's Second Appearing**. They were called Shakers because of their ecstatic shakings in worship. The movement was founded in England about 1747 and taken to North America in 1774 by Ann Lee, the wife of a Manchester blacksmith, known as Mother Ann. She said God would appear in a female aspect, which her followers identified with her. She founded a colony in New York, and eventually 18 colonies existed in several states. They believed in separation from the world in farm communities, simple dress and liv-

Shaker furniture is still admired for its beautiful simplicity.

ing conditions, celibacy, and faith healing. New members were supplied to the colonies through conversion and adopting orphans, but the Shakers' doctrine of celibacy led to their virtual extinction in the 20th century.

Sherman, William Tecumseh (1820–1891)

A Union general in the **Civil War**, best remembered for his ruthless march through Georgia. He served in the **Mexican War** and was superintendent of the Military Academy of Louisiana when the Civil War began. He resigned to return to the US Army and fought at the first Battle of **Bull Run** in 1861 and **Shiloh** in 1862. Two years later he beseiged, captured, and burned Atlanta, then marched through helpless Georgia, laying it waste. Despite the widespread destruction he inflicted as he marched to the sea, he was conciliatory in victory, offering terms that had to be repudiated by President Andrew **Johnson**. He succeeded Grant as commander of the army in 1869.

❝ There is many a boy here to-day who looks on war as all glory, but, boys, it is all hell. ❞

William Sherman, speech at Columbus, Ohio, 11 August 1880

Shiloh, Battle of

A Union victory during the **Civil War**, fought on 6 and 7 April 1862 near Shiloh Church in Tennessee. It saw the failure by the Confederates to stop Gen Ulysses S **Grant**, who then took control of the Mississippi valley. On 6 April a Confederate force of 40,000 under Gen Albert Sidney Johnston attacked Grant's army and in a few hours threw back the entire Union line. Johnston was killed, however, and replaced by Gen Pierre **Beauregard**. Grant reinforced his troops overnight and threw in an attack at 6 a.m. next morning. By this time the Confederates had

One area held by Union soldiers during the Battle of Shiloh, a bank along a road, was called 'the hornet's nest' by the Confederates because of the deadly fire stirred up each time they attacked it.

lost more than a quarter of their original force and were slowly forced back until making their escape. Both sides had lost more than 10,000 soldiers.

Sioux

A member of the largest group of Plains Indians, numbering about 103,000 (1990) in the USA and 60,000 in Canada (1991), and now mostly living on reservations in North and South Dakota and Nebraska. They are also called Dakota, which means 'allies'. They were originally located in Minnesota but moved about 1650 to the Dakotas. Here they took up a way of life centred on buffalo hunting. When gold was discovered in the Black Hills of South Dakota in 1874 and thousands of miners invaded their territory, US troops were sent to remove the Sioux. This led to the Battle of **Little Bighorn** in 1876 in which Lt-Col George **Custer** and and his 259 men were all killed by the **Sioux** and **Cheyenne** led by two **Sioux** chiefs, **Crazy Horse** and **Sitting Bull**. The Sioux were finally defeated on 31 October that year, and the **Ghost Dance** spiritual movement ultimately led to a massacre of the Sioux by US troops at **Wounded Knee** on 29 December 1890.

- In 1973 the Sioux occupied the site of Wounded Knee which raised the awareness of the American Indian Movement (AIM)
- Gold, uranium, coal, oil, and natural gas have been found on their reservations
- The Sioux pressed for and were awarded $160 million compensation in 1980.

Sitting Bull (*c.* 1834–1890)

A chief of the Sioux people who joined with **Crazy Horse** to lead the Sioux and Cheyenne in the massacre of Lt-Col George **Custer** and his men at the Battle of **Little Bighorn** in 1876. He was pursued by the US Army and forced to flee to Canada. He was allowed to return in 1881 and toured in the Wild West show of 'Buffalo Bill'. Sitting Bull, whose Indian name was Tatanka Iyotake, settled on a Dakota reservation and was killed during his arrest on suspicion of involvement in Indian agitations.

Sitting Bull *Sioux Indian chief Sitting Bull fought a rearguard action against white incursions into Indian lands. He defeated Gen Custer at the Battle of Little Bighorn, on 25 June 1876.*

slavery

The first black slaves landed in an English colony in North America (Virginia) in 1619. In the American South, slavery became a mainstay of its plantation economy. While the Northern states abolished slavery from 1787 to 1804, the Southern states protected the 'peculiar institution', as they called it. Slavery became an issue in the economic struggles between Southern plantation owners and Northern industrialists in the first half of the 19th century. That struggle ended with the **Civil War**, although it was not fought primarily on the slavery issue. Abraham **Lincoln**, however, saw the political advantages of promising freedom to Southern slaves, and the **Emancipation Proclamation** was enacted in 1863. This was reinforced by the 13th Amendment to the **Constitution of the United States** that officially abolished slavery, being ratified on 6 December 1865 after the war.

> ❝ The Southern newspapers, with their advertisements of Negro sales and personal descriptions of fugitive slaves, supply details of misery that it would be difficult for imagination to exceed. ❞
>
> **Frances Anne Kemble**, British actress, *Journal of a Residence on a Georgian Plantation in 1838–1839*, 1863

Smith, John (1580–1631)

An Englishman who, after an adventurous early life, took part in the colonization of Virginia, founding the first settlement of **Jamestown** in 1607 and acting as president of the colony in 1608 and 1609. He explored New England in 1614, which he named, and published pamphlets on America and an autobiography. His trade with the Indians may have kept the colonists alive in the early years. During an expedition among the American Indians he was captured, and his life is said to have been saved by the intervention of **Pocahontas**, the daughter of the chief, Powhatan.

social security

The term 'social security' was first applied officially in the USA in the Social Security Act of 1935, passed to provide insurance to retired employees and unemployment compensation. It was part of the **New Deal** announced by President Franklin D Roosevelt. Through the years, **Congress** added extra benefits, such as survivors insurance in 1939, disability insurance in 1956, and health insurance in the form of Medicare in 1965. The Social Security Administration in Baltimore, Maryland, is responsible for the programme. Like other countries, US social security protection is being threatened by the increased financial needs of an ageing population.

sod house

A small house built by Western settlers in the 19th century. It was commonly called a 'soddy', a name also sometimes given to its owner. Some of the houses were partly dug into a hill. Earth was cut into brick shapes for the walls, with spaces left for the windows and doors. The roof was also made of sod with the grass still growing. Settlers often built sod houses quickly to meet the obligation to improve the property that was required for free land under the Homestead Act.

Sons of Liberty

The name adopted by American colonists who opposed the **Stamp Act** of 1765. Merchants, lawyers, farmers, artisans, and labourers joined what was an early instance of concerted resistance to British rule, causing the repeal of the act in March 1766. The Sons of Liberty met under 'Liberty Trees' and erected 'Liberty Poles' topped by a 'Liberty Cap'. Their protest helped initiate a general desire for independence.

The Sons of Liberty took their name from a speech made by Col Isaac Barré in the British Parliament on 13 February 1765, when he said British agents sent to the colonies had 'caused the blood of these sons of liberty to recoil within them'.

Sooners

Homesteaders who rushed into the Oklahoma Territory to choose free land before the legal date allowed. Then on 22 April 1889, marshals held back the long line of horsemen and wagons until the official gun was fired at noon, sending about 50,000 settlers stampeding towards the land. By the end of the day, all 810,000 hectares/2 million acres were occupied. (It had been taken from the **Indian Territory**.) The following year, the land rush was repeated in South Dakota.

People in Oklahoma are still called Sooners, the state's official nickname is the Sooner State, and the University of Oklahoma's football team is called the Sooners.

Southeast Asia Treaty Organization See *SEATO*.

Spanish–American War

A brief war in 1898 between Spain and the USA over Spanish rule in Cuba and the Philippines. The war began in Cuba when the US battleship *Maine* was blown up in Havana harbour, allegedly by the Spanish. Other engagements included the Battle of Manila Bay, in which the US Navy under Commdr George **Dewey** destroyed the Spanish fleet in the Philippines, and the taking of the Cuban port cities of El Caney and San Juan Heights (in which the **Rough Riders** led by Theodore **Roosevelt** were involved). The defeat of Spain made the USA a colonial power: the Treaty of Paris ceded the Philippines, Guam, and Puerto Rico to the USA, and Cuba became independent. The USA paid $20 million to Spain, which lost its colonial presence in the Americas.

spoils system

The patronage system of granting offices and favours to supporters of the party in office was first extensively used by President Andrew **Jackson** in the 1830s. It also occurred under Republican administrations after the Civil War, reaching a peak with the presidency of Ulysses S **Grant** from 1869 to 1877. In the 20th century, civil-service posts in large cities have often been filled on the recommendation of newly elected political leaders,

The term 'spoils system' is derived from an assertion in 1832 by Democratic senator William Marcy (later secretary of state): 'To the victor belong the spoils.'

as seen by the **Democratic Party** 'machine' of Richard Daley, the powerful mayor of Chicago from 1955 to 1976.

Spotsylvania, Battle of

An indecisive engagement during the **Civil War**, from 8 to 19 May 1864 at Spotsylvania Court House in Virginia. The Confederate army under Gen Robert E **Lee** had entrenched themselves at this important road junction blocking Union general Ulysses S **Grant's** route to Richmond. Grant attacked on 10 May but was thrown back. Union major general Winfield Hancock followed with no better result, and another attack by Col Emory Upton's brigade left 1,000 Union dead on the field. On May 12, Hancock joined with Maj-Gen Ambrose Burnside in a successful attack with 18,000 men, but a fierce Confederate counterattack forced a hand-to-hand struggle at the 'Bloody Angle'. For another week, Grant threw men at Lee's defensive entrenchments but could not break them. The Union had lost 18,399 men to the Confederate losses of about 10,000.

Square Deal

The name for President Theodore **Roosevelt's** domestic programme, especially his plan to control large companies with **antitrust laws**. He introduced the term in 1902 during a speech. Roosevelt then used the Sherman Antitrust Act to haul more than 30 of the nation's most powerful corporations before the courts, including United States Steel and the Standard Oil Company.

> ❛A man who is good enough to shed his blood for his country is good enough to be given a square deal afterwards. More than that no man is entitled to, and less than that no man shall have.❜
>
> **Theodore Roosevelt**, speech at Springfield, Illinois, 4 June 1903

stagecoach

The American stagecoach is most remembered for its dangerous journeys through the **Wild West** in the 19th century. Commonly called a stage, it was drawn by one to three pairs of horses.

A trip from St Louis, Missouri, to San Francisco, California, took about 25 days, travelling at a top speed of eight km/five mi per hour. Stagecoaches carried up to nine passengers and also moved goods and the mail. Versions included the light 'mud coach' the strong Troy coach, and the Concord luxury coach that Mark Twain called 'an imposing cradle on wheels'.

To protect against robbers and American Indians, stagecoach companies often hired a man with a gun to sit next to the driver. Americans still say they are 'riding shotgun' if they are next to the driver in a car, and that they are sitting in the 'shotgun seat'.

Stamp Act

An act of the British Parliament in 1765 that sought to raise enough money from the American colonies to cover the cost of their defence. The act taxed (by requiring an official stamp) all publications and legal documents published in British colonies.

> ❛We hope your Honour will join with us in an Endeavour to secure that great badge of English liberty, of being taxed only with our own Consent...❜
>
> New York General Assembly, message to the colony's governor, September 1764, after hearing of plans for the Stamp Act.

Refusal to use the required tax stamps and a blockade of British merchant shipping in the colonies forced repeal the following year. The controversy helped to precipitate the **American Revolution**. The act provoked vandalism and looting in America, and the Stamp Act Congress meeting in New York City from 7 to 25 October 1765 (the first intercolonial congress) declared the act unconstitutional, with the slogan 'No taxation without representation'.

'Star-Spangled Banner, The'
The national anthem of the United States was written by the lawyer Francis Scott Key during the **War of 1812**. He was a prisoner aboard a British ship that was bombarding Fort Henry at Baltimore, Maryland, throughout the day and night of 13 September 1814. When dawn broke, Key was amazed to see the large American flag still flying over the fort and penned his verse on the back of an old envelope. It was printed in the *Baltimore American* newspaper on 20 September. His brother-in-law, Judge J H Nicholson, suggested the poem be set to the music of an old British drinking song, 'Anacreon in Heaven'. 'The Star-Spangled Banner' was an immediate success, but Congress did not officially designate it as the national anthem until 3 March 1931.

'THE STAR-SPANGLED BANNER'

Oh, say can you see by the dawn's early light
What so proudly we hailed at the twilight's last gleaming?
Whose broad stripes and bright stars thru the perilous fight,
O'er the ramparts we watched were so gallantly streaming?
And the rocket's red glare, the bombs bursting in air,
Gave proof through the night that our flag was still there.
Oh, say does that star-spangled banner yet wave
O'er the land of the free and the home of the brave?

START
The abbreviation and common name for the Strategic Arms Reduction Treaty, peace discussions dealing with disarmament, initially involving the USA and the Soviet Union (from 1992 the USA and Russia) and from 1993 including Belarus and Ukraine. It began in 1983 with talks in Geneva that led to the signing of the **INF Treaty** of 1987. Two years later proposals for reductions in conventional weapons were added to the agenda. The START

treaty was signed in Moscow on 31 July 1991, agreeing to reductions of about 30% in strategic nuclear weapons systems, and more significant cuts were agreed in 3 January 1993 (START II).

Star Wars See *SDI.*

State of the Union Address
The annual speech of the president of the United States to the US **Congress**. He reviews the successes and policies of his administration and sets out its new plans and programmes. The address is required by the **Constitution of the United States**, which says the president 'shall from time to time give to the Congress Information of the State of the union...' That time has traditionally been set early in the new session of Congress that begins on January 3, with the president addressing a joint meeting of both houses.

states' rights
The interpretation of the **Constitution of the United States** that emphasizes the powers retained by individual states. In 1832 South Carolina developed the doctrine of nullification, claiming the right to overrule federal laws against its own interests. The practice of slavery and the right to secede from the Union were claimed under this doctrine by Southern states that formed the **Confederate States of America**. Southern states continued to champion the idea in the 20th century, as shown by the formation in 1948 of the States Rights' Party, called the **Dixiecrats**. States' rights have since become stronger throughout the nation, beginning with the administration of Ronald **Reagan**.

Statue of Liberty
The famous monument on Liberty Island in New York harbour that has become a symbol of liberty. Its official title is the Statue of Liberty Enlightening the World.

The 92-m/302-ft statue was presented to the US people by the French and dedicated

Statue of Liberty *The Statue of Liberty.*

in 1886, marking the centenary of American Independence and commemorating the alliance between the USA and France during the **American Revolution**. It was the first sight for most immigrants arriving by ship to **Ellis Island**. The statue, by the French sculptor Frédéric-Auguste Bartholdi and designed by Gustave Eiffel, represents a woman holding a fiery torch in her upraised right hand and a tablet inscribed with '4 July 1776' (the date of American Independence) in her left. It was declared a national monument in 1924 and a World Heritage Site in 1984.

> 6 Give me your tired, your poor,
> Your huddled masses yearning to breathe free,
> The wretched refuse of your teeming shore.
> Send these, the homeless, tempest-tost to me,
> I lift my lamp beside the golden door! 9
>
> **Emma Lazarus**, part of her sonnet engraven on the
> pedestal of the Statue of Liberty.

Steinem, Gloria (1934–)
A US journalist and liberal feminist. She emerged as a leading figure in the US women's movement in the late 1960s and was also involved in radical protest campaigns against racism and the Vietnam War. She co-founded the Women's Action Alliance in 1970 and *Ms* magazine. In 1983 a collection of her articles was published as *Outrageous Acts and Everyday Rebellions*.

> 6 We are becoming the men we wanted to marry. 9
>
> **Gloria Steinem**, *Ms* magazine, July/August 1982

Stones River, Battle of
An inconclusive but bloody battle of the **Civil War** from 31 December 1862 to 2 January 1863 along Stones River near Murfreesboro, Tennessee. It was also called the Battle of Murfreesboro. Confederate general Braxton Bragg, with nearly 38,000 troops, attacked Maj-Gen William Rosecrans' force of more than 43,000, causing damage but meeting stiff resistance. No fighting

took place on New Year's Day, but on 2 January the Confederates attacked a hill and lost about 1,500 men within minutes. Bragg decided to withdraw and was later surprised to read that both sides called it a Union victory.

On the dark and cold New Year's Eve after the first day's battle, one side's military band began to play 'Home, Sweet Home' and the opposing band joined in, bringing silence among the homesick soldiers of both armies.

Stowe, Harriet (Elizabeth) Beecher (1811–1896)

A US suffragist, abolitionist, and author. Her antislavery novel *Uncle Tom's Cabin* was first published serially in 1851 and 1852. The inspiration came to her in a vision in 1848, and the book brought immediate success. It was radical in its time and did much to spread antislavery sentiment, but in the 20th century was criticized for sentimentality and racism. Born in Litchfield, Connecticut, Stowe was a daughter of Congregationalist minister Lyman Beecher, and in 1836 married C E Stowe, a professor of theology. In 1853 Stowe visited Britain to lecture on the slavery question.

Strategic Arms Limitation Talks See *SALT*.

Strategic Arms Reduction Talks See *START*.

Strategic Defense Initiative See *SDI*.

Stuyvesant, Peter (c. 1592–1672)

A Dutch colonial leader in America. He was appointed director general of New Netherlands in 1646 and arrived there the following year. He reorganized the administration of the colony and established a permanent boundary with Connecticut by the Treaty of Hartford in 1650. Forced to surrender the colony to the British in 1664, Stuyvesant remained there for the rest of his life. Born in Holland, he first worked as an official of the Dutch West India Company. He was governor of Curacao in 1643.

Stuyvesant retired to his farm called 'the Bouwerie' which is now the Bowery section of Manhattan in New York City.

suffragist

A woman who fought for the right to vote in the USA. The name 'suffragette' was often used. The US suffragist movement officially began at the Seneca

Falls Convention in 1848. Elizabeth Cady Stanton and Susan B **Anthony** founded the National Woman Suffrage Association in 1869. At about the same time, Lucy Stone formed the American Woman Suffrage Association. The two groups merged in 1890 as the National American Woman Suffrage Association. The perseverance of this group and others led to the ratification of the 19th Amendment in 1920 that gave US women the right to vote.

Sugar Act

The popular name for the British Revenue Act of 1764. It was Parliament's first effort to raise money to help pay for the cost of protecting and defending the American colonies. The Act cut the duty on molasses from sixpence to threepence a gallon, but added new duties on such foreign (non-British) items as sugars, coffee, wines, and textiles. At a protest rally in Boston on 24 May 1764, James Otis criticized 'taxation without representation'. Protest continued throughout the colonies, including boycotts of British goods, so the Act was sometimes not enforced.

superpower

The term that was used to describe the USA and the USSR from the end of **World War II**, when they emerged as significantly stronger than all other countries. With the collapse of the Soviet Union in 1991, the USA is, arguably, now the world's sole superpower, both militarily and economically.

Supreme Court

The highest US judicial tribunal, composed since 1869 of a chief justice (William H Rehnquist from 1986) and eight associate justices. Appointments are made for life by the president, with the advice and consent of the Senate, and justices can be removed only by **impeachment**. The court has considerable power and can rule on whether a law passed by **Congress** is unconstitutional. Its many important decisions include *Brown v Board of Education* of Topeka ruling against **segregation** and *Roe v Wade* supporting **abortion**.

Tammany Hall

The **Democratic Party** organization in New York City. It originated in 1789 as the Society of St Tammany, named after the building in which it met. It was dominant from the 1830s until the 1930s and gained a reputation for corruption and the rule by bosses. Its domination was broken by Mayor La Guardia in the 1930s and Mayor Edward Koch in the 1970s.

Taylor, Zachary (1784–1850)

The 12th president of the USA in 1849 and 1850, a Whig. Taylor was born in Virginia but grew up in frontier Kentucky. A veteran of the **War of 1812** and a hero of the **Mexican War**, he was known as 'Old Rough and Ready'. In the latter war, Taylor advanced into Mexico in 1846 and won several battles and a promotion to major general. By fall he had taken Monterrey and in February 1847 had defeated Santa Anna at Buena Vista. After becoming president, he died of cholera after less than one and a half years in office. His short term was dominated by controversies over the **slavery** issue, with Taylor supporting the antislavery elements.

> ❝ His whole life has been a series of military services, ending in a blaze of glory. He is, according to his own frank and honest declarations, utterly unskilled in matters of state and divested of all experience of civil affairs. ❞
>
> **United States Magazine and Democratic Review**, June 1850, assessing President Taylor a month before he died

Teapot Dome Scandal

A US political scandal that revealed the corruption of President Warren G Harding's administration. It centred on the leasing of naval oil reserves in 1921 at Teapot Dome, Wyoming, and Elks Hill, California, without competitive bidding, as a result of bribing the secretary of the interior, Albert B Fall. Fall was tried and imprisoned in 1929.

Tennessee Valley Authority (TVA)

A US government corporation founded in 1933 to develop the Tennessee River basin (an area of some 104,000 sq km/40,000 sq mi), mainly by building hydroelectric power stations. The TVA was associated with the **New Deal** of President Franklin D **Roosevelt**. Its major functions were to provide cheap electricity to a seven-state area, control destructive flooding on the lower Mississippi River and to provide employment during the **Great Depression**. There are now 50 dams incorporated into a massive river-control system, along with 11 thermal power stations and two nuclear-powered plants.

territory

The political form taken by 31 of the 50 US states before they obtained statehood. The first such area was the Northwest Territory whose ordinance in 1787 set the pattern for the development of future territories. Each region, placed under a territorial governor, could elect a legislature when it had a population of 5,000 and then apply for statehood when it reached 60,000. The last US territory to become a state was Hawaii on 21 August 1959.

Tet Offensive

In the **Vietnam War**, a prolonged attack beginning 30 January 1968 by 80,000 communist Vietcong against Saigon (now Ho Chi Minh City) and other South Vietnamese cities and hamlets, as well as the US Marine base at Khe Sanh. About 32,000 Vietcong were killed by mid-February, and their soldiers were finally forced to withdraw. The Tet Offensive, however, brought into question the ability of the South Vietnamese army and their US allies to win the war and added fuel to the antiwar movement in the USA. **See also:** *Khe Sanh siege.*

Texas Rangers

A law enforcement body in Texas first formed as a 10-man unit in 1823 by Stephen F Austin to protect settlers from **American Indians** and Mexicans. The Rangers operated as cavalrymen, winning fame during the **Mexican War** and the **Wild West** era. They became part of the Texas Highway Patrol in 1935.

Texas Revolution

A war for independence from Mexico organized by Texan settlers from the USA. The Mexican government had encouraged them to immigrate but then tried to stop the rush of settlers. Led by Stephen F Austin, the Texans proclaimed their independence on 20 December 1835. To put down the revolt, Mexican general Santa Anna led a force of 4,000 troops who besieged the **Alamo** and killed all of its defenders on 6 March 1836. As soon as 21 April, however, Gen Sam Houston's soldiers (crying 'Remember the Alamo!') launched a surprise attack on Santa Anna on the banks of the San Jacinto River, and the Mexican general signed a declaration of Texas independence in return for his release.

Thanksgiving

A national holiday in the USA (fourth Thursday in November) and first celebrated by the **Pilgrim** settlers in Massachusetts after their first harvest in 1621. It was proclaimed a national holiday in 1863. The current date has been celebrated, by act of Congress, since 1942. The original day of thanksgiving was proclaimed by Plymouth governor William Bradford after the Pilgrims had survived their first winter, owing largely to help from their Indian ally Massasoit. Canada also celebrates Thanksgiving, on the second Monday in October.

thirteen colonies, the

The 13 original American colonies belonging to Britain until their representatives signed the **Declaration of Independence** in 1776. After winning the **American Revolution**, they became the original 13 United States of America. The colonies, all in the east, were Connecticut, Delaware, Georgia, Maryland, Massachusetts, New Hampshire, New Jersey, New York, North Carolina, Pennsylvania, Rhode Island, South Carolina, and Virginia. They were united first under the **Articles of Confederation** and then under the **Constitution of the United States**.

Tippecanoe, Battle of

A battle on 7 November 1811 in which Gen William Henry Harrison defeated Shawnee Indians led by Chief Tecumseh. The fighting, which took place near the Tippecanoe River in the

Chief Tecumseh and his brother, The Prophet, promised their Shawnee warriors that they would be magically protected from the bullets of the soldiers during the battle.

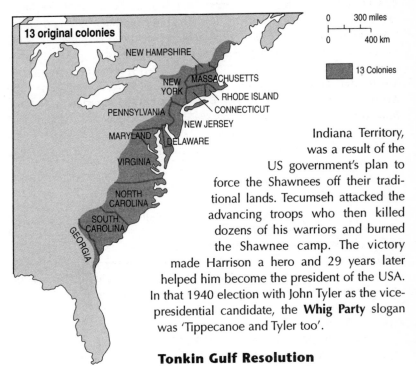

13 original colonies

NEW HAMPSHIRE
NEW YORK
MASSACHUSETTS
RHODE ISLAND
CONNECTICUT
PENNSYLVANIA
NEW JERSEY
MARYLAND
DELAWARE
VIRGINIA
NORTH CAROLINA
SOUTH CAROLINA
GEORGIA

0   300 miles
0   400 km

13 Colonies

Indiana Territory, was a result of the US government's plan to force the Shawnees off their traditional lands. Tecumseh attacked the advancing troops who then killed dozens of his warriors and burned the Shawnee camp. The victory made Harrison a hero and 29 years later helped him become the president of the USA. In that 1940 election with John Tyler as the vice-presidential candidate, the **Whig Party** slogan was 'Tippecanoe and Tyler too'.

Tonkin Gulf Resolution

A resolution passed on 7 August 1964 by the US **Congress** that formed the basis for the considerable increase in US military involvement in the **Vietnam War**. It resulted from the Tonkin Gulf Incident from 2 to 5 August when two US destroyers (USS C *Turner Joy* and USS *Maddox*) were supposedly fired on by North Vietnamese torpedo boats. The US ships sunk two of the boats and bombed their nearby bases. The resolution allowed President Lyndon **Johnson** to 'take all necessary steps to repel any armed attack'. It was repealed 1970 in the light of evidence that the Johnson administration deceived Congress about the incident.

Tory See *Loyalist*.

town meetings

A form of local government established in colonial New England. All the voters in a town gathered to elect its officials, decide on taxes and other financial matters, and discuss other local affairs. The meetings became mandatory in the 19th century. A few small communities still hold town meetings for all residents, and some larger towns have kept the idea but only elected representatives attend the meetings.

Townsend Acts

Acts by the British Parliament in 1767 concerning the American colonies. The most controversial was the Revenue Act that placed duties on tea, glass, paper, lead, and paint imported into the colonies. American merchants began refusing to handle British goods, and Sam **Adams** led the demands for 'no taxation without representation'. On 12 April 1770, one month after the **Boston Massacre**, the British

Charles Townsend earned the nickname of 'the weathercock' because he kept changing his political views through several governments.

taxed only tea (and that led to the **Boston Tea Party** in 1773). The Acts were named after the British chancellor of the Exchequer, Charles Townsend, who initiated them. He died three months later.

Trail of Tears

The name given to the route travelled by 16,000 **Cherokee** in 1838 from their ancestral lands in North Carolina, Georgia, Tennessee, and Alabama to **Indian Territory** under the Indian Removal Act of 1830. Held initially in stockades by the US army, they were forced to march under military escort nearly 1,600 km/1,000 mi in winter with little food. Over 4,000 died from disease, hunger, and exposure. The Trail of Tears became a national monument in 1987.

transcontinental railroad

The first US railway to stretch from east to west was completed on 10 May 1869 at Promontory Point, Utah, when tracks being laid by the Union Pacific and Central Pacific railroads were connected. At a festive ceremony, a symbolic golden spike was driven in with a silver hammer. The two companies each used over 1,200 men in a competition to lay the most track. The Union Pacific's crew of mainly Irish immigrants laid 1,747 km/1,086 mi from Omaha, Nebraska, and the Central Pacific, using mostly Chinese workers, put down 1,110 km/690 mi from Sacramento, California. The railroad was the beginning of the end for the cattle drive, **wagon train**, and **stagecoach**.

Truman, Harry S (1884–1972)

The 33rd president of the USA from 1945 to 1953, a Democrat. Born in Lamar, Missouri, Truman served in France during **World War I** and returned to enter politics, becoming a US senator in 1934. In January 1945 he became vice-president to Franklin D **Roosevelt**, and president when Roosevelt died in April. That same year, Truman took part in the **Potsdam Conference** and used the atom bomb against Japan. In 1947 he launched the **Marshall Plan** to restore Western Europe's economy and also initiated the Truman Doctrine, a policy for helping countries threatened by communism. He sent troops to Korea in 1950 when the communists invaded, but sacked Gen Douglas **MacArthur** when the general's policy threatened to start World War III.

> 6 The buck stops here. 9
>
> **Harry S Truman**, sign on his presidential desk

Truth, Sojourner (c. 1797–1883)

The adopted name of Isabella Baumfree, later Isabella Van Wagener, a US antislavery and women's-suffrage campaigner. Born a slave, she ran away and became involved with religious groups. In 1843 she was 'commanded in a vision' to adopt the name Sojourner Truth and 'travel up and down the land, showing the people their sins and being a sign unto them'. She worked as a fund-raiser for

Sojourner Truth was honoured in 1996 when NASA named their Mars rover vehicle 'Sojourner'.

the North during the **Civil War**, and President Abraham **Lincoln** appointed her in 1864 to the Freedman's Relief Association. **See also:** abolitionism.

Tubman, Harriet Ross (1821–1913)

A US abolitionist who was active in the **Underground Railroad**, helping more than 300 slaves escape to the North and Canada. Born a slave in Maryland, she escaped herself in 1849 to Philadelphia (where slavery was outlawed). During the **Civil War** she was a spy and scout for the Union army. She spoke

Harriet Tubman's nickname was 'Moses' because she led her people to freedom.

against slavery and for women's rights, and founded schools for emancipated slaves after the war. **See also:** *abolitionism.*

Turner, Nat (1800–1831)

A US slave and Baptist preacher who led 60 slaves in a revolt in August 1831 that killed at least 55 slave-owners. Believing himself divinely appointed, Turner instigated the Southampton Insurrection in Southampton County, Virginia. After hiding for six weeks, Turner was caught and hanged with 16 other slaves who had taken part in the uprising. The terror he created led to restrictive legislation in the South, including a prohibition against educating slaves. (Turner had learned to read.)

Tuskegee Institute

A college established for black Americans in 1881 in Tuskegee, Alabama, by Booker T Washington, who became its first principal. Many of its students were former slaves. George Washington **Carver** taught agriculture and developed many uses for the peanut while there. Now named Tuskegee University, the private school had 3,023 students and a faculty of 306 in 1998.

TVA See *Tennessee Valley Authority.*

UN See *United Nations*.

Uncle Sam

The official nickname for the US and its government. It was coined during the **War of 1812** by opponents of US policy. He is depicted with a white beard and wearing a tall hat with stars around it, and a red, white, and blue suit. His name was probably derived from the initials 'US' placed on government property, but some believe it came from 'Uncle Sam' Wilson of Troy, New York, who supplied beef to the US Army during the war. In 1961, the US government officially adopted the name as its symbol.

Uncle Sam *Uncle Sam.*

- The earliest recorded use of the nickname was in the *Troy Post* on 7 September 1913.

- The first use of the name in a book was in *The Adventures of Uncle Sam* (1816) by 'Frederick Augustus Fidfaddy, Esq.'.

- Just before the **Civil War** the expression found its way into dictionaries as the nation's accepted nickname.

- The figure of Uncle Sam became well known in both world wars on recruiting posters, pointing at the viewer and saying 'I WANT <u>YOU</u>'.

Underground Railroad

A secret network established in the North before the **Civil War** to provide sanctuary and assistance for escaped black slaves. The name was first used about 1830, but the system was not underground or a railroad. Safe houses ('stations'), transport facilities, and guides ('conductors') existed to lead the slaves ('passengers') to safety in the North and Canada. It is estimated that up to 100,000 slaves used the network, but the number may have been exaggerated. Those who helped run the 'railroad' included former slave Harriet **Tubman** and the white abolitionists Susan B **Anthony** and Levi Coffin.

United Nations (UN)

The United Nations charter was drawn up in 1945 in San Francisco, California, by 51 states as a successor to the League of Nations, which the USA never joined. It was based on proposals made at the Dumbarton Oaks Conference in 1944 in **Washington, DC**. The name 'United Nations' was coined by the US president Franklin D **Roosevelt**. The US is a permanent member of the UN's powerful Security Council, along with Britain, Russia, France, and China. The first military action taken by the Council was in June 1950 when the US led a UN force to repel the invasion of

In September 1997 the US media magnate Ted Turner donated $1 billion to the UN, to be paid over ten years.

South Korea by North Korean communists. The UN also responded promptly to the Iraqi invasion of Kuwait in 1990. In 1994 it used the threat of **NATO** air strikes to provide safe havens for refugees in Bosnia-Herzegovina and in 1999 sanctioned NATO air strikes against the Serbs to successfully pressure them into withdrawing from Kosovo.

U-2 Incident

A diplomatic incident in 1960 involving a US military reconnaissance aeroplane, the U-2, used in secret flights over the USSR from 1956 to photograph military installations. One was shot down over the USSR and the pilot, Gary Powers, was captured and imprisoned. The U-2 affair led to the cancellation of a proposed meeting in Moscow between President Dwight **Eisenhower** and Soviet premier Nikita Khrushchev, and it led to a greatly increased Soviet arms spending in the 1960s and 1970s.

- Gary Powers was exchanged two years later for a US-held Soviet agent
- The U-2, designed by Richard Bissell, flew higher (21,000 m/70,000 ft) and further (3,500 km/2,200 mi) than any previous plane
- In 1962 U-2 flights revealed the construction of Soviet missile bases in Cuba.

Valley Forge

The site in Pennsylvania 32 km/20 mi northwest of Philadelphia, where George **Washington's** army spent the bitter winter of 1777–78 in great hardship during the **American Revolution**. Of the 10,000 men there, hundreds died, and the rest suffered from lack of rations and other supplies. Although some deserted, the colonial soldiers demonstrated both their loyalty and endurance. During the winter, the army was expertly trained by a Prussian officer Friedrich Wilhelm von Steuben, who spoke no English.

Vanderbilt, Cornelius (1794–1877)

A US industrialist who made a fortune in steamships and (from the age of 70) by financing railways, during which he gained control of the New York Central Railroad. He defeated stock raids and take over attempts by other financiers in the process of amassing a fortune of more than $100 million, being labelled one of the 'robber barons'. Despite his wealth, he did not engage in any philanthropic activities until very late in his life, when he gave $1 million to what would become Vanderbilt University.

Vespucci, Amerigo (1454–1512)

The Florentine merchant whose name was given to the Americas as a result of the widespread circulation of his tales of his explorations. A geographer, Martin Waldseemüller, first added the name to a map in 1507. Vespucci's accounts of the voyage from 1499 to 1501, however, include descriptions of places he could not possibly have reached (the Pacific Ocean, British Columbia, and Antarctica).

Vicksburg, Campaign and Siege of

In the **Civil War**, a series of failed Union attacks on Vicksburg, Mississippi, followed by a long but successful siege. Vicksburg was a well-fortified town guarding the Mississippi River from its heights. The first Union attempt to take it in June 1862 was by a small force of about 5,000 with a fleet of gunboats. Two Union corps under Brig-Gen John A McClernand laid siege in January 1863 without success and assaulted the town on 22 May, failing

Vanderbilt
Family Tree

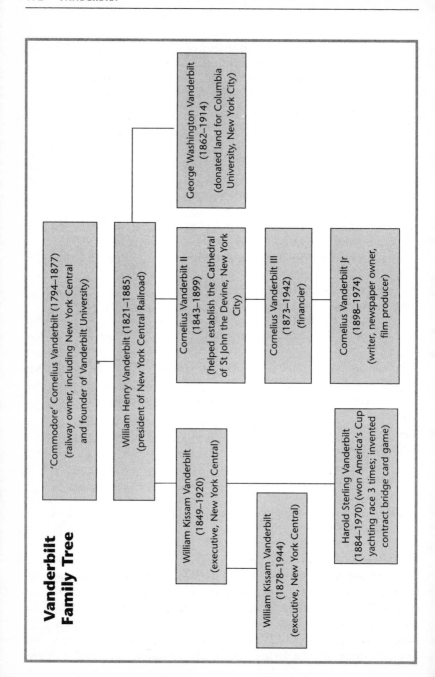

'Commodore' Cornelius Vanderbilt (1794–1877) (railway owner, including New York Central and founder of Vanderbilt University)

William Henry Vanderbilt (1821–1885) (president of New York Central Railroad)

George Washington Vanderbilt (1862–1914) (donated land for Columbia University, New York City)

Cornelius Vanderbilt II (1843–1899) (helped establish the Cathedral of St John the Devine, New York City)

Cornelius Vanderbilt III (1873–1942) (financier)

Cornelius Vanderbilt Jr (1898–1974) (writer, newspaper owner, film producer)

William Kissam Vanderbilt (1849–1920) (executive, New York Central)

William Kissam Vanderbilt (1878–1944) (executive, New York Central)

Harold Sterling Vanderbilt (1884–1970) (won America's Cup yachting race 3 times; invented contract bridge card game) spectacularly and being relieved by Maj-Gen Ulysses S Grant. With 70,000 troops, Grant pressed the town hard and Lt-Gen John C Pemberton, the Confederate commander, surrendered his 25,000 men and 90 guns on 4 July 1863. The capture of the town split the Confederacy in two.

- Because Union ships on the Mississippi could not pass the guns at Vicksburg, Maj-Gen Grant tried to dig a canal through the Louisiana bayou but high water defeated him.

- The Union forces dug a tunnel under the Confederate line and exploded 2,200 pounds of powder, but the Confederates had established a second line of defence to stop the planned attack.

- The starving troops and civilians in Vicksburg turned to eating mule meat, which was officially approved by a Confederate order.

- Grant set the prisoners free on their promise never to fight again, a promise seldom kept.

Vietnam War

The war from 1954 to 1975 between South Vietnam troops, supported by US forces from 1961 to 1975, and communist North Vietnam. Korean and Australian forces were also deployed. It cost the lives of over 58,000 Americans and about 200,000 South Vietnamese soldiers, 1 million North Vietnamese soldiers, and 500,000 civilians. Following the Vietnamese defeat of the French in 1954, US involvement in the country grew until 1 million US troops were involved. In 1961, President John **Kennedy** decided against using combat units but sent 'advisers'. President Lyndon Johnson used the **Tonkin Gulf Resolution** in 1964 to take unlimited action. US resolve was seriously shaken in February 1968 by the communist **Tet Offensive**. In the USA,

The Vietnam Veterans Memorial, dedicated on 13 November 1982 in Washington, DC, is a black granite wall 76 m/250 ft long that contains the names of over 58,000 Americans killed or missing in the war.

the draft and high war casualties resulted in demonstrations that forced Johnson to abandon re-election plans. President Richard **Nixon** first expanded the war to Laos and Cambodia but finally phased out US involvement. His national security adviser Henry **Kissinger** negotiated a peace treaty in January 1973 in Paris with North Vietnam, and all US troops had left Vietnam by March. The communists soon conquered the South and united the nation. Although US forces were never defeated, Vietnam was considered a humiliating political defeat for the Americans.

von Braun, Wernher Magnus Maximilian (1912–1977)

The German-born rocket engineer who invented the Saturn rocket (*Saturn V*) that made the **Apollo moon landing** possible in 1969. He had been responsible for Germany's rocket programme in **World War II** that developed the V1 (flying bomb) and V2 rockets. In the last days of the war in 1945, von Braun and his staff, not wishing to be captured in the Soviet-occupied part of Germany, travelled to the West to surrender to US forces. In the 1950s he was part of the team that produced rockets for US satellites and early space flights by astronauts. He also devised the space shuttle concept.

> ❝ It will free man from the remaining chains, the chains of gravity which still tie him to this planet. ❞
>
> **Wernher von Braun**, quoted in *Time* magazine, 10 February 1958

W

wagon train

A long line of covered wagons was considered the safest way for settlers to travel west in the 19th century. The movement of large numbers of settlers in a wagon train offered protection from Indian attacks, natural disasters (flooding rivers, sand storms), and accidents (broken wheels, injured horses). The trains also moved military supplies and goods. The main type of wagon was the large Conestoga wagon pulled by horses, mules, or oxen. It was called a prairie schooner because its shape resembled a ship.

One of the worst failures of a wagon train occurred in 1846 when George Donner's group of over 30 settlers became lost in the Sierra Mountains of California. Camping there during the harsh winter, half died and the others resorted to cannibalism to survive.

wagon train *Settlers crossing the Plains in covered wagons.*

Wallace, George Corley (1919–1998)

The governor of Alabama who opposed the integration of black and white students in the 1960s. He contested the presidency in 1968 as an independent (the American Independent Party) and in 1972 campaigned for the Democratic nomination but was shot at a rally and became partly paralysed. He was governor from 1963 to 1967, 1971 to 1979, and 1983 to 1987, elected the last time with black support after he moderated his **segregation** stance. His wife Lurleen Burns Wallace was elected governor in 1967 but died in office the following year.

War of 1812

A war between the USA and Britain caused by British interference with US trade as part of the economic warfare against Napoleonic France. British **impressment** took US sailors from American ships, and a blockade was imposed on US shipping. President James **Madison** authorized the beginning of hostilities against the British on the high seas. US forces failed twice in attempts to invade Canada. In 1813 the US won the battle of Lake Erie, but the following year British forces occupied **Washington, DC**, and burned the White House and the Capitol. The Americans halted an attack on Baltimore, Maryland, and the war went into a stalemate. A treaty signed in Ghent, Belgium, on 22 December 1814 ended the conflict. Before news of peace reached Gen Andrew **Jackson**, he had defeated the British at the Battle of **New Orleans** in 1815.

War on Poverty

The name given by President Lyndon **Johnson** to his programme to help America's poor. He first used the term in his 1964 **State of the Union Address** to **Congress**, and two months later requested $962 million to begin the campaign. Poverty in the USA was then defined as earning less than $3,000 a year for a family of four. Johnson's 'war' created such programmes as Medicaid providing medical care for the needy, the Job Corps for young people, the Volunteers in Service to America (VISTA), and the Community Action Program.

> 6 For the first time in our history, it is possible to conquer poverty. 9
>
> **Lyndon B Johnson**, speech to the US Congress, 16 March 1964

War Powers Act

Legislation passed in 1973 restricting the US president's powers to deploy US forces abroad for combat without prior Congressional approval. The president is required to report to both Houses of Congress within 48 hours of having taken such action. **Congress** may then restrict the continuation of troop deployment despite any presidential veto. The act was passed over the veto of President Richard **Nixon** and aimed at restricting the president's use of US forces without Congressional declaration of war. Its provisions generally have been ignored by both Congress and presidents.

Warren Commission

The special US commission that investigated the assassination of President John F **Kennedy**. The chairman was Earl Warren, the chief justice of the US **Supreme Court**, and the six-man committee included the US Congressman (later president) Gerald **Ford**. The commission's 296-word 'Warren Report' published on 24 September 1964 said Lee Harvey Oswald had been the sole gunman and there was no conspiracy. It also called for better protection for the president and vice-president, recommended that the assassination of either become a federal crime, and criticized the **FBI** for not informing the Secret Service that Oswald, a communist activist, was in Dallas during the president's visit.

Washington, Booker T(aliaferro) (1856–1915)

A US educationalist and pioneer in higher education for black people in the South. He was the founder and first principal of the **Tuskegee Institute** in Alabama in 1881.

Washington was born in Franklin County, the son of a slave. After emancipation he went with his family to West Virginia and in 1892 attended the Hampton Normal and Agricultural Institute in Virginia. As principal of Tuskegee Institute, he emphasized the virtues of industrial training rather than liberal arts education.

Washington, George (1732–1799)

The commander of the colonial forces during the **American Revolution** and the first president of the USA from 1789 to 1797, a Federalist. He is known as 'the father of his country'. George Washington was born in Westmoreland County, Virginia. He was a land surveyor who fought for the British against the French during the **French and Indian War**. He sat in the **Continental Congress** and on the outbreak of the American Revolution was chosen commander in chief of the Continental army. He led his troops through many setbacks to final victory, accepted the surrender of British general Charles Cornwallis at Yorktown in 1781. After the war Washington retired to his Virginia estate, Mount Vernon, but in 1787 re-entered politics as president of the Constitutional Convention in Philadelphia. Elected US president in 1789, he shaped the powers of the new office. He was widely criticized for signing **Jay's Treaty** in 1794 that resolved differences with Britain. Washington was re-elected in 1793 but refused to serve a third term, setting a precedent that stood until 1940. He made a

Washington *George Washingon, by Peale.*

famous farewell address, warning the country to remain aloof from European quarrels.

- George Washington had a furious temper but was so shy he sometimes trembled when speakin
- He had to borrow money to travel to his first inauguration in New York City
- Washington suggested he be addressed as 'His Mightiness the President of the United States' (until the speaker of the House laughed him down).

Washington, DC

The capital of the USA in the District of Columbia on the Potomac River. The District is an area of 174 sq km/69 sq mi ceded by Maryland and Virginia in 1788 and 1789 (although the Virginia portion was returned in 1846). The site was chosen by President George **Washington**, and the city, the first planned national capital, was designed by French architect Pierre L'Enfant. It was originally named Federal City, but was renamed in honour of the first president. Congress first convened in the Capitol on 1 December 1800. During the **War of 1812**, the British invaded the city in 1814 and burned down the White House and the Capitol. During the 19th century,

Washington
Family Tree

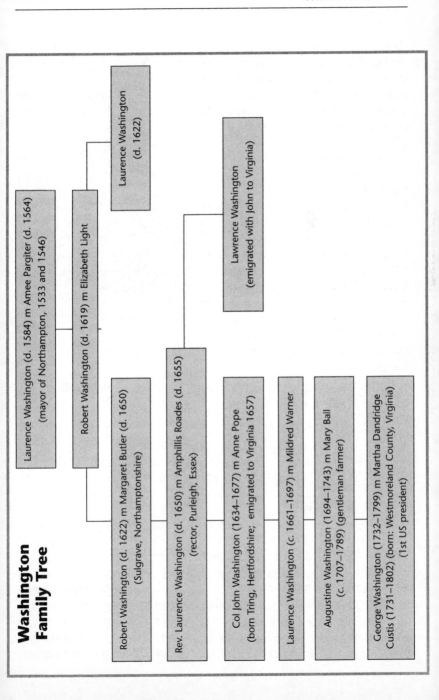

Laurence Washington (d. 1584) m Amee Pargiter (d. 1564)
(mayor of Northampton, 1533 and 1546)

Robert Washington (d. 1619) m Elizabeth Light

Laurence Washington
(d. 1622)

Lawrence Washington
(emigrated with John to Virginia)

Robert Washington (d. 1622) m Margaret Butler (d. 1650)
(Sulgrave, Northamptonshire)

Rev. Laurence Washington (d. 1650) m Amphillis Roades (d. 1655)
(rector, Purleigh, Essex)

Col John Washington (1634–1677) m Anne Pope
(born Tring, Hertfordshire; emigrated to Virginia 1657)

Laurence Washington (c. 1661–1697) m Mildred Warner

Augustine Washington (1694–1743) m Mary Ball
(c. 1707–1789) (gentleman farmer)

George Washington (1732–1799) m Martha Dandridge
Custis (1731–1802) (born: Westmoreland County, Virginia)
(1st US president)

Washington became a beautiful city of wide avenues, white stone and marble buildings, and over 300 statues or memorials. Pennsylvania Avenue, between the White House and the Capitol, is the city's ceremonial street. National monuments and buildings include the White House, Capitol, the Washington Monument, the Lincoln Memorial, the Jefferson Memorial, and the Vietnam Veterans Memorial. The city's estimated population in 1997 was 528,964, but the metropolitan area had a population of 3,923,600 in 1990.

Washington, Treaty of

A treaty signed in 1871 in **Washington, DC**, between the USA and Britain to negotiate the Alabama Claims against Britain for the damage done by the Confederate ship *Alabama* and 10 other Confederate ships built in England. The treaty established an international tribunal that in 1872 awarded $15,500,000 for damages by the *Alabama, Florida*, and *Shenandoah*, which Britain paid in gold. The Treaty also put together fishing and trade agreements between the USA and Canada.

Watergate

A US political scandal that led to the resignation of President Richard Nixon.

It was named after the building in **Washington, DC**, that housed the headquarters of the Democratic National Committee in the 1972 presidential election. Five men, hired by the Republican Committee for the Re-election of the President, were caught after breaking into the headquarters. Investigations revealed that the White House was implicated in the break-in and there was a 'slush fund' used to finance unethical activities, including using the CIA and the Internal Revenue Service for political ends. Nixon resigned rather than face **impeachment** for obstruction of justice and other crimes. Others involved, including former US attorney general John Mitchell and several senior White House staff, went to jail.

Wayne, Anthony (1745–1796)

An officer in the **American Revolution** and an Indian fighter whose nickname was 'Mad Anthony' because of his daring tactics. He took the Hudson River fort of Stony Point from the British on 15 July 1779 and participated in the **Yorktown surrender**. After the war, Wayne secured a treaty in 1795 with Indians, making possible the settlement of Ohio and Indiana. He also built Fort Wayne, Indiana.

Webster, Daniel (1782–1852)

A US politician and orator who negotiated the Webster-Ashburton Treaty in 1842 that fixed the boundary between Maine and Canada. His 'seventh of March' speech in the Senate in 1850 helped secure a compromise on the slavery issue. Webster was born in Salisbury, New Hampshire. He sat in the US House of Representatives from 1813 to 1827 and in the Senate from 1827–41 and 1845–50, at first as a Federalist and later as a Whig. He was secretary of state from 1841 to 1843 and from 1850 to 1852. Webster argued that **Congress** was powerless under the **Constitution of the United States** to interfere with slavery, and he maintained that the break-up of the Union would produce an even greater evil.

> ❝I was born an American; I will live an American; I shall die an American. ❞
>
> **Daniel Webster**, speech on the Compromise Bill in the US Senate, 17 July 1850

Webster, Noah (1758–1843)

A US lexicographer whose books on grammar and spelling and *American Dictionary of the English Language* (1828) standardized US English. Webster learned 26 languages and began the scientific study of etymology. Following the American Revolution, he was prompted by patriotic sentiment to create schoolbooks that would impart that sentiment to young students. His *Blue-Backed Speller* sold nearly 100 million copies in a century. In 1833 he published a revision of the *Authorized Version of English Bible*.

Wells Fargo

A famous **stagecoach** company in the 19th century. It carried up to 15 passengers (as well as gold, goods, and the mail) on transcontinental journeys that lasted 25 days, stopping at stage stations every 18 to 30 miles. A major route was between New York and San Francisco. The company began as a bank established in 1852 by Henry Wells and William G Fargo. They bought the **Pony Express** in 1861 and the Overland Mail Company in 1866. Wells Fargo merged in 1918 with other companies to become the American Railway Express Company.

Western Union

A US telegraph company established in 1851 and later providing a vital service to the Union army during the **Civil War**. It took over the US Telegraph Company in 1866 to become a monopoly, and its technology caused the demise of the **Pony Express**. Thomas Edison was later hired to develop a telephone, but Western Union had to sell the design to the National Bell Telephone Company, which had prior rights. Western Union now sends its message by satellites.

Westmoreland, William Childs (1914–)

The US general who served as commander of US forces from 1964 to 1968 during the **Vietnam War**. He was an aggressive advocate of expanded US military involvement there. Born in Spartanburg County, South Carolina, Westmoreland was a 1936 graduate of West Point military academy where he was superintendent from 1960 to 1963. He ended his active military career as army Chief of Staff from 1968 to 1972.

Whig Party

A US political party opposed to the autocratic presidency of Andrew **Jackson** from 1834. The Whig presidents were W H Harrison in 1841, Zachary **Taylor** in 1849–50, and Millard Fillmore from 1850–53. The party diverged over the issue of slavery: the Northern Whigs joined the **Republican Party** and the Southern or 'Cotton' Whigs joined the **Democratic Party**. The title was taken from the British Whig Party which supported Parliament against the king. During the **American Revolution**, colonial patriots described themselves as Whigs, while those remaining loyal to Britain were known as Tories, or **Loyalists**.

Whiskey Rebellion

A rebellion from June to November 1794 of settlers in western Pennsylvania against a federal excise tax on whisky that was passed in 1791. Led by Scotch-Irish farmers who made whisky from their grain, the protesters destroyed the whisky stills of those who paid the tax, and they tarred and feathered US tax collectors. President George **Washington** ordered 13,000 militiamen into the area, and the revolt immediately collapsed.

Two of the rebellion leaders were charged with treason, but George Washington pardoned them because he said one was insane and the other was a 'simpleton'.

White House

The official residence of the president of the USA, in **Washington, DC**. It is a plain three-storeyed edifice of grey sandstone, built in Italian Renaissance style from 1792 to 1799 to the designs of Philadelphia architect James Hoban. He also restored the house after it was burned down by the British in 1814 during the **War of 1812**; it was then painted white to hide the scars. The building, containing about 100 rooms, was completely restored from 1948 to 1955, when it was discovered that the structure had become unsound. The president's study is known from its shape as the **Oval Office**.

The name White House, first recorded in 1811, is often adapted to refer to other residences of the president: for example the Little White House, at Warm Springs, Georgia, where Franklin D **Roosevelt** died; and the Western White House, at San Clemente, California, where Richard **Nixon** had a home.

Whitewater scandal

A long-running financial scandal that dogged the US presidency of Bill **Clinton** from 1992. It relates to activities during the 1980s when Clinton was governor of Arkansas and became involved, along with his wife Hilary, in the Whitewater Development Corporation, an Arkansas property venture. The scandal involved allegations of sham land deals, tax benefits, and suspicions over the mysterious death, in July 1993, of White House deputy counsel Vincent Foster. Kenneth Starr, the special prosecutor (Independent Counsel) investigating the allegations since August 1994, broadened the investigation to include allegations of sexual harassment made against the president by Paula Jones, a former Arkansas state employee. This line of query eventually led to the revelation of Clinton's improper relationship with a White House intern, Monica Lewinsky, and to his unsuccessful **impeachment** by Congress.

Whitney, Eli (1765–1825)

A US inventor who in 1794 patented the cotton gin, a device for separating cotton fibre from its seeds. It allowed the South to develop cotton as a major cash crop that would perpetuate the institution of **slavery**. Also a manufacturer of firearms, Whitney created a standardization system that was the precursor of the assembly line. Whitney was born in Westborough, Massachusetts, and studied law at Yale. His cotton gin was so easy to copy and manufacture that he eventually gave up defending his patent and in 1798 turned to the manufacture of firearms in New Haven, Connecticut, pioneering interchangeable parts in the first example of **mass production**.

Wilderness, Battle of the

An indecisive battle fought during the **Civil War** on 5 and 6 May 1864 in a wooded areas known as 'The Wilderness' 24 km/15 mi west of Fredericksburg, Virginia. It was the first direct confrontation between Confederate general Robert E **Lee** and Union general Ulysses S **Grant**. Initial Union success was reversed by Confederate reinforcements, and soon the Confederates had routed a Union corps. Grant brought up reinforcements and the next day broke through the Confederate lines, only to be stopped by a concentration of artillery. The day ended with Lee pressing hard, but Grant crossed the Rapidan River and the Battle of **Spotsylvania** began.

> ❛ My God, Gen McGowan! Is this splendid brigade of yours running like a flock of geese? ❜
>
> **Gen Robert E Lee**, to Brig-Gen Samuel McGowan as he watched McGowan's men retreating, quoted in Shelby Foote's *The Civil War*, 1958

Wild West, the

The western frontier of the USA between 1850, when westward expansion began, and 1890, when the west coast region was settled. This was the era of the great cattle drives and **gold rushes**. Cowboy legends began during this period, including the lawmen 'Wild Bill' **Hickok** and Wyatt **Earp** and the lawless Jesse **James** and '**Billy the Kid**'. Our images of the Wild West, however, owe more to **Hollywood** than to reality.

Williamsburg

A historic town in southeast Virginia between the James and York rivers. It was established in 1632 as Middle Plantation and then renamed after King William III of England. It served as the capital of the colony of Virginia from 1699 to 1779. Much of it has been restored to its 18th-century appearance as Colonial Williamsburg, a major tourist attraction. The College of William and Mary, one of the oldest in the USA, was founded there in 1693.

Wilson (Thomas) Woodrow (1856–1924)

The 28th president of the USA from 1913 to 1921, a Democrat. He kept the USA out of **World War I** until 1917 and in January 1918 issued his **Fourteen Points** as a basis for a just peace settlement. At the peace conference in Paris he secured the inclusion of the League of Nations in individual peace treaties, but these were not ratified by **Congress**, so subsequently the USA did not join the League. He was awarded the Nobel Peace Prize in 1919. Born in Virginia, Wilson graduated from Princeton University and studied law at the University of Virginia. He became president of Princeton University in 1902. In 1910 he became governor of New Jersey. Elected US president in 1912, he initiated anti-trust legislation and secured valuable social reforms in his progressive 'New Freedom' programme. He strove to keep the USA neutral during World War I but the German U-boat campaign forced him to declare war in 1917. In 1919 he suffered a stroke from which he never fully recovered.

> ❝ The world must be made safe for democracy. ❞
>
> **Woodrow Wilson**, address to Congress, April 1917, asking for a declaration of war against Germany

Winthrop, John (1588–1649)

An American colonist and first governor of the Massachusetts Bay Colony. A devout Puritan and one of the founders of the Massachusetts Bay Company in 1628, he served as Massachusetts governor or deputy governor until his death. He first arrived in New England with a large group of settlers in 1630. He was a founder of the city of Boston in the same year. Winthrop was born in Suffolk, England, and was educated at Cambridge University. He studied law at Gray's Inn and became a barrister in 1628.

Works Progress Administration See *WPA*.

World War I

At the outbreak of World War I, there had been much sympathy for Germany in the USA, compounded by the British maritime policy which interfered with US shipping. This changed on 7 May 1915 when a German U-boat (submarine) sunk the liner *Lusitania* with the loss of 1,200 lives, including 128 Americans. The Germans called off widespread U-boat attacks until 13 January 1917, but then soon sank six US vessels. Although President Woodrow **Wilson** had tried to follow a policy of strict neutrality, the USA formally declared war on 6 April. The first contingent of American troops landed in France on 25 June 1917 under Maj-Gen John **Pershing**, and the US navy sent vessels to escort Atlantic convoys. The increased strength of the Allied troops overpowered the Germans, whose government sent a note to President Wilson on 4 October, asking for an armistice and declaring Germany's acceptance of his **Fourteen Points** as a basis for peace discussions. The armistice was signed between Germany and the Allies on 11 November 1918, and fighting ceased on the Western Front at 11 a.m. the same day. The total American casualties in the war were 320,710, including 116,708 deaths.

World War II

Before the USA entered World War II, President Franklin D **Roosevelt** gradually shifted the country's traditional isolationist position of 1939 into 'the arsenal of democracy'. The **Lend-Lease Agreement** was signed on 11 March 1941, enabling the USA to supply war materials to Britain and it allies. After Japanese carrier-borne aircraft bombed **Pearl Harbor** on 7 December 1941, the USA entered the war. The Japanese onslaught was halted in 1942 by the American victories in the Battle of the **Coral Sea** and the Battle of **Midway**. The Americans took control of the Pacific War in 1943 by winning the Battle of Guadalcanal. In the Atlantic, German U-boats were still taking a heavy toll of Allied shipping until a large number of US Liberator aircraft were made available for convoy escort work. In Europe, the **D-Day** invasion of Normandy on 6 June 1944 began the final push into Germany, with the Battle of the Bulge in December being the Germans' last major effort to avoid defeat. The German leader Adolph Hitler committed suicide on 30 April 1945 and Germany surrendered on 7 May. The war in the Pacific came to an abrupt end later that year after the USA dropped atomic bombs on Hiroshima on 6 August and Nagasaki three days later. Japan surrendered on 14 August. The total American casualties in the war were 1,079,162, including 407,316 deaths.

Wounded Knee

The last engagement of America's **Indian Wars**, a massacre of an Indian village. Wounded Knee is the site on the Oglala Sioux Reservation in South Dakota where the confrontation took place. On 15 December 1890, Chief

Sitting Bull had been killed, supposedly resisting arrest. On 29 December, the US 7th Cavalry surrounded a group of Indians involved in the **Ghost Dance** movement (aimed at resuming Indian control of North America with the aid of the spirits of dead braves). The troops gunned down around 200 Indians, including women and children; 29 soldiers were killed.

In 1973 the militant American Indian Movement, in the siege of Wounded Knee from 27 February to 8 May, held hostages and demanded a government investigation of the Indian treaties.

WPA

The abbreviation and common name for the Works Progress Administration, part of the **New Deal** of President Franklin D **Roosevelt**. It was established in 1935 and later renamed the **Works Projects Administration**. WPA was a government initiative to reduce unemployment during the **Great Depression**. It provided useful work for 8.5 million people during its eight-year existence, mainly in construction projects, at a total cost of $11 billion. It was discontinued only in 1943 when the change to a war economy eliminated unemployment.

Wright, Orville (1871–1948) and Wilbur (1867–1912)

US aviator brothers who flew the first successful heavier-than-air aircraft with an engine on 17 December 1903 on Kill Devil Hill near Kittyhawk, North Carolina. Orville piloted the 13-horsepower plane, named 'Flyer', after winning the toss of a coin. There were four short flights, the longest being for 59 seconds over a distance of 260 m/852 ft. The brothers had constructed the plane in their bicycle workshop and had spent over $1,000 before the flight. They also built their own wind tunnel to test it. Three years later, they were able to make a flight that lasted more than an hour. The Flyer has been in the Smithsonian Institution in **Washington, DC**, since 1948.

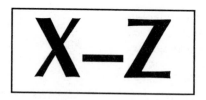

XYZ Affair

An incident in 1797 and 1798 in which the French were accused of demanding a $250,000 bribe before agreeing to negotiate with US envoys in Paris. The proposed negotiations were part of an attempt to resolve a crisis in Franco-US relations caused by the war in Europe and by French raids on American shipping. Three French agents (referred to by President John Adams as X, Y, and Z) held secret talks with the envoys over the money. The event fuelled anti-French feelings in the USA, led to increased US military spending, and nearly caused a war.

Yalta Conference

A strategic conference held from 4 to 11 February 1945 in Yalta (a Soviet holiday resort in the Crimea) by the main Allied leaders in **World War II**. At this, the second of three key meetings between the 'Big Three' – Winston Churchill (Britain), Franklin D **Roosevelt** (USA), and Joseph Stalin (USSR) – plans were drawn up for the final defeat and disarmament of Nazi Germany, the post-war partition of Europe, and the foundation of the **United Nations**.

Yankee

A colloquial (often disparaging) term for an American. Outside the USA the term is applied to any American. It was originally a disparaging term for a Dutch freebooter, later applied to English settlers by colonial Dutch in New York. During the **Civil War**, the term was applied by Southerners to any Northerner or member of the Union Army and is still used today to refer to Northerners. A 'real yankee' is a person from the New England states, especially someone descended from a colonial-founding family. The word has also come to connote craftiness and business acumen, as in 'yankee ingenuity'.

Yorktown surrender

The surrender on 19 October 1781 at Yorktown, Virginia, by British general Charles Cornwallis, ending the **American Revolution**. His 8,000 troops had been surrounded there since 28 September by George **Washington's** 9,000 troops and 7,000 French. When British ships bringing reinforcement were unable to pass the French fleet, Cornwallis was forced to surrender.

Yorktown surrender *The surrender of Lord Cornwallis at Yorktown.*

> ❝ I have the mortification to inform your Excellency that I have been forced to give up the posts of York and Gloucester, and to surrender the troops under my command. ❞
>
> **Gen Charles Cornwallis**, message to Sir Henry Clinton, British commander in chief, 20 October 1781

Zenger, John Peter (1697–1746)

A German-born American colonial printer and newspaper editor. He emigrated to New York in 1710, established his own press in 1726, and became active in local political affairs. In 1733 he founded the *New York Weekly Journal* through which he publicized his opposition to New York governor William Cosby. In 1734 he was arrested for seditious libel. Acquitted by a jury in 1735, he published *A Brief Narrative of the Case* and *Trial of John Peter Zenger* (1736) and remained a spokesman for the principle of freedom of the press.

Appendix

North America: chronology

BC

c. 100000–40000 Mongoloid Asian peoples migrate into North America. Settlement spreads south and east.

c. 9000 Marmes man, earliest human remains.

c. 7000–1400 Civilization develops.

300 Earliest Moundbuilder sites.

AD

c. 1000 Leif Ericsson reaches North America. First known European settlement, of Norsemen in 'Vinland', a part of Newfoundland.

12th–14th centuries Height of the Moundbuilder and Pueblo cultures.

1492 Columbus sails from Spain to the West Indies, so named because he mistakes them for the East Indies; for the same reason, the American Indians he encounters are called 'Indians'. The permanent settlement of North America by Europeans begins.

1513 Ponce de Leon of Spain explores Florida in search of the Fountain of Youth.

1540–42 Francisco Coronado explores southwest region of North America.

1565 First Spanish settlements in Florida.

1585 First attempted English settlement in North Carolina.

1607 First permanent English settlement, Jamestown, Virginia.

1620 The Pilgrim Fathers found Plymouth Colony.

1624 Dutch form the colony of New Netherlands; taken by England in 1664.

1733 Georgia becomes the thirteenth British colony on the east coast.

1763 British victory over France in the Seven Years' War secures territory as far west as the Mississippi River.

1765 British first attempt to levy tax in American colonies with the Stamp Act.

1773 Boston Tea Party – colonists board ships and throw cargoes of tea into the sea in protest at the import duty.

1775 Beginning of American Revolution (War of Independence).

1776 Declaration of Independence.

1781 Americans defeat the British at the Battle of Yorktown. The rebel states form a loose confederation, which is codified in The Articles of Confederation.

North America: chronology (*cont.*)

1783	Britain recognizes the independence of the 13 colonies in the Treaty of Paris, and the USA now extends from the Atlantic seaboard to the Mississippi River.
1787	The Founding Fathers devise a new constitution for the USA.
1789	George Washington is elected first president of the USA.
1791	The Bill of Rights guarantees individual freedom.
1803	The Louisiana Purchase of land from France doubles the area of the USA.
1812–14	French trade blockade of British shipping sparks the War of 1812.
1819	The USA buys Florida from Spain.
1846-48	The USA wins the Southwestern states from Mexico in the Mexican War.
1860	Abraham Lincoln is elected president.
1861	The USA buys Alaska from Russia.
1861–65	The Civil War brings about the end of slavery.
1865	Abraham Lincoln is assasssinated.
1869	Railway opens linking east and west coasts.
1876	Sioux Indians defeat US troops at the Battle of Little Big Horn.
1898	Hawaii cedes itself to the USA.
1903	The USA leases the rights to the Panama Canal Zone.
1914	Panama Canal completed.
1917	USA enters World War I.
1920	Women receive the right to vote. The sale of alcohol is prohibited until 1933.
1929	The Wall Street Crash – the stock market collapse leads to the Great Depression, creating 13 million unemployment by 1933.
1941	USA enters World War II following the Japanese attack on the US fleet at Pearl Harbor.
1947	Truman Doctrine – pledges US aid for countries threatened by communism. Start of the Cold War between the USA and the USSR.
1948	Formation of Organization of American States (OAS).
1949	Formation of NATO.
1950-53	The USA leads a UN force in the Korean War forcing North Korean invaders out of South Korea.
1954	Racial segregation in schools is deemed unconstitutional, start of the campaign to secure civil rights for Black Americans.
1961	The USA backs the abortive 'Bay of Pigs' invasion of Cuba by anti-Castro Cuban exiles.
1963	President Kennedy is assassinated.
1969	US space launch is the first to put a person on the Moon.
1960s–70s	Opposition to the Vietnam War causes domestic discord in the USA.
1973	The Vietnam War ends for the USA with a ceasefire agreement and withdrawal of troops.

North America: chronology (*cont.*)

1974	Watergate Scandal, evidence of domestic espionage forces President Richard Nixon to resign.
1983	The USA invades Grenada to preserve constitutional government.
1989	The USA and Canada sign a free trade agreement. The USA invades Panama and takes its leader, General Noriega, into custody.
1990	President George Bush declares an end to the Cold War.
1990–91	Gulf War: US-led coalition, joined by Britain and other nations, drives the invader Iraq from Kuwait.
1992–93	The USA, Canada, and Mexico reach accord on North American Free Trade Agreement (NAFTA), aimed at ending tariffs, and the treaty is signed.
1999	The USA leads NATO's bombing of Serbian troops in Kosovo, forcing their withdrawal.
1999	The USA returns the Panama Canal and its zone to Panama.

US Presidents

Year elected/ took office	President	Party	Losing candidate(s)	Party
1789	1 George Washington	Federalist	no opponent	
1792	re-elected		no opponent	
1796	2 John Adams	Federalist	Thomas Jefferson	Democrat–Republican
1800	3 Thomas Jefferson	Democrat–Republican	Aaron Burr	Democrat–Republican
1804	re-elected		Charles Pinckney	Federalist
1808	4 James Madison	Democrat–Republican	Charles Pinckney	Federalist
1812	re-elected		DeWitt Clinton	Federalist
1816	5 James Monroe	Democrat–Republican	Rufus King	Federalist
1820	re-elected		John Quincy Adams	Democrat–Republican
1824	6 John Quincy Adams	Democrat–Republican	Andrew Jackson	Democrat–Republican
			Henry Clay	Democrat–Republican
			William H Crawford	Democrat–Republican
1828	7 Andrew Jackson	Democrat	John Quincy Adams	National Republican
1832	re-elected		Henry Clay	National Republican
1836	8 Martin Van Buren	Democrat	William Henry Harrison	Whig
1840	9 William Henry Harrison	Whig	Martin Van Buren	Democrat
1841	10 John Tyler[1]	Whig		
1844	11 James K Polk	Democrat	Henry Clay	Whig
1848	12 Zachary Taylor	Whig	Lewis Cass	Democrat

US Presidents (*cont.*)

Year elected/ took office	President	Party	Losing candidate(s)	Party
1850	13 Millard Fillmore[2]	Whig		
1852	14 Franklin Pierce	Democrat	Winfield Scott	Whig
1856	15 James Buchanan	Democrat	John C Fremont	Republican
1860	16 Abraham Lincoln	Republican	Stephen Douglas	Democrat
			John Breckinridge	Democrat
			John Bell	Constitutional Union
1864	re-elected		George McClellan	Democrat
1865	17 Andrew Johnson[3]	Democrat		
1868	18 Ulysses S Grant	Republican	Horatio Seymour	Democrat
1872	re-elected		Horace Greeley	Democrat–Liberal Republican
1876	19 Rutherford B Hayes	Republican	Samuel Tilden	Democrat
1880	20 James A Garfield	Republican	Winfield Hancock	Democrat
1881	21 Chester A Arthur[4]	Republican		
1884	22 Grover Cleveland	Democrat	James Blaine	Republican
1888	23 Benjamin Harrison	Republican	Grover Cleveland	Democrat
1892	24 Grover Cleveland	Democrat	Benjamin Harrison	Republican
			James Weaver	People's
1896	25 William McKinley	Republican	William J Bryan	Democrat–People's
1900	re-elected		William J Bryan	Democrat
1901	26 Theodore Roosevelt[5]	Republican		
1904	re-elected		Alton B Parker	Democrat
1908	27 William Howard Taft	Republican	William J Bryan	Democrat
1912	28 Woodrow Wilson	Democrat	Theodore Roosevelt	Progressive
			William Howard Taft	Republican
1916	re-elected		Charles E Hughes	Republican
1920	29 Warren G Harding	Republican	James M Cox	Democrat
1923	30 Calvin Coolidge[6]	Republican		
1924	re-elected		John W Davis	Democrat
			Robert M LaFollette	Progressive
1928	31 Herbert Hoover	Republican	Alfred E Smith	Democrat
1932	32 Franklin D Roosevelt	Democrat	Herbert C Hoover	Republican
			Norman Thomas	Socialist
1936	re-elected		Alfred Landon	Republican
1940	re-elected		Wendell Willkie	Republican

US Presidents *(cont.)*

Year elected/ took office	President	Party	Losing candidate(s)	Party
1944	re-elected		Thomas E Dewey	Republican
1945	33 Harry S Truman[7]	Democrat		
1948	re-elected		Thomas E Dewey	Republican
			J Strom Thurmond	States' Rights
			Henry A Wallace	Progressive
1952	34 Dwight D Eisenhower	Republican	Adlai E Stevenson	Democrat
1956	re-elected		Adlai E Stevenson	Democrat
1960	35 John F Kennedy	Democrat	Richard M Nixon	Republican
1963	36 Lyndon B Johnson[8]	Democrat		
1964	re-elected		Barry M Goldwater	Republican
1968	37 Richard M Nixon	Republican	Hubert H Humphrey	Democrat
			George C Wallace	American Independent
1972	re-elected		George S McGovern	Democrat
1974	38 Gerald R Ford[9]	Republican		
1976	39 James Earl Carter	Democrat	Gerald R Ford	Republican
1980	40 Ronald Reagan	Republican	James Earl Carter	Democrat
			John B Anderson	Independent
1984	re-elected		Walter Mondale	Democrat
1988	41 George Bush	Republican	Michael Dukakis	Democrat
			Ross Perot	Independent
1992	42 Bill Clinton	Democrat	George Bush	Republican
1996	re-elected		Bob Dole	Republican
			Ross Perot	Reform

[1] Became president on death of Harrison.

[2] Became president on death of Taylor.

[3] Became president on assassination of Lincoln.

[4] Became president on assassination of Garfield.

[5] Became president on assassination of McKinley.

[6] Became president on death of Harding.

[7] Became president on death of F D Roosevelt.

[8] Became president on assassination of Kennedy.

[9] Became president on resignation of Nixon.

United States of America: states

State	Nickname(s)	Abbreviation	Capital	Area (sq km)	Area (sq mi)	Population (1995)	Joined the union
Alabama	Heart of Dixie/ Camellia State	AL	Montgomery	134,700	51,994	4,253,000	1819
Alaska	Mainland State/ The Last Frontier	AK	Juneau	1,531,100	591,005	603,600	1959
Arizona	Grand Canyon State/ Apache State	AZ	Phoenix	294,100	113,523	4,217,900	1912
Arkansas	Bear State/Land of Opportunity	AR	Little Rock	137,800	53,191	2,483,800	1836
California	Golden State	CA	Sacramento	411,100	158,685	31,589,200	1850
Colorado	Centennial State	CO	Denver	269,700	104,104	3,746,600	1876
Connecticut	Constitution State/ Nutmeg State	CT	Hartford	13,000	5018	3,274,700	1788
Delaware	First State/Diamond State	DE	Dover	5,300	2,046	717,200	1787
Florida	Sunshine State/ Everglade State	FL	Tallahassee	152,000	58,672	14,165,600	1845
Georgia	Empire State of the South/Peach State	GA	Atlanta	152,600	58,904	7,200,900	1788
Hawaii	Aloha State	HI	Honolulu	16,800	6,485	1,186,800	1959
Idaho	Gem State	ID	Boise	216,500	83,569	1,163,300	1890
Illinois	Inland Empire/Prairie State/Land of Lincoln	IL	Springfield	146,100	56,395	11,829,900	1818
Indiana	Hoosier State	IN	Indianapolis	93,700	36,168	5,803,500	1816
Iowa	Hawkeye State/Corn State	IA	Des Moines	145,800	56,279	2,841,800	1846
Kansas	Sunflower State/ Jayhawker State	KS	Topeka	213,200	82,295	2,565,300	1861
Kentucky	Bluegrass State	KY	Frankfort	104,700	40,414	3,860,200	1792
Louisiana	Pelican State/Sugar State/Creole State	LA	Baton Rouge	135,900	52,457	4,342,300	1792
Maine	Pine Tree State	ME	Augusta	86,200	33,273	1,241,400	1812
Maryland	Old Line State/Free State	MD	Annapolis	31,600	12,198	5,042,400	1788
Massachusetts	Bay State/Old Colony	MA	Boston	21,500	8,299	6,073,550	1788
Michigan	Great Lakes State/ Wolverine State	MI	Lansing	151,600	58,518	9,549,400	1837

United States of America: states (cont.)

State	Nickname(s)	Abbreviation	Capital	Area (sq km)	Area (sq mi)	Population (1995)	Joined the union
Minnesota	North Star State/Gopher State	MN	St Paul	218,700	84,418	4,609,500	1858
Mississippi	Magnolia State	MS	Jackson	123,600	47,710	2,697,200	1817
Missouri	Show Me State/Bullion State	MO	Jefferson City	180,600	69,712	5,323,500	1821
Montana	Treasure State/Big Sky Country	MT	Helena	381,200	147,143	870,300	1889
Nebraska	Cornhusker State/Beef State	NE	Lincoln	200,400	77,354	1,637,100	1867
Nevada	Sagebrush State/Silver State/Battleborn State	NV	Carson City	286,400	110,550	1,530,100	1864
New Hampshire	Granite State	NH	Concord	24,000	9,264	1,148,300	1788
New Jersey	Garden State	NJ	Trenton	20,200	7,797	7,945,300	1787
New Mexico	Land of Enchantment/Sunshine State	NM	Santa Fé	315,000	121,590	1,685,400	1912
New York	Empire State	NY	Albany	127,200	49,099	18,136,100	1788
North Carolina	Tar Heel State/Old North State	NC	Raleigh	136,400	52,650	7,195,100	1789
North Dakota	Peace Garden State	ND	Bismarck	183,100	70,677	641,400	1889
Ohio	Buckeye State	OH	Columbus	107,100	41,341	11,150,500	1803
Oklahoma	Sooner State	OK	Oklahoma City	181,100	69,905	3,277,700	1907
Oregon	Beaver State/Sunset State	OR	Salem	251,500	97,079	3,140,600	1859
Pennsylvania	Keystone State	PA	Harrisburg	117,400	45,316	12,071,800	1787
Rhode Island	Little Rhody/Ocean State	RI	Providence	3,100	1,197	989,800	1790
South Carolina	Palmetto State	SC	Columbia	80,600	31,112	3,673,300	1788
South Dakota	Coyote State/Mount Rushmore State	SD	Pierre	199,800	77,123	729,000	1889
Tennessee	Volunteer State	TN	Nashville	109,200	42,151	5,256,100	1796
Texas	Lone Star State	TX	Austin	691,200	266,803	18,724,000	1845
Utah	Beehive State/Mormon State	UT	Salt Lake City	219,900	84,881	1,951,400	1896
Vermont	Green Mountain State	VT	Montpelier	24,900	9,611	584,800	1791

United States of America: states (*cont.*)

State	Nickname(s)	Abbre- viation	Capital	Area		Population (1995)	Joined the union
				sq km	sq mi		
Virginia	Old Dominion State/ Mother of Presidents	VA	Richmond	105,600	40,762	6,618,400	1788
Washington	Evergreen State/ Chinook State	WA	Olympia	176,700	68,206	5,430,900	1889
West Virginia	Mountain State/ Panhandle State	WV	Charleston	62,900	24,279	1,828,100	1863
Wisconsin	Badger State/America's	WI	Madison	145,500	56,163	5,122,900	1848
Wyoming	Equality State Dairyland	WY	Cheyenne	253,400	97,812	480,200	1890
District of Columbia (Federal District)	–	DC	Washington	180	69	554,300	estab- lished by Act of Congress 1790–91